TRENDS IN MANAGEMENT THINKING
1960–1970

TRENDS IN
MANAGEMENT THINKING
1960-1970

Harold R. Pollard

B.Com., M.B.I.M.
Formerly Senior Lecturer in Management Studies
Peterborough Technical College

GULF PUBLISHING COMPANY
BOOK DIVISION
HOUSTON, LONDON, PARIS, TOKYO

William Heinemann Ltd
15 Queen Street, Mayfair, London W1X 8BE
LONDON MELBOURNE TORONTO
JOHANNESBURG AUCKLAND

© H. R. Pollard 1978

First published 1978
This edition published by
Gulf Publishing Company
1978

ISBN 0–87201–880–6

Printed in Great Britain by
Cox & Wyman Ltd, London, Fakenham and Reading

Foreword

Regrettably management and organization studies are not disciplines, at least not yet. As a result researchers and writers use a wide and often contradictory vocabulary and the work of one expert often relates to that of others, even in the same subject matter area, only obliquely. In other words it is not even easy to know who agrees or disagrees, what ideas are mutually consistent and which are contradictory.

Fortunately there is something of a solution to the problem faced by the outsider, be he (or she) a student or manager seeking to gain some understanding of these vital fields. A thoughtful and insightful Englishman, Harold Pollard, has taken it upon himself to read (and obviously reread) a number of works which help form the foundation for modern management thought. He then 'translates' these diverse works into good, straightforward English and provides an engaging running commentary in the tradition of a fine essayist.

But let me not be misunderstood, these are not vague ramblings but careful and extraordinarily clear condensations of what must, in some cases, be what the author wished he had said. Pollard knows these fields and is thus able to provide a quite accurate although simplified review. One good writer is so much easier to follow than a whole series of authors with separate backgrounds and styles. Pollard's book is a fine improvement on the more typical 'readings' that leave the reader with the need to jump from one style and framework to another without the aid of a carefully chosen, homogeneous style of exposition.

I hope this innovation continues. As one of the authors 'reprocessed' I can testify as to the accuracy and validity of the work.

Columbia University   L. SAYLES

v

Preface

"If it be true that 'good wine needs no bush'
'tis true that a good play needs no epilogue".

A Midsummer Night's Dream. Shakespeare.

Yet Shakespeare provided an epilogue. But to an author and, more particularly, to his potential readers a new book needs a 'prologue' or, to be more precise, a Preface. Why? One good reason is to state as clearly as possible the reason for the book's existence. Only if this is known will the would-be reader look further and the author justify his work.

The field of management as a subject to be studied has developed at an exponential rate over the past quarter of a century, especially in the United States. At the same time the number of books on it has increased to keep pace with the increase of knowledge. As so often happens the solution to one set of problems merely presents us with another. And it is this new problem which this book attempts in some way to answer.

Put briefly the problem is that there are now so many, many books on so many aspects of management that the student cannot begin to read even a reasonable cross-section; the professor providing a reading list knows before he starts that his list is either incomplete or impossible; and the practising manager wanting to find what might be relevant to his job does not know where to begin. That the problem exists there can be no doubt. How far this book meets the needs of this situation is for others to judge.

During the decade 1960–70 it seemed that significant advances were being made in managerial thinking in a number of different directions. Toward the end of the 70s these should, in so far as they have stood the test of time, have moved into the accepted world of the student, the teacher and the manager. But, to present all of the surviving ideas of the decade would have been an impossible and self-defeating task.

The solution adopted has been the concept of 'Satisficing' as put forward by March and Simon in Chapter 20 of this book. Given certain limitations on the size of the book I laid down the minimum criteria which it was hoped to meet. The first was three different approaches in which significant advances seemed to have been made and the second a cross-section of seven or eight books under each approach which seemed to give

vii

a reasonable picture. When the minimum criteria seemed to have been reached I stopped. It was as simple as that.

Obviously there are big dangers in this method. As only three approaches are used—Organization-Structure, Further Psycho-sociology and Decision and Control—other approaches are left out. Again under each approach a handful of authors leaves a multitude out. There can be no answer to the complaint that 'X' should have been included and 'Y' left out. Yet, hopefully, by presenting the essence of some twenty significant books within the covers of one book I may make the task of getting a general picture a more realistic one and also lead my readers back to the original sources when they would like more detail. This, then, is the reason for the book.

No book can be written without the help of many other people and to them I must express my thanks. In particular these go to Professor Leonard Sayles of Columbia University for providing the Foreword to the book and to Professor Chris Argyris of Harvard and Professor Herbert A. Simon of Carnegie-Mellon both of whom provided help and guidance for which I am extremely grateful. These three and many others of the authors about whom I have written have been good enough to read 'their' chapters before publication and to give their blessing.

Without the tolerance and service provided by the staff of the British Management Library, in particular Miss Dare, the task would have been impossible. My thanks are due to them. Mrs Beaumont and Mrs Winter, both of Denby Dale, showed great patience and skill in surmounting the difficulties inherent in converting a difficult manuscript into a presentable typescript. They deserve my sympathy and gratitude. To the unknown person who will, in due course, relieve me of the chore of providing an index to the book I here and now say thank you in advance. My wife, by her support, tolerance and practical help has gone far beyond what used to be known as 'wifely duty' and deserves far more than a passing mention.

Finally to the authors whose ideas and works form the core of this book and without whom it could never have been written I can only say 'Thank you all for making it possible.'

Denby Dale
Yorkshire
England   H. R. POLLARD

Acknowledgments

The author wishes to acknowledge his indebtedness to the following for kind permission to include extracts from the books quoted and to others for brief quotations whose source is acknowledged in the text:

Prentice-Hall Inc.
Modern Organizations, by A. Etzione (1964)
Organizational Psychology, by E. H. Schein (1970)
A Behavioural Theory of the Firm, by R. M. Cyert and J. G. March (1963)
The Social Science of Organizations, edited by H. J. Leavitt (1963)

Tavistock Publications Ltd
Systems of Organization, by E. J. Miller and A. K. Rice (1967)

John Wiley and Sons Inc.
Integrating the Individual and the Organization, by C. Argyris (1964)

McGraw-Hill Book Company
Managerial Behaviour, by L. Sayles (1964)
Organizations in Action, by J. D. Thompson (1967)
New Patterns in Management, by R. Likert (1961)
The Human Organization. Its Management and Value, by R. Likert (1967)

Heinemann Educational Books Ltd
A Theory of Organizations, by D. Silverman (1970)

The Macmillan Company
Jonathan Livingston Seagull, by R. Bach (1970)

Gulf Publishing Company
The Managerial Grid, by R. R. Blake and J. S. Mouton (1964)

Contents

Introduction

If there is one thing that is certain in a world that is changing as fast as ours in the last quarter of the twentieth century it is that 'certainty' is a relative term. What is today's mumbo jumbo was yesterday's fact. Today's fiction will be tomorrow's fact.

This is so trite and so obvious that it should not need saying. But is it so obvious? And if it were what consequences would it bring?

Nowhere today, and for the rest of this century at least, are these two questions more important than in the field of management. Is it obvious to all men and women holding managerial or supervisory jobs today that, in the lifetime of the managers at or near retiring age, the whole industrial and commercial world has changed more than in the lifetime of several generations of their forbears? Is it obvious that most of that change has taken place in the last twenty-five years? Is it obvious that, as one American general said, 'If it flies, it is obsolete'? Is it obvious that we are most of us so busy running to keep up with ourselves that we cannot see, let alone understand, what is happening around us?

It would be tedious and unnecessary to go on. But why bring these questions up at all? In the seventeenth century James Duport wrote in Latin that, 'Whom God would destroy He first sends mad'. Two questions hang over us today – 'Is the world rapidly going mad?' and 'Why, if every other civilization the world has ever known has collapsed and largely disappeared, why should not Western industrial civilization also be destroyed or destroy itself?' The pessimist would answer 'yes' to the first question and 'no reason at all' to the second. The optimist would hope that both questions can be proved wrong. But which, if either, is the realist? And what, in any case, has all this to do with the rest of this book?

At the risk again of seeming trite and obvious two facts should be clear beyond all possible doubt. The first is the universal existence and overwhelming power of 'the organization' in today's world, whether it be the small business, the multi-national corporation, the trade union, the university, the Civil Service, the Government of whatever colour. All are organizations, all impinge on the life of the individual at ever-increasing points. If organization collapses civilization as we know it goes with it.

The second fact is that the central core, the brain, the nervous system of organizations consists of its managers. Without them organizations cannot exist, without a better performance from them than we seem to get today the whole structure will collapse like a house of cards. In 1942 James Burnham, in his book *The Managerial Revolution*, put forward the idea of a managerial elite who would carry the full burden of responsibility for society. Fantasy in 1942 – near-fact in 1976, but not obvious fact to all.

A tremendous amount of work on the meaning of management has been written since 1960, the approximate date when *Developments in Management Thought*, written by the present author, stopped. The next generation of managers must have at least the basic guidelines on what was written between 1960 and 1970. Because no one could possibly find the time or, perhaps, the inclination to read through it all, a few of these ideas have been brought within the covers of one book.

While the decade 1960–70, give or take a few years either way, produced such tremendous growth in research and writing on management it is equally true to say that much of this growth was into narrower and narrower special, sectionalized aspects. In this it was only following the pattern of every other aspect of human knowledge that had gone before it. There is nothing wrong in this, in fact it is all to the good. To draw a parallel, medical science has only progressed as rapidly as it has over the past century because some doctors have spent more and more time learning and discovering about particular 'bits' of the body or about particular diseases. But the general practitioner has to know enough about the broad sweep of medical science to recognize when he has a patient he can successfully treat himself and when the patient should be referred to a specialist and, equally important, to which specialist. It was, I believe, Chris Argyris who hinted in one of his books that management might develop the same way with 'general practitioner' managers backed up by teams of 'specialists' in particular fields.

It is with this idea of a general view in mind that this selection of unspecialized approaches is put forward. It is not and cannot be exhaustive. It is my hope that it may be helpful even if only by drawing attention to other work which could have been a better selection than mine.

PART I

Organization and Structure

I

An Overview

In general terms it was fairly widely accepted before 1960 that organization was a neat, well-ordered subject arranged around Fayol's Scalar Chain and Heirarchy and Urwick's 'drawing office job'.[1] Its fundamental base was a logical division of the work to be done and the responsibilities to be carried between individuals as depicted by neat rectangles linked by straight lines on an organization chart.

But it was equally true that Lord Wilfred Brown[2] was about to publish some very revolutionary ideas based on his own personal experience and it was also true that for some time psycho-sociologists had been writing about the 'informal' organization opposed to, or at best, parallel to the 'formal' organization.

One of the major conflicts of the lecture theatre and the discussion group in the 1950s and 60s was the difference between 'organization' as expounded by the lecturer or discussion leader and the practising managers' overtly expressed or covertly held opinions that 'it ain't necessarily so', that his daily experience bore little relationship to the 'theory' of the academic.

Due to a number of causes the subject of organization and the structure of firms received a great deal of attention during this period. The glaring differences between theory and practice and the urgent need for a theory which did fit the facts were undoubtedly major causes. The post-war surge towards larger and larger firms encouraged consultancy, field research and much closer contact between academics and managers. New problems needed new solutions, 'dead' theories needed new approaches. New solutions and new approaches appeared in plenty in the 1960s or thereabouts.

Part I contains a selection, albeit brief, of these new approaches. To repeat the caution in the *Introduction* the selection is neither complete nor optimum. It is hoped, however, that it gives some reasonable cross-section of the lines of development.

The next seven chapters tell their own story but a few brief comments will set the stage.

3

Burns and Stalker (1961) emphasized the relation between different environmental conditions and different forms of organization and structure. They abolished once and for all the idea that there is one best form of organization, one best pattern of relationships within the firm. The 'best' is that which is best suited to the firm's particular environment. Relatively stable environments need 'mechanistic' organization, relatively dynamic, changing ones are best met with 'organic' structures. Burns and Stalker demonstrated the effects of political and status systems and of the conflict between professional expertise and general line management.

Blau and Scott (1962) were two amongst many who introduced into organization theory the concepts of social structure and social culture thereby abolishing the arid formality of organization as a purely impersonal thing. This led them to the concept of 'total' organization or the combination of the formal and informal aspects of organization into a single interacting whole instead of two aspects which could be studied in isolation.

Etzioni's approach (1963) was one of attempted reconciliation of outstanding conflicts which were only too real in practice and too much ignored in theory. One was the apparent conflict between the need for rationality in organization and the need for human satisfaction in the work situation. Another was the question of whether conflict itself between individuals and between groups in the organization was inimical to success. He gave a fresh look to the problems of power within the organization and of the side effects and hidden costs involved in organization itself.

In 1967 Miller and Rice brought together some of the generalizations based on empirical studies carried out under the aegis of the Tavistock Institute for Human Relations over more than a decade. Chiefly these centred on the relationships between the task needs, the social and psychological needs of workers and the effects of both on organization structure. From this they deduced the 'socio-technical system', an approach towards a complex 'systems' view of organization without getting lost in the labyrinth of a pure 'systems' approach.

By the mid-60s there were so many new approaches, so many new points of view that some drawing together, some reconciliation seemed to be needed. Lawrence and Lorsch (1967) attempted this mammoth task. Their review of different theories, including purely classical ones, places the different approaches into a continuum which matches different points with different circumstances. Overall this is developed into a Contingency Theory in which the form and structure of organization is contingent upon the environment in which it exists and, in particular, upon the degree of certainty or uncertainty in that environment. Central to this theory is the matching of the degrees of differentiation and integration in the organization to the needs of its environment.

Thompson (1967) was, at the same time, taking the question of organization further into 'systems' theory. He introduced concepts of closed and open systems as both appropriate to organization structure and dependent upon the degree of uncertainty. Open systems are necessary at the boundaries of the organization to absorb uncertainty in order that its central technological core can operate successfully as a closed system.

Towards the end of the decade there seemed to be signs that the approach which regarded organization as an analogy of a natural system might develop into a comprehensive, all-embracing theory of organization. In fact, it has not done so. Reflection has shown that the analogy is not close enough to hold absolutely. Similarities there are in plenty, but there are also too many differences.

Perhaps it is fitting, then, to end Part I with Silverman (1970), a British sociologist who rejects out of hand the 'systems' approach. It seems impossible to get away from the question of whether his book is an analysis of organization and structure rather than of sociology, or whether sociology itself is a study of human organization.

The core of his argument is that organization is the result, not of deliberate planning, but of the meanings which individuals and groups assign to the events and states of affairs around them. These ascribed meanings form the frame of reference on which action and, therefore, organization is based.

The neat certainties of Fayol's order and Urwick's drawing board have gone for ever, shattered into myriads of new facets. Each facet shows some reflection of reality, perhaps accurate, perhaps distorted. It is still too soon to tell when and where the true picture will emerge.

References

   (1) Urwick, L. *The Elements of Administration* (London: Pitman, 1943).
   (2) Brown, W. *Exploration in Management* (London: Heinemann, 1960).

5

T. Burns and G. M. Stalker
1961

In the last quarter of the twentieth century knowledge, above all, should be international. But differences of language, of social culture, of background, of history leave most of us with at least some vestiges of national pride and prejudice. In a British book, written by a British author there may be a little appropriateness in starting with the consideration of the work of two British researchers and authors.

The Management of Innovation may seem an odd title to start Part I of this book, with its heading 'Organization and Structure', but we are concerned with the contents and their significance rather than niceties of title. Burns and Stalker looked at and analysed real-life organizations to try to find out why, in practice, there should be such wide differences in the pattern, structure, and operation of firms. Their answers were and still are of great significance.

Throughout the book there is a constant interweaving of illustration, hypothesis and conclusion. For our purposes we shall be concerned mostly with conclusions with just enough illustration to make the mixture digestible.

The sociological viewpoint with which the work started was an attempt to study a firm as a 'community of people at work'.[1] The conclusion that a study of the firm should be embedded in a wider sociological study of the small town in which it was situated shows very clearly the main line of thought. Even as early as this, however, other organizational factors began to show, e.g. managerial practices and their results and, perhaps more importantly, the discovery of conflict between Research and Development managers and line managers. The latter is the hint about what is to come – a detailed study of the relationship between organization structure and the environment in which it works. Deliberately or because it was the way the research developed the sociological basis seems to retire to the background.

The second study of a firm showed an organization structure and management practices which ran counter to almost every preconceived notion from classical management theory. In spite of, or as Burns and

Stalker 'heretically' suggest perhaps because of, this state of affairs the firm was both technically and commercially successful. Could it be that carefully defined jobs, specified relationships, formal channels of communication and authority were not always the crucial factors in success? Could it possibly be that what really mattered was that the adaptation of the relationships between individuals to meet the technical and commercial requirements of the organization's environment was the really significant factor in success?

'Mechanistic' and 'Organic' organizations

To test out such a suggestion in practice needed a rather special combination of circumstances. Ideally it would be a group of similar firms, well established, with a reasonably stable pattern of successful organization, who through no fault of their own were pitchforked into an entirely new environment making different demands on them from the environment in which they had 'grown up'. A near perfect situation was immediately to hand for Burns and Stalker. A number of firms in the electronics industry moved on to their doorstep under a Government-sponsored scheme to attract new and developing technologically based industry to Scotland. The firms had grown up in the secure and reasonably stable atmosphere of Government war-time and post-war contracts where production was of prime importance. With the post-war run-down these contracts had stopped. The firms were in a new physical environment but, much more importantly, were also in a new technical environment where their own research into and development of new products was essential and a new marketing function to find new customers and translate their needs into the firms' languages was absolutely vital to success. Instead of production to Government specification the required pattern became marketing – development – production or research – marketing – development/adaptation – production. To complete the picture the rate of technological development in the industry as a whole was accelerating fast.

Burns and Stalker observed and analysed what was going on in the different firms. Their immediate conclusions were that none of the firms set up adequate marketing functions, that few managed to build up and incorporate proper research and development departments, that conflicts over power and status between 'new' and 'old' departments were widespread and that purely management problems were only too often converted into personality struggles between managers. In general the old order remained, the organization failed to adapt to the new environment and relative commercial failure was the result.

It could not all have been as negative as this because the only really valid conclusions possible would be that a successful form of organization in one environment may not work successfully in another and a change of environment does not necessarily produce a suitable change in organization. The real leap forward lies in postulating two fundamentally different extremes of organization patterns at the two ends of a scale and the two extremes of environment to which they are most suited. 'Mechanistic' organization goes best with a stable environment and 'organic' organization with a developing, changing and unstable one.

'Mechanistic' systems of organization tend very much to resemble classical theory. Tasks and problems are broken down into constituent parts which can be assigned to a department, a section and finally an individual. Sectionalized like this the individual task becomes separated from the real tasks of the organization as a whole. The individual sees and does, more or less, his own task, and the job of ensuring that it fits in with and furthers the organizational tasks is, at all levels except the Managing Director, a job for someone higher up. Tasks are (supposedly) well-defined, interaction between people is up and down the heirarchy, the instruction is the normal guide to behaviour and the fount of knowledge is at the top. They are suitable for, and effective in a stable or very slowly changing environment that is reasonably predictable, which does not produce new information at such a rate that it cannot reach the top, and where there is time to build up stable patterns of behaviour and relationships.

Under 'organic' systems of organization tasks and problems cannot be neatly divided and parcelled out. They are too numerous, they involve too many different aspects at once, they relate directly to the main tasks of the organization and the required knowledge is likely to be spread throughout the organization at all sorts of levels. So under this system the line heirarchy has much less power, jobs are not clearly and closely defined and, in fact, will change their content to suit the immediate situation. Communications will be a criss-cross pattern across specialities, across departments and often directly between quite different levels in the heirarchy. Decision making is no longer the prerogative of the man higher up but tends to go to the individual or the group of individuals who possess the particular knowledge necessary for the particular problem in hand. As a system of organization it matches a constantly and, perhaps, violently changing and developing environment.

Perhaps a word of caution should be given here. These are two more or less adequate descriptions of two extremes, as are the conditions to which they are suitable. Real life is not just black and white but most frequently a shade of grey somewhere between the two.

Reverting for a moment to the Scottish electronics firms, Burns and Stalker could not evade the question of why, if their 'mechanistic' systems were not suitable to the new conditions, they did not change. Their diagnosis is that the established members of the firms were also members of sub-groups whose interests they supported against threats from the newcomers. In addition, they would, at the individual level, regard their rank, status and prestige as being very important. From this diagnosis they suggest that in every firm parallel with the working organization there will be a political structure of alliances between groups and/or members to further aims which may not agree with organizational ones and a status system which all who possess a satisfactory (to them) level of status will try to preserve. The changed conditions for the Scottish electronic firms required for success new internal patterns of organization, structure, communication and decision making. They required the integration of scientists with different ways of thinking. Burns and Stalker say that these were resisted, not by open conflict, but by intricate manoeuvres and counter moves in discussions and decisions on the future structure and policies of the firms. A further reason for resisting change was the possibility that it might disrupt existing status patterns between managers.

In contrast, a somewhat later study of eight English firms in the same industry and facing the same problems from the changed environment showed both successful and unsuccessful adaptations to the situation. All the firms were larger than the Scottish ones but the significance, if any, of this is not mentioned. The really important factor was that some of the firms already had an 'organic' form of organization, while others were 'mechanistic'. Within the 'organic' firms change from any direction was already seen as affecting the firm as a whole and all individuals in it, in some way or other. So changes in organization, tasks and growth tended to be seen as the firm's reactions to new situations. Conflict was not eliminated but was handled by open discussion against the background of the needs of the firm as a whole. The 'mechanistic' firms, on the other hand, generally adopted a completely different strategy. Their answer was to set up a new department or section to deal with the new problems so at least partially isolating them and leaving the rest of the work, status and political systems untouched. To deal with the problems at the boundaries of the new department and the old ones liaison posts were created to avoid direct contact. This is in complete contrast to the behaviour of the 'organic' systems where the paramount aim was to find solutions which were practicable from all points of view and also met the needs of the organization as a whole. These involved using a common language comprehensible to all and establishing direct contacts at all levels.

A further insight suggested here is that the bounds set by individuals as to how far instructions, requests, information from others would be

9

acceptable form a continuous measure from one extreme to the other. In 'organic' situations they would be relatively wide, in 'mechanistic' ones relatively narrow. Obviously this will lead to different amounts of communication and inter-relationship between individuals and between departments and is one explanation of differences in organization structure.

Two final conclusions to this section are that 'organic' systems are becoming more and more appropriate and necessary as the general rate of change in society steps up and that to work an 'organic' system the individuals comprising it must be prepared willingly to accept a greater commitment to the organization, less control over their immediate working environments, an ability to cope effectively with and resolve conflicts and, in general, the capacity to live with increased stress and anxiety. This is one of the prices of progress.

Organization and change

It is not too difficult to assume by now that Burns and Stalker are prepared to generalize the problems of their electronics firms into the suggestion that the rate of change in technology and society generally is now such that innovation in organization is essential if we are to survive.

They suggest that the technological changes of, say, the last two centuries have benefited the few at the expense of the many. This surely must be relative rather than absolute. They seem to be on safer ground when they suggest that our ability to handle technological advance has outrun our ability to manage effectively the social changes that have inevitably been brought about by improved technology. In organization the inability is shown most clearly in the difficulties between the scientists required by technology and the generalists required in line management, also in the growth in size of firms, consequent upon technology, which makes any overall view almost impossible of achievement.

The main problem, change, and the main thesis 'organic' organization, have in this case already been stated, at least by implication. Burns and Stalker now turn their attention to a more detailed development of particular aspects.

The first backtracks a little on the assertion just made. It describes in some detail the structure and practices of two firms, one 'mechanistic', the other 'organic'. They conclude each firm showed a structure which was specifically related to its needs, was economical in terms of resources required to meet its aims and each was successful. So although the general pattern must be one of development, change and uncertainty, there are still industries and areas where reasonably stable conditions make 'mechanistic' organization the appropriate pattern. The environment is the independent variable and organization and management processes should be the dependent variable adapted to suit the circumstances. But, however desirable and necessary changes may be to meet changing and new conditions, things do not always work out as they should.

The simple fact that the firm must employ whole people and not just the required set of characteristics is the first difficulty. While their contract of employment, whether written or assumed, and their more or less defined job description commit workers and managers to further the ends of the firm, they cannot help bringing personal aims and purposes in with them. So far as these aims and purposes can be met by furthering the aims of the firm all well and good. When they cannot, the individuals either singly or in groups may seek to meet them by actions which disrupt or even prevent the creation of the required organization structure. One very common form of this behaviour is the informal group, outside the official structure of the firm, committed to furthering the personal aims of its members, which may cut across and frustrate the aims of the firm especially if the latter are for change. (As an aside and away from the trend in Burns and Stalker's thinking at this moment, informal organization is not essentially and necessarily opposed to official purposes. It can be, and often is, used to short-circuit cumbersome official organization structure in order to get the job done. Perhaps the most glaring example of this occurs when a trade union threatens to 'work to rule', i.e. to work strictly according to agreed procedures, formal organizational practices, instead of to its members' informally determined codes of conduct. The chaos which often results shows the importance of 'informal' practices in meeting 'official' objectives.)

Returning to the main argument the informal organization is subdivided into two aspects, the political system and the status structure. These are directly linked with the 'central source of visible power'.[2] This 'source' is the man at the top of the heirarchy under consideration. Saying this does not make him the supreme, let alone the only source of power in the organization. He may influence it positively by instructions, persuasion, guidance and advice, he may influence it negatively by permissive tolerance, by careless ignorance, by withdrawal into an ivory tower. He cannot avoid exerting some influence but that influence, however great, will always be affected by the political structure and the status system below him. It may back and reinforce his influence, it may very severely restrict it with a range of possibilities in between. Again things are seldom all black or white.

Having placed this restriction on the power of the top man by showing the effectiveness of political systems and status in controlling adaptation, Burns and Stalker rather seem to ignore them. The function of the top man is qualitatively different from that of other managers below him. He should set the basic mission of the organization, create a social organization capable of carrying out the mission. With or without others he directs the use of resources, determines tasks and, in particular, decides the rate of change in the conditions of the task. 'In our terms, leadership at the top or direction, involves constant pre-occupation with the technical and commercial parameters of the situation in which the concern has to operate and with the *adjustment* of the internal system to that external situation.'[3] (My italics.) Either the Scottish managing directors failed to understand their function or the political and status systems were too strong for them.

Beyond that, the top man should ensure by precept and example that the working situation is such that it calls forth from each member enough commitment to the organization, effort and involvement, to ensure that its purposes are achieved. These two aspects of the top job correspond to the rate of change in the external environment and the extent of the pursuit of private objectives by members of the organization.

Models of the working organization
Presumably as a support to the logicality of their 'organic' system Burns and Stalker review briefly the changes that have taken place in the models of organization used by other writers. The large complex bureaucracy of Weber (1948) is seen as a logical development from the one boss small-scale business and as appropriate to the conditions and available knowledge of its day. The model of bureaucracy leads on to a split in ideas. Gouldner is the foundation of a rationalistic view of bureaucracy while Selznik is regarded as the supporter of a natural system model. The natural system theory assumes that organizational goals are only some of the needs to which the organizational system is orientated. In particular a natural system strives to reach an equilibrium in which survival is a main objective and in doing so becomes an end in itself at the expense of organizational goals.

More recent approaches, recent that is in 1961, adopted two main lines which lead right into 'organic' systems of organization. In brief one line was that organization was *both* a bureaucracy and, at the same time, a community of people with individual needs to fulfil, and that in practice bureaucracy obtains informal co-operation and spontaneous reciprocity from its members by ignoring its own rules. The other line used dynamic models of organization whose purpose was to adapt to change instead of the earlier static models which regarded change and irregularity as a deviation from theory.

'Organic' systems are Burns and Stalker's version of an organization structure suitable for dealing with rapid change. At the heart of any such system lies the decision-making process.

Decision making

Any organization in a rapidly changing environment must make many decisions which are not simply routine but are what Simon calls 'non-programmed'. To do this successfully it must have developed a managerial system which can cope with considerable uncertainty, which has a common culture and a code of conduct which all, or at least the vast majority, of its managers accept.

Under relatively stable conditions programmed decisions will be vastly in the majority and, as previously noted, the trend in all decision-making in a 'mechanistic' organization will be to reduce or eliminate uncertainty. Decision-making systems under the two different sets of conditions will have quite different characteristics. These have mostly appeared at earlier points in this chapter but a brief gathering together will not be out of place here:

'Mechanistic' characteristics

(i) Specialization of task and hence of problems.

(ii) Concentration on specialized task rather than organizational task.

(iii) Co-ordination of tasks and their relevance achieved by hierarchy.

(iv) Precise definition of each role and its area of responsibility.

(v) Hierarchic (up and down the line) authority, control and communication.

(vi) Other results of hierarchical structure – concentration of knowledge at the top, vertical interaction, control by instructions and decisions from above.

(vii) Insistence on loyalty to the organization and obedience to seniors.

(viii) Prestige and individual importance resting largely on internal knowledge within the organization.

'Organic' characteristics

(i) All specialized knowledge and experience is contributed to the common (organizational) task.

(ii) Individual tasks are realistically related to common task and continually adjusted and re-defined by changes in common task and interaction with other members at any level.

(iii) Responsibility is an individual, personal problem which cannot be pushed up, down or sideways. Individual commitment goes beyond strictly definable limits.

(iv) Authority, control and communication patterns form networks that cut across functions, departments and levels and concentrate on the point where the specialized knowledge and expertise required at the moment may be.

(v) Power and knowledge are not automatically assumed to lie at the top of the hierarchy.

(vi) Communication between individuals tends to take the form of information and advice rather than instructions and decisions.

(vii) The commitment required from the individual is towards the overall task and beliefs rather than loyalty and obedience.

The two lists of characteristics lead on to a third list of corollaries which follow from the differences. Some are obvious but the following may not be quite so self-evident:

(i) An hierarchy will exist in an 'organic' system but it will be based on seniority and not on knowledge and authority both of which will be widely spread and have a relevance related to each situation as it arises.

(ii) The 'organic' system will have a common fund of shared beliefs about the values and goals of the organization to which all subscribe.

(iii) The increased commitment required by and the uncertainty existing in 'organic' systems may create stresses and strains for individuals.

(iv) The specialization and inward looking practices of 'mechanistic' systems are more likely to create internal rivalry and dissension.

(v) 'Organic' systems assume that individuals are prepared to work with anyone else to meet organizational aims irrespective of rank or department and that at all levels people are prepared to ask or to answer the question 'Why?'.

(vi) Both sets of characteristics are statements of the extreme positions and in real life organizations will lie somewhere in between them. For success under stable conditions the organization should be towards the 'mechanistic' end; under rapidly changing conditions towards the 'organic' end. Neither set is in itself right or better; it is only more or less appropriate to a given set of circumstances.

Political systems and status structure

Political systems arise when managers come together in groups to support common aims, to resist change or to defeat a common 'enemy'. In the cases studied by Burns and Stalker all three purposes were involved.

The common aim among line managers was to maintain the relative certainty of the organization and their patterns of behaviour and relationships, the common 'enemy' were the scientists and marketing men with different ideas and different cultures whose generalized function was to bring about change. By forming political systems and so supporting each other line managers were able to forward their own sectional aims while still claiming to be acting in the interests of the firm. Such schemes by altering or creating power blocks have a very considerable bearing on the outcome of decision-making. The status system is similarly important because any threat to it will be resisted by the people concerned.

Professionalism and conflict

It is inevitable that people like scientists with a professional training as engineers, chemists or whatever have within their profession a common culture, a common body of knowledge and, to a large extent, a common language which is more or less incomprehensible to the generalist. When adaptation to change involves bringing into the organization specialists of this kind inevitably it produces problems. The main one is undoubtedly the barrier between the specialist and the line manager. Not only do the specialist and his department create new technical problems which cross the boundaries with production but they present them in a new language and a new setting which challenges everything for which line management has stood. Under 'mechanistic' systems conflict is inevitable and the 'obvious' solution of geographically separating research departments and laboratories from the Works only makes matters worse by making the communication problem much more difficult and the creation of 'longhaired, impractical' stereotypes even more likely. This, in fact, is just what happened in Scotland and made the necessary adaptation impossible. By implication only an 'organic' system can cope effectively with such a situation.

Managerial conduct

The first impression of Part III of the book is that Burns and Stalker are wandering away from their main theme. Rather, perhaps, they are returning to their opening theme of sociology.

One of the main factors determining whether an organization is towards the 'mechanistic' or the 'organic' end of the spectrum is the extent to which the Managing Director can interpret the outside world, adapt the organization to suit the conditions and obtain the required amount of commitment from all members of his team. By his actions and beliefs and their interaction within the total internal situation he sets the framework of the organization and the framework of decision within which managers work. Coupled with this are tendencies for junior managers to ascribe better information to seniors by virtue of their position and for 'organic' systems of organization to revert to 'mechanistic' ones. As an aside this question of reversion is not explicitly justified. From the ideas and concepts put forward in the book there would seem to be two possible arguments for it. The first is that the additional stress for managers under 'organic' systems becomes unbearable and in order to reduce it they create more certainty by reverting. The other would seem to be that political systems and status structures are not destroyed but driven underground by 'organic' systems and that sooner or later they reassert themselves. Neither argument seems entirely satisfactory but this is not the place to follow them through.

Returning to the Managing Director, he is alone at the top of the hierarchy, a unique position which he may try to exploit or escape from. If he exploits his situation with the consent of his followers this results in charismatic leadership and the possibility of rapid and effective change in the firm. Exploitation without consent will isolate him even further, reduce the information fed to him and its accuracy, and produce political systems openly or secretly working against him. Escape from isolation by involving his senior managers in effective joint decision-making is called 'leading' and sets a pattern for similar behaviour right down the organization. The other forms of escape, having an under-cover informer or playing off one group against another can only disrupt the organization.

For the Managing Director the definition, maintenance, and control of standards of admissible conduct should always be a major concern. Under 'organic' systems it must be.

References

(1) Burns, T. and Stalker, G. M. *The Management of Innovation* (London: Tavistock Publications, 1961), p. 1.
(2) Ibid, p. 101.
(3) Ibid, p. 102.

Bibliography

BOOK BY T. BURNS AND G. M. STALKER
The Management of Innovation (London: Tavistock Publications, 1961).

3

P. Blau and W. R. Scott
1962

Formal Organizations by Blau and Scott is a useful book for our purpose in that it brings together a number of ideas from other sources which might not warrant being dealt with separately. In addition it contains conclusions derived from their own research work which Blau and Scott put forward with the qualification, 'Hence [as useful comparative studies of formal organizations were not available] all of our conclusions are inferential and must be considered only suggestions, not confirmed propositions'.[1] There is a stress on the dynamic aspects of formal organizations rather than the static approach of earlier days.

Introduction

The *Introduction* lays down a few standard concepts on which the rest of the book is based. In the broadest sense an organization is a social unit established to attain certain goals. The characteristics of a social organization are structure, shared beliefs, norms or expected standards of behaviour, social interaction, influence, co-operation, social relations and status. The network of social relations is called social structure and the shared beliefs social culture. Once an organization is established, it tends to assume an identity of its own, independent of the people who comprise it.

While a formal organization will have been delibe ratelyset up to achieve certain specified goals, the actions of and interaction between the people comprising it do not all conform to the achievement of those goals. Formal, and supposedly rational, organization and procedures will always be matched by unofficial or informal organizations and standards. The total organization must consist of the combination of, and interaction between formal and informal aspects, and it is impossible to understand it properly without considering the results of this combination and interaction.

Nature and types of formal organization

Like many other writers on organization about this time Blau and Scott use Max Weber as their base. His analysis of formal organization in terms of bureaucracy is described in terms of authority or systems of legitimate social control.

Authority is defined as 'the probability that one actor in a social relationship will be in a position to carry out his own will despite resistance'.[2] This definition does not seem to tie up with the other qualifications laid down, such as the statement that authority is to be distinguished from power, influence and persuasion and that the test of authority is that the person submitting to it shows voluntary compliance and in doing so suspends his own judgement. Other forms of social control, e.g. persuasion, may develop into authority when those over whom they are exercised come to accept them as legitimately equivalent to it.

The traditional form of authority derives from early forms of rights due to heredity and, later, possession of property. Charismatic authority is the result of a dominant and attractive personality or other similar characteristic of the leader which causes other people to follow him. Legal or legitimized authority is the right to command others which is the result of acceptance of established social norms. Such norms are designed to control the conduct of members of an organization in the rational pursuit of its specified goals.

Weber's distinctive characteristics of bureaucracy are given as

   (i) Division of labour, specialization, the use of expertise.

   (ii) Hierarchical structure of clearly defined authority positions.

   (iii) Formally established system of rules and regulations covering members' decisions and behaviour in all anticipated circumstances.

   (iv) Officials (members) of the organization deal with clients, other officials, and employees in an impersonal way.

   (v) Technical qualification as the basis for promotion.

Although Blau and Scott start with these brief extracts from Weber they are far from happy about adopting his conclusion that organization based on his principles would produce maximum rationality in decision-making and maximum administrative efficiency. In fact they see it as a theoretical model of an ideal type in an ideal world and very unlikely ever to be realized in practice. More criticism follows with the suggestion that it is 'an admixture of a conceptual scheme and a set of hypotheses'.[3] The hypotheses should be separated out so that they can be tested for validity in practice. Finally the very aspects that Weber claims as advantages for bureaucracy Blau and Scott see as possible real handicaps and the undeniable fact of informal organization, they suggest, is completely ignored by Weber.

The second model put forward is Simon's (1958) version of the organization as a structure primarily designed to ensure rational decision-making. Once again the informal organization is missing from the model. So it seems is Simon's concept of *bounded* rationality (*see* Chapter 19).

A hint of a new direction in thinking is given by using Parsons (1960) as their third model. According to this model every social system must solve four problems simultaneously:

(i) Adapting to the demands of the environment in which it exists and actively transforming the external situation.
(ii) Defining its own objectives and mobilizing the resources needed to carry them out.
(iii) Maintaining adequate integration of its internal relationships.
(iv) Maintaining its own motivational and cultural patterns over periods of time.

In addition to these requirements the organization must have technical, managerial and institutional hierarchies. The hints here are towards an open-ended system theory in which an organization exists in, reacts to and interacts with a surrounding environment at many points.

The social structure of workgroups

The emphasis on the workgroup as an important aspect of organization is due to systematic research following on from the Human Relations School of the 1930s, 40s and early 50s. Blau and Scott consider that the School missed the real point by treating the group as if it had the same attributes as the individual. The group is more than the sum of a number of individuals.

The line of approach is the process of interaction within the group and between the group and its environment, the group being taken to mean the informal, spontaneous one which may, and often does, cut across the formal groups of organization. The main aim of the informal group is given as protecting the interests of the group as a whole against any action by management or other groups which is seen by the group as threatening it. Cohesion or solidarity within the group provides social support to its members and makes any stress resulting from actions undesired by management more tolerable. It may also increase some forms of worker satisfaction and reduce labour turnover and absenteeism. So far as it does, it will be due to loyalty towards workmates rather than towards the firm. Whether or not cohesion within the group has any effect on productivity depends on the aims and norms of the group. If these are to support organizational objectives all well and good. If they run counter to or are neutral towards organizational objectives at best they will have no effect, at worst they will disrupt or even stop production altogether.

The question of status for the individual within the informal group may derive from individual power or prestige. These may be based on seniority, knowledge, expertise, or from popularity arising from more personal attributes. High status within the group makes the individual more effective in determining aims and conduct for the group. Low status is usually accorded to those who resist the group pressures to conform to its norms and objectives. But as not all norms and objectives will have equal importance to the group the pressure to conform will be greater in the case of those that are higher up the group's scale of preferences.

Group cohesion is given as relating to the strength of the network of social bonds that hold the group together. Group solidarity relates to the degree of mutual support and collective strength within the group in relation to the environment surrounding the group. Usually homogeneous groups of generally similar individuals will possess greater solidarity than heterogeneous ones. But heterogeneous ones can also show solidarity (especially in the face of a perceived threat from outside).

The effective power and solidarity of a group in relation to its environment will depend, among other things, on the importance of its official function in achieving the organization's objectives. The greater the importance the greater its power.

While it may not be obvious from that which has been said above, Blau and Scott give their opinion that the findings of research work on informal groups are often complex and contradictory. But, as they said right at the beginning, organization can only be realistically considered as the combination of formal organization and informal organization. The essential point is the interaction of the two. The tendency has been to consider them separately.

Processes of communication
Communication is, of course, a universal activity in one form or another between people at all times in their lives with the exception of a few religious orders and hermits. Within an organization it is formalized as social interaction and is measured by its total amount, its frequency, who initiates it, the degree of reciprocity and its direction, upwards, downwards or sideways, among the members. Based on experimental work it is suggested that communication has three aspects – error correction, social support, and competition – but this list is obviously far from complete. Error correction arises from the assumptions that it is always easy to see and to tell others about their mistakes and that they will accept the criticism. Social support aspects provide approval for ideas and allay anxieties. The competitive aspects of communication which, in effect,

come to individual striving for status and recognition, can further organizational aims or retard them. It is suggested that co-operation is a more powerful aid in achieving desired results.

Communication which is between different levels tends to reduce the impact of all three aspects. It is difficult to correct the errors of superiors or to compete for status from a lower level in the hierarchy. But a reduction in the status difference between levels, usually achieved by more democratic forms of leadership, should improve communication especially if the leader genuinely shows that he is willing and wants to listen. On the other hand one piece of research is quoted as showing that co-ordination is improved if the free flow of ideas from any and every source is reduced. So emphasis on formal status is better if co-ordination of effort is the priority but if correct solutions are required, the freer the communication channels the better.

Lateral communication between equals has been shown to reduce anxiety, improve self-confidence and lead to better decision-making. However, if such lateral communication among peers is one-sided, e.g. A always goes to B for help while B seldom, if ever, goes to A, then it will produce patterns of informal status and dependency. If it is reciprocal, A to B and B to A, it has no harmful side effects.

All this leads to a paradox in terms of co-ordination and effective operation. Free-flowing communication is necessary for the best solutions to problems and, therefore, the most effective operation. But co-ordination is also needed for effective operation and this involves hierarchy and status differentials. These tend to restrict the necessary flow of communication especially when status differentials are high and easily visible. Blau and Scott regard this as an unavoidable dilemma in the dynamic process of operating in an organization.

The role of the supervisor

The legal authority of a superior over his subordinates is an implied condition of the contract of employment. Ultimately, however, its usefulness for attaining organizational ends is limited by the degree of acceptance by the subordinate, who may leave the employment, go on strike, or work as far below the optimum standard as he or his group feels that he can get away with. Authority by itself is recognized as being insufficient to ensure efficiency and the emphasis has shifted to leadership and motivation.

Two styles of supervision are given as:

   (i) Domination by the assertion of power through the use or threat of punishment.

   (ii) Putting subordinates under obligation to conform because the supervisor provides help, information, support, and backing for his subordinates against outside threats.

But both domination and obligation when related to group behaviour, as against individual behaviour, depend on the group accepting conformity to the supervisor's commands or wishes as a norm in its code of conduct and enforcing it on its own members. The extent of this acceptance is limited by the values enshrined in the legal contract, the cultural ideologies, the restraints (or permissiveness) of the social environment, and the respect and loyalty earned by the supervisor. Blau and Scott here make the rather curious distinction of defining the supervisor's authority which rests on legal position as 'formal' and that which rests on respect, loyalty, and group values as 'informal'.

Authoritarian supervision relies mainly on close, detailed supervision of subordinates, a strict non-personal approach, a rigid maintenance of procedures, and more orders being given. It can and sometimes does produce high output but this may not be maintained over long periods (cf. Likert Chapter 15). It may produce such side effects as absenteeism and high labour turnover. On the other hand it may lower worker satisfaction and reduce output down to the minimum acceptable level, or even below it, as when a strike ensues.

'Human relations' type supervision may involve the supervisor in too close personal relationships with his subordinates so that he becomes indulgent and unable to enforce standards. Emotional detachment and some social distance are considered essential if the supervisor is to maintain the balance between that which management requires from him and his obligation to look after the interests of the group.

The appropriate form of supervision is a function of the total circumstances of group and environment. There is no one right and best way for all cases. Three things are essential, however, in all supervision. The supervisor must have some degree of independence from his superior, his actions must be and be seen to be reasonably consistent, and his approach must accord with his character. The phoney supervisor is soon recognized, usually with disastrous consequences.

Managerial control

It is perhaps somewhat typical of the early 1960s that the ideas under this heading seem to be rather confused and even contradictory. As they will be either developed or dropped as we work our way through the decade they will only be briefly mentioned at this stage.

Where a superior controls many subordinates, in other words has a wide span of control, supervision will tend to be less close and the independence of subordinates that much greater. Other aspects which affect the amount of checking on the performance of subordinates are the time span of decision at the level concerned, the position in the hierarchy, and the physical proximity of superior and subordinates.

The use of specialist staff as experts in particular fields of the manager's work is still the cause of conflict and really satisfactory ways of incorporating them into the management structure have still to be found. Conflicts between line managers themselves also occur. If they derive from self-interest whether personal or departmental they will almost certainly be harmful to the organization as a whole. But if they arise through genuine differences of opinion on what is best for the organization they will be helpful provided adequate, satisfactory methods for resolving conflicts exist.

Impersonal control, not in Weber's sense of non-personal impartiality, but in the sense of built-in mechanisms and procedures may obtain conformity without the inter-personal friction involved in having one person *over* another. Examples given are the assembly line, direct reporting of results to the person responsible for them and not to his superior, and automation.

The idea of creating industrial democracy by involving workers in management decisions is challenged on the grounds that it is often only pseudo-democracy.

Organizational dynamics

It is appropriate that Blau and Scott should conclude their book with some thoughts on organization and change, as the change from a static to a dynamic theory of organization is probably the 'great divide' between the 1950s and before and the 1960s and after. On the question of change they distinguish between adjustment to changed circumstances, which is self-sufficient when made, and dilemma, where any choice between alternatives only satisfies some aspects and leaves others unsatisfied or raises new problems to create new dilemmas. Formal organizations and the study of them are faced with dilemmas.

The growth of industry and commerce has led to the greater differentiation of business organization and structure away from other forms of structure in society. Business organization has become a relatively autonomous sub-system of society with principles of organization peculiar to itself. The growth within a business organization is, however, seldom evenly distributed among all its parts and, in addition, its tendency has always been towards greater sub-division and complexity. This growth and increased complexity have involved a more than proportionate increase in administrative/managerial staff. Blau and Scott think this growth in staffing has not been overdone and that it is due to changes in the form of organization and to increased complexity. There are, however, dangers in increased bureaucracy and the changing of means into ends in themselves.

Whether the organization moves forward and outward or turns inward on itself depends on its relationship with its own particular environment. If this is favourable, the organization will use its present aims as stepping stones to new and wider ones. If it is hostile, the organization will tend towards regressive, inward-looking behaviour.

Bureaucratic forms of organization, although based on rules and regulations designed to cover all eventualities, cannot possibly foresee all possible future circumstances. There will therefore always be some area of operations where informal practices will not only arise but are essential if the organization is going to function. At a later date these may be formalized into new rules.

Formal organizations are always involved in three dilemmas, the problem of an hierarchy strong enough to achieve co-ordination without stifling adequate communication, the resolution of the conflict between line authority and staff expertise, and having adequate planning without stifling initiative.

Change, Blau and Scott conclude, will always be with us. Solving one problem may produce learning on how better to solve the next but it will not prevent the next arising. Conflict of interests between groups and between individuals will always exist and lead to change.

Within the organization people come and go and there is a proverb about 'new brooms'. Finally, they suggest, conflict between democratic freedom and effective industrial performance will not be resolved without further changes in the forms and practices in organization.

References

(1) Blau, P. and Scott, W. R. *Formal Organizations* (London: Routledge and Keegan Paul, 1963), p. 223.

(2) Ibid, p. 27. [Quoted from *The Theory of Social and Economic Organization* Henderson, A. M. and Parsons, T. (trans.) and Parsons, T. (ed.) (Glencoe, Ill: Free Press and Falcon's Wing Press, 1947), p. 152.]

(3) Ibid, p. 33.

Bibliography

BOOK BY P. BLAU AND W. R. SCOTT
Formal Organizations (London: Routledge and Kegan Paul, 1963).

4

A. Etzioni
1964

The struggle that was emerging in the 1960s to solve the problem created by the two schools of management thought is very clearly shown in *Modern Organizations*. Etzioni goes directly to the core of the problem with the title of his first chapter – 'Rationality and Happiness. The Organization Dilemma'.

A number of broad generalizations set the scene. In Western industrial society the emphasis is on the universal use of organization structures and on the moral values of rationality, effectiveness and efficiency. The organization is the most rational and efficient social grouping known, bringing together, as it does, the wide range of human attributes and skills and the other non-human resources required, money, machines, buildings, etc. At the same time the organization 'continually evaluates how well it is performing and tries to adjust itself accordingly in order to achieve its goals'.[1] Organizations, it is claimed, are capable of meeting the needs of society and individuals more efficiently than smaller social groupings. But, Etzioni admits that the increased efficiency achieved by size and rationality has involved social and human costs. The organization is tending to become the master rather than the servant of the individual and society. As it does so, frustration and alienation from the organization become typical attitudes.

However, the picture is not as black as it seems. These 'hidden' costs of frustration, alienation and unhappiness are being recognized as a brake on efficiency, and modern industry generally realizes that human beings are its main source of energy so the aim is to reduce these unwanted side effects and hidden costs and so improve efficiency still further. The fundamental problem is to 'construct human groupings that are as rational as possible and at the same time produce a minimum of undesirable effects and a maximum of satisfaction'.[2] The precise wording of this quotation is particularly interesting because of the form it gives to the solution of the problem of the two approaches to management. The grouping is to be as rational (efficient) as possible but undesirable effects and satisfaction

25

are to be minimized and maximized respectively. As these are all to be achieved simultaneously it would seem that efficiency is the last in the queue.

Last but not least in these introductory generalizations comes Etzioni's definition of organization which he adopts from Parsons. 'Organizations are social units (or human groupings) deliberately constructed and re-constructed to seek specific "goals".'[3] Its characteristics are given as division of labour, power structures, communication channels, and patterns of responsibility. All these are deliberately planned with the purpose of achieving organizational goals; direction, control and review by power centres; and changes in membership over time. These are, of course, the usual characteristics of formal organizations spelt out a little more explicitly than is sometimes the case. But the informal aspects of organization are not specifically mentioned and the inclusion of the phrase 'deliberately planned' must rule them out.

The organizational goal

Organizational goals are states of affairs to be realized in the future and guidelines for managerial and operational activity. Actually Etzioni uses the phrase 'organizational activity' which seems to separate him immediately from the Classical view of organization as a static framework. It is a dynamic, ongoing process striving for a goal which, once reached, ceases to be a goal and becomes a past achievement. In addition goals are a source of justification for actions and standards by which to assess effectiveness and efficiency.

A goal is a 'guiding image' which has a sociological effect on organizational action and reaction. This immediately raises the very difficult problem of whose 'image'. In the days of the one-man business the answer was easy – the boss's. Etzioni rules out all individuals and, for that matter, all single groups, including top management. A goal or a series of goals is something which the 'organization as a collectivity'[4] is trying to bring about. It may take form through consultation, through conflict, sometimes by imposition by a power group of its will over the rest. To a greater or a less extent all members and groups are assumed to have at least a minimal influence on its formation or modification. This neatly and accurately gets round the need to assume that the organization must have a personality of its own to make it possible to separate organizational goals from personal ones. It is on possibly dangerous ground in assuming such a wide spread of influence. A realistic reminder is included that things are not always as they seem and that the way resources are deployed may be a better guide to the actual goals being aimed at than the 'official' statements of what the goals are, and also that personal and sub-unit goals may differ from and conflict with organizational goals.

There would seem to be some back-tracking from the rather ideal statement of universal influence in the suggestion that 'virtually all organizations have a formal, explicitly recognized organ for setting initial goals and their amendment'.[5] There is also a reservation that in practice goals may be the result of power politics between groups or individuals, or may be conditioned by the external values of society relating to appropriate behaviour. As an afterthought environmental forces are given an important role in determining organizational objectives. This is perhaps an early pointer to the systems analysis of a later date, although in its context it is applied to legislation and trade unions that impose limits on freedom.

Efficiency and effectiveness are differentiated in the usual way, effectiveness being the degree of attainment of objectives and efficiency the measure of the resources used. This measure is cost and specifically includes long-term as well as short-run items. Rationality in organizations puts extra emphasis on efficiency but because costs can only be measured for certain items, usually short-term ones, attention often becomes concentrated on these at the expense of other non-measurable but ultimately more important items. This and the fact that many so-called accurate costs are, in fact, very far from accurate and may depend on assumptions that can be challenged mean that apparent short-term rationality may, in the long run, be anything but rational.

Etzioni has by no means finished with goals yet. The displacement of goals is even more dangerous. This can happen in various ways. Ends can become means, sectional and individual goals can take precedence over organizational ones, empire building can distort real aims and internal problems of organization can disrupt achievement. When its goal is attained the organization must find a new one or disintegrate. A new goal may also be looked for if the current one is not being successfully met.

Attention now turns specifically to multi-purpose organizations, those having more than one goal. On the one hand multi-purpose organizations may be more efficient and effective in reaching each and all of their goals because the greater variety attracts higher quality members and gives them more scope. But on the other hand multiple goals may compete for scarce resources, create problems of priorities and create stresses and strains among members.

At this point Atzioni seems to break loose. So far, he says, he has only given views which are widely held and which do not go far enough. There was a hint in the suggestion that goals were ideals. He now argues that measuring achievement against goals produces social criticism rather than scientific study and, in any case, it has little real significance as few organizations really achieve their goals and a low level of achievement is the more usual state of affairs. This point of view he calls the 'goal model' of an organization.

His alternative is the 'system model' which is based on the comparison of one organization with another in terms of the effective use of its resources. 'System models' are of two kinds – survival models and effectiveness models. The survival model only considers whether the basic requirements of the organization are being met while the effectiveness model goes further, evaluates change in the organization over time and relates this to its ability to meet goals as compared with its earlier states or with other organizations. This is really moving into the dynamic sphere.

Classical theory

It seems that few books of about this time would have been complete without an attack on Classical theories. Etzioni adds little that is new except to bring into the argument what he calls the Neo-Classical School of Simon, Smithburg and Thompson. These gentlemen are largely concerned with formal organization but they do go beyond this by discussing the means by which values, goals and sub-goals can be implemented.

A brief discussion of the hoary problem of centralization versus decentralization suggests that this is really a question of whether decisions should be taken at a higher or lower level, shows the factors involved and suggests ways of achieving either. Both, it seems, have the usual advantages and disadvantages.

Decision theory also comes into the Neo-Classical School as being based on formal organization. Etzioni regards it as an important new addition to theory although at the time of writing (1964) it was 'at present largely a non-organizational theory that deals with decisions made by individuals'.[6]

Simon's concept of division of labour on decision-making and March and Simon's ideas on search behaviour and satisficing are mentioned, but Etzioni maintains that, although there is a great distance between Taylor and Simon, both focus on formal organization and so are, perhaps, the two extreme ends of Classical theory.

From Human Relations to the Structuralists

The Human Relations approach is a reaction to the formalism and lack of humanity of the Classical School. The conclusion reached is that this new approach has been supported by a considerable body of research findings, has been widely publicized and has had considerable influence in modifying the management practices of America and some other countries.

While Human Relations and the Classical School are diametrically opposed in method of approach both assumed that greater efficiency and greater happiness were compatible. Progress beyond the ideas of both of them has been achieved by taking one concept from each and combining these with a flat contradiction of another.

Together these give the Structuralist Approach which moves forward to greater realism and validity by assuming that:

(i) Alienation and conflict in organizations are inevitable, sometimes desirable.

(ii) They can produce useful results for the organization.

(iii) There is a real relationship between the formal organization and the informal one.

(iv) The true nature of organization is the combination and inter-action of both.

While these are the main assumptions of the Structuralists they need some expansion. An organization is a large, complex social unit consisting of many sub-groups that interact and have some interests in common and others that are incompatible. In consequence the sub-groups co-operate in some spheres and compete in others. Two major groups, each of which may consist of some or many sub-groups, are management and workers. Management's aim is to get the workers to work up to a standard which management regards as optimum or, at least, as satisfactory. Its efforts to do this alienate the workers because, while work may be made more pleasant it cannot be made 'satisfying in any absolute sense'.[7] (Author's comment: This view of work put as baldly as this certainly has some general validity but it is not by any means universal. Etzioni states that two sources from which the Structuralists derive their ideas are Max Weber and Karl Marx so the parentage of this view of work is, presumably, obvious.) Marx's influence can also be seen in the statement that work is a power struggle between groups with some interests in common and some incompatible ones.

Conflict is assumed to have important social and organizational functions. Where genuine differences of belief, opinion and interests are brought out into the open and faced their resolution can produce an organization that is better adapted to its environment. If they are not brought out and solved they will lead to further alienation and psychological withdrawal.

Finally the Structuralists claim that the informal group, the sacred cow of Human Relations, is by no means as common as is suggested and should not be studied in isolation. Their future is the study of the total organization, the interaction of the organization and its environment, the study of simultaneous membership of multiple groups, and the extension of organization theory into non-industrial units.

Bureaucracies, structure and legitimation

After a very brief description of Weber's main points about bureaucracy Etzioni says that Weber introduces 'a whole new dimension to the study of organizational discipline'.[8] This new dimension is that power is the ability to induce others to accept orders, legitimation of power rests in its acceptance by those over whom it is exercized because it matches their own values, and authority is the operational link between power and acceptance.

The acceptance of authority within the bureaucratic organization depends on the reliance upon rules, competence, the hierarchy and impersonality. Management at all levels below the top owes its right to power to a scrupulous following of bureaucratic values, to being 'bureaucrats'. But the top man must not be a bureaucrat bound by the rules for he is the one man who must create and, when necessary, amend the rules.

Charismatic leadership based on personality, knowledge, or experience can also be acceptable as well as leadership based on democracy. It is possible for an organization to move from working under one style to the other given time for the many adjustments needed.

Organizational control and leadership

This and the next two sections are claimed to be the application of the Structuralist approach to give insight into the strains and stresses within organizations and the means used to alleviate them.

The first problem is that of managerial control. Strain arises here because the aims of management (e.g. high productivity, low waste, low costs, high profits) conflict with the aims of the worker (e.g. high wages, lack of pressure from above, minimum involvement). Organizations having specific purposes to serve are planned, structural, and complex self-reviewing bodies which make informal control inadequate and reliance on identity of interests impossible. Deliberate means of control therefore have to be set up by management and these are based on the distribution of rewards and sanctions according to performance. This right of distributing rewards and sanctions puts power into the hands of managers. Power may be coercive, the use or threat of physical force, utilitarian, the use of material rewards, chiefly money wages, or normative-social, the use of symbols, prestige, esteem, love and acceptance. Alienation is said to be at its greatest with coercive power and to diminish as power moves towards normative-social while commitment to the organization goes in the opposite direction. The form of power used seems to vary, becoming more normative-social in the higher ranks of the hierarchy. The response to power depends not only on the form used but also on the social and cultural personalities of the people involved. Somewhat curiously Etzioni omits any reference to the response depending on the expectations and norms of the people over whom power is exercized.

The claim is made at this point that organizations which differ in the form of control used and in the level of alienation or commitment also differ significantly in organization structure.

Leadership and control

Power to control others may rest on the specific position held in an organization, on personality, or on personality plus position. Formal leaders come under the first or third categories, informal leaders can only rely on personality but personality here must presumably be taken to include such things as knowledge, experience, expertise, informal status, and so on.

Control broadly has to be exercized in two areas. The first covers instrumental activities and relates to the input and allocation of resources. The second covers those areas called expressive activities and relates to inter-personal relations, acceptance of and adherence to norms. Different leaders may control different areas or aspects. In fact Etzioni goes so far as to suggest that official control (the hierarchy) is concerned with the instrumental control of production and efficiency and is not normally concerned with the norms and patterns of relationship set up by workers and informal leaders unless these interfere with the work and efficiency. The degree of alienation or of commitment is given as a vital element in determining the pattern of leadership despite the fact that this seems to be a circular argument. In analysing types of leadership a short time ago the type was suggested as the determinant of the degree of alienation. It would be better to describe them as mutually interacting with some bias towards the style and leadership having the more primary and greater influence. Where the norms of the workgroups and those of the official leadership are closer together the social relationships between them are likely to be better.

Organizational control and other correlates

While the questions of leadership and norms may usually take pride of place in considering control there are other factors which may have a vital influence on it.

The selection of new members to join the organization or indeed of existing ones to be removed altogether or to be transferred into other parts of the organization can, if done effectively, have a considerable influence on the amount of control required. Etzioni goes so far as to say that a large proportion of deviant acts are produced by a relatively small proportion of members. So the selection of the right person for the job can potentially considerably reduce the amount of control and therefore of resources, of time, and of effort needed.

Another factor is called 'socialization'. This seems to be a blanket word for indoctrination and training and involves adapting and altering the members' personal qualities 'to make them similar to those required for satisfactory performance of organizational roles'.[9] The nearer socialization can bring the individual to matching the precise needs of the organization the fewer resources will be required for the control activities. The ethical question of the right of the organization to modify and mould people in this way to get what, in the ultimate, is a conditioned response is not mentioned.

The pervasiveness of norms and their acceptance are further factors in control requirements. It seems here that only the official norms of the hierarchy are under consideration as a wide scope and widespread acceptance of norms are shown as leading to a low level of official control being required.

While Etzioni admits that the study of control has a long way to go he seems to put forward one tentative hypothesis which could have very interesting consequences. It is that in the modern (Western) world people move very easily out of one social unit into another, e.g. work and home or community activities. These areas are very different in their scope and the demands they make on the individual. The work situation is said to be rational and exacting while the non-work situations are supposedly non-rational and relaxing. The individual will be able to withstand tensions at work because he can release them in non-work activity. Although the difference in the situations may be tenable as a probable assumption, the ease of carry-over may be more debatable and seems to need considerable research to justify the conclusion.

Administrative and professional authority

Restated in classical theory terms this is the Line-Staff conflict and a problem which in those terms has never been satisfactorily resolved provided Lord Wilfred Brown[10] is excluded from the Classical School. Etzioni considers that all the problems he has raised so far are due to the failure to match personalities and personal aims with organizational requirements and goals. Realistically he assumes that this matching, while it could be improved, will always remain incomplete and therefore a problem. Beyond this, however, there is a further range of problems which arise from the differences in outlook, background, training and experience of line managers responsible for operations and specialists concerned in much greater detail with one specialized aspect of operations. The necessary use of both these types in the hierarchies of complex organizations makes conflict inevitable.

Authority based on position in the hierarchy creates the 'power of position' which exercizes control over lower ranks. Authority based on professional knowledge and expertise creates the 'power of knowledge'. This may have no direct control over anybody except a relatively few specialists in the same field and even there the power is actually one of 'position' in a frequently small branch of the hierarchy.

In theory, if not always in practice, the 'power of position' can be transferred from one person to another by the process of promotion or transfer. The 'power of knowledge' is based on individual, personal knowledge and cannot be transferred. The two tend to work with different bases for their conduct. The line manager's base is compatibility with organization rules and regulations and the direct or indirect approval of his superior. For the professional specialist the base for conduct is the correctness of the action as shown by the knowledge available within his profession. The one works to internal, organizational rules, the other to outside, professional rules. The problem, of course, is to generate needed specialist knowledge and to use it in the organization without destroying the latter's structure.

Having stated the problem Etzioni does nothing to provide new solutions. He stresses that the goals of business are consistent with administrative (line) orientations while the goals of the specialist usually conflict with them. Traditional line and staff type organization with the staff advising the line management and the latter retaining the right of veto, or staff having limited authority over carefully defined, limited areas or aspects of operations are both Classical solutions and are something of an anti-climax to a book which professes to reject most of Classicism.

Organization and the social environment
With one chapter left Etzioni begins to flirt gently with ideas which precede Systems theory. He suggests as three burning questions of 1964:
  (i) Under what social conditions do modern organizations rise and develop?
  (ii) What is society's role in regulating relations between them?
  (iii) How will the relations between society and organizations change in the future?

In reply to the first he maintains that differentiation between individuals and between functions are essential pre-requisites of developing social institutions devoted to specialized functions. These are organizations and are artificial social units, with norms and structures designed to fit their specific goals. In the more complex societies a second order of complex institutions has arisen to control the first order. The rationality of modern society has put the stress on the practical, on efficiency, and on the long-term view.

Within this world modern man is different from earlier pre-industrial man. The claim is that he has developed a tolerance for the stratification of his life, for moving easily from one social structure to another, for frustration, an ability to defer immediate for future gratification, and an orientation towards achievement. The description may be somewhat overstated at some points and the applicability of any aspect to a particular individual may vary, but there must be a basic truth in it for present-day industrial society to exist.

The book concludes with the suggestion of three patterns of trends under the main different sociological areas of the world. In the less-developed areas the trend is towards greater differentiation, towards many and deep conflicts with tradition, towards a greater variety and number of encompassing organizations. In totalitarian societies extreme centralization has been tried and is being replaced by a trend towards decentralization, autonomy and liberalization. In modern (so-called) democratic, industrial societies the move is towards more and wider central controls to restrict the freedoms of the last two centuries. In industry itself the emphasis is shifting from organizational demands to greater stress on personal and social values.

References
(1) Etzioni, A. *Modern Organizations* (Englewood Cliffs N.J.: Prentice Hall, 1964), p. 1.
(2) Ibid, p. 2.
(3) Parsons, T. *Structure and Process in Modern Societies* (New York: Free Press, 1960), p. 17.
(4) Etzioni, A. op. cit., p. 6.
(5) Ibid, p. 7.
(6) Ibid, pp. 29–30.
(7) Ibid, p. 42.
(8) Ibid, p. 51.
(9) Ibid, p. 70.
(10) Brown, W. *Exploration in Management* (London: Heinemann, 1960).

Bibliography
BOOK BY A. ETZIONI
Modern Organizations (New Jersey: Prentice Hall, 1964).

5

E. J. Miller and A. K. Rice
1967

As a nation that produced so many of the great inventions of the world from Watt's earliest steam engine through the Industrial Revolution to Whittle's jet engine and beyond, Britain may be forgiven for taking pride in being a 'practical' nation and one which has always managed to get there by compromise and 'muddling through'. It must have been a British manager who invented the sentence, 'That's all right in theory but . . .' And there is little doubt that British contributions to management theory are relatively few.

One of the few sources has been the Tavistock Institute for Human Relations. Men such as Emery, Trist, Rice and Miller, to name the four best known, have undoubtedly achieved a world reputation for the work that they did in the 1950s and 60s. Long-wall coal mining and the Ahmedabad cotton mills are household words in current management thought. But it is in keeping with the ideas of the previous paragraph that they were primarily practical attempts to solve practical problems and any advance in theory was a by-product.

The first real attempt to draw some of the work done by members of the Institute together and to 'develop a theory of organization that reconciles tasks, human activities and organization within one general framework'[1] is Miller and Rice's *Systems of Organization*. Earlier work by Tavistock researchers had thrown up concepts such as primary tasks, socio-technical systems, human needs as constraints on performance, organization as a tool for task performance, and a simple open-systems approach. Miller and Rice drew on these concepts, backed by empirical research to test them, to write *Systems of Organization*. While the book must be included, it does appear to present major problems. The worst is a question of judgement as to how much to include and how much to leave out. While this must be a personal opinion it does seem that at times the logic behind the book is faulty and even contradictory. To include the contradictions would be confusing, to leave them out would give only a partial and personal view of Miller and Rice's thesis. It is a difficult decision but, on balance, it seems better to leave them out. Long descriptions of field tests and experiments are also omitted.

The Preface to the book is much longer than usual and contains so many fundamental ideas that it must be included to set the scene. The first one that underlies all their thinking is that personal and group needs are significant constraints on task performance and, presumably, on the attainment of organizational objectives. Where, as in the changeover to long-wall mining methods, human needs become sufficiently frustrated then task-performance suffers. They quote the psycho-sociologists of the early 1960s as 'concerned with . . . the need to modify "task-centred" organizations in the interests of human need'.[2] They go on to suggest themselves that the assumption that 'the "right" organization would satisfy both task and social needs'[3] when applied in practice inevitably led to a compromise on one or both aspects. But when real attempts were made to match task and human needs, as at Ahmedabad and in British coal-mining, then it had proved possible to obtain a better match with greater human satisfaction and greater productivity.

A major difficulty in getting this reconciliation is taken from Schein's ideas (1965). It is that the organization required to carry out the tasks of operation requires only a part of the human being's total resources, so co-ordination is of tasks not of people. From the narrow point of view of task performance any one of a number of people having the specific aptitudes required for the task will do equally well. But as each will have other differing characteristics from the point of view of overall organizational performance it may matter a great deal which one is employed.

This question of employing only part of a whole human being while trying to fit the whole person into organization theory led to the concepts of formal and informal organizations as meeting organizational and human needs respectively. Miller and Rice speculate that perhaps this split was of less importance when change took place more slowly and the integration of task and human needs had sufficient time to keep up. Recently, as the rate of change of technology has increased, organization in all its aspects, industrial, social, and political, has been unable to keep pace. However one might question this idyllic view of the past there can be no doubt about the assessment of the present. Also with the earlier hint about open-systems approach the singling out of technology as the dominant force belies the complex interaction of many variables in the system.

This theme of the duality of organization – task needs and human needs – is developed a stage further to the general proposition that all enterprises need three parallel forms of organization – one to control task performance, a second to ensure the commitment of its members to the objectives of the enterprise, and a third to control the relations between the task and the 'sentient' systems. A 'sentient' system means a system which demands and receives loyalty from its members and is here taken to mean the informal organization, although logically it could also be the formal system. Miller and Rice appear to take it for granted that human needs conflict with organizational ones. But they do, in fact, admit that there can be the *special case* where task and sentient boundaries or systems coincide.

These two concepts of task systems and groups on the one hand and sentient systems and groups on the other are central to much of what follows. 'An effective sentient system relates the members of an enterprise to each other *and* to the enterprise in ways that are relevant to the skills and experience required for task performance.'[4] Rather curiously 'task performance' is not qualified but there does seem to be an implication that effective performance is meant.

Studies by Tavistock members are said to have shown that the concepts of Classical theory with its base in relative stability were inadequate to deal with rapid technical, social, and economic change. A new 'culture' is needed in which continuous change in organization, in roles, in group membership can become a steady state.

Finally research which had crossed the recognized boundaries in formal organization and those between the organization and its environment had shown that the idea of boundary regulation was an essential aspect of management control.

These, then, are the central ideas around which Miller and Rice formulate their theory of Systems of Organization.

Systems of activity and their boundaries

An enterprise consists of a series of activities by which the processes of input, throughput and output are carried out. Throughput is the process of transforming the resources which are brought into the enterprise as inputs (materials, plant, people, money, etc.) into the commodities or services which are exported (sold) back to the environment as outputs of the system. Activities that directly affect the output such as manufacturing or transport are classified as operating. Maintenance activities supply resources to the operating activities and maintain and service them. Regulatory activities are concerned with the direction, co-ordination and control of the other two. Activities of all kinds build up into systems and sub-systems which are to some extent self-contained, have boundaries and therefore relate to other sub-systems and systems by transactions across boundaries. These need controlling in the interests of the enterprise as a whole or some major part of it.

A system is described as a complex of activities that is required to convert an input into an output. A task-system is the complex of activities together with the human and physical resources needed to perform the activities. The term system implies a complex which has some in-built form of unity which separates and differentiates it from other systems and provides it with a boundary which separates it from its environment. But at the same time this separation of systems and sub-systems involves some degree, large or small, of interdependence between them.

Very small, undifferentiated systems may have no internal boundaries. The larger and more complex the system becomes the more it will be differentiated into the three major activities of operating, maintenance, and regulatory, the more each one will be further differentiated into sub-systems, sub-sub-systems and so on, and the more each one will break down into its own internal system of input, throughput and output.

For the system as a whole its environment is the whole or some part of the world outside. For the sub-systems or sub-units the environment includes the other sub-systems which make up the next higher system or sub-system and, at one or more removes, the world outside.

The difference between a system and an aggregate of activities is that the former is regulated with some specific common purpose or purposes in mind. To some extent all systems are self-regulating but this may be very limited and not directed towards the system's real objectives. Regulation to be effective must be purposeful. (This is not to say that purposeful, automatic self-regulation cannot be built into a system.) There are two types of regulating activity. One is monitoring which occurs within a system or sub-system and is used to check performance. The other is boundary-regulation which relates a system or sub-system to its environment by controlling the boundary input and output transactions. Boundary-regulation is external to the system or sub-systems being regulated and requires a definite break or discontinuity of activity to give an area in which it can operate. It can be differentiated into an hierarchy of levels arrived at either by division and sub-division as one goes down from the complete system or by building up from the simplest undifferentiated sub-unit to combinations of such units into a higher order of sub-unit which has a boundary, then combining a number of these sub-units into a sub-unit or unit of the next higher order and so on until the complete system becomes the unit. At each higher level a boundary exists involving decisions of a higher and still higher level of abstraction.

Individuals, groups and their boundaries
The individual is an essential form of resource without which the organization could neither exist nor function. He or she is a person having

many of the characteristics of an 'open' system interacting with the environment. The tendency among individuals to interact by forming groups is vital because of the many different forms of activity which groups can undertake which may favour, be neutral to or antagonistic to the organization.

Miller and Rice suggest, but do not seem to carry through, the idea that theories of systems and of human behaviour are analogous and that both are needed in a complete theory of organization.

The view of the individual put forward here is a much more optimistic one than, say, that of Argyris. Personality is derived from and the result of biological inheritance and the sum of experience to date acquired in the family, at school, at work and from other interactions with the society in which the individual lives. Few would disagree so far, but it is perhaps dubious whether all would agree that through these experiences individuals 'can work out their own development'[5] or that 'Through these areas of conduct [within the family, society and at work] they satisfy their physiological and psychological needs and defend themselves against the stresses and strains of having to come to terms with the realities of their environment'.[6] From this they grow to maturity.

Behaviour of the individual is affected by expectations about the outside world, the hopes and fears which they produce, 'inborn influences' [*sic*], controls based on early contacts with authority, and crude distinctions between things and people which are regarded as good and favourable and others which are bad and damaging. (Author's comment: The idea of maturity does not seem to have survived very well so far.) But maturity returns again as the ability to recognize the difference between objective outside reality and the personal, subjective, and internal view of it. Maturity also shows in the capacity to recognize what should be accepted and what should be rejected in the outside world. This is the boundary control area between the individual as a system and his environment. And so back to apparent ambivalence because individuals project their feelings arising from subjective 'good or bad' in themselves on to others outside and so cause a major barrier to understanding the relationships between individuals and tasks. Finally at the individual level a love–hate relationship is said to exist between managers and managed which is linked with their mutual dependence on each other to get the job done. This leads to defensive behaviour on both sides in order to avoid the consequences of their mutual hostility.

Moving from the individual to the group Miller and Rice seem to consider mostly the informal or spontaneous group. In order to perform a real task, presumably the one set by management as a means towards organizational objectives, the group have to relate to and come to terms with reality, to behave as rational human beings. Presumably this implies effective performance of the task set.

A group develops an emotional climate which is determined by its attitudes and beliefs about its members and about the task it has to perform. In addition it develops an inner purpose deriving from individual contributions to the group and feelings about the group and the outside environment. Individual contributions are assumed to be rational but attitudes towards the organization may help or hinder task performance. Again there are the possibilities of conflict between members within the group and between the group as a whole and its environment. Boundary transactions are assumed to exist between the member and the group and the group and its environment.

A group requires leadership for two purposes, one to achieve task performance and the other to express group opinions and generally act as communication link with the environment. Both functions may or may not be carried out by the same person.

The effective face-to-face small group is given as consisting of between eight and sixteen members. A group of this size can sustain close personal relationships, provide feelings of security, of help and of belonging to the individual, require conformity of behaviour from members and yet enable each member to feel that he has a worthwhile contribution to make towards the assumptions and beliefs of the group.

At this point Miller and Rice turn to the formal organization group with two generalizations which do not seem to be entirely justified although they must be accepted in the development of their theory. The first is that the large organizational group consists of sub-groups which may be formal and/or informal. The second is that the formal group has a membership and a purpose 'consistent with the requirements of the enterprise'[7] and the informal group is 'directed to other ends'[8] other, that is, than those of the formal organization.

Internally the large (organizational) group has the following characteristics:

(i) Relationships between individuals.

(ii) Relationships within and between the sub-groups comprising it.

(iii) Individuals' overt needs and unconscious strivings.

(iv) Small group tasks and the group assumptions that hold them together.

(v) Individuals and groups who at one and the same time act at conscious and sub-conscious levels and in accordance with both task and internal assumptions.

(vi) Leadership functions at different levels that confirm the identities

of their groups and relate the internal aspects of the group or
sub-group with its environment.

(vii) Activities rather than formal positions which determine leadership which need not be the prerogative of one person.

(viii) The possibility of conflict between task leadership and leadership based on group norms and assumptions.

In order to complete the group concept the idea of sentience is re-
introduced. Belonging to a group involves for the individual at least some
and maybe much emotional commitment. The level of commitment or
loyalty is the measure of sentience. Around the group is the boundary
area dividing it from other groups and the rest of the environment. The
appropriate leader must communicate and make transactions for the
group across this boundary as it cannot survive in isolation. As these
transactions could threaten the sentience and even the existence of the
group the group protects its boundary by imposing conditions on the
leader as to the frequency and nature of transactions he may enter into on
their behalf.

Task priorities and restraints

Miller and Rice take the modern view that the primary task of any
organization is 'the task that it must perform if it is to survive'.[9] But this
is immediately modified to some extent. There may be conflict between
the ideas of the constituent (operating) system and the superordinate
(controlling) system of the organization. Conflict may also arise between
the organization's view of its primary task and the environment's view in
which case the latter will impose constraints. With survival as the main
purpose paradoxically it may be necessary to elevate some ancilliary task
to the position of temporary primary task if survival is to be possible at all.

Resources of all kinds are the very tools by which the purposes of the
organization are carried out but the nature of the resources possessed and,
in particular, the shortage or absence of key resources may be major
constraints on feasible objectives. Human resources in particular are
singled out as a constraint because members' values derived from
membership of other groups are 'unlikely always to be in harmony with
those (values) attached to work'.[10] Where the large, complex organization
has multiple tasks the performance of one will act as a constraint on
others if there is no definite priority established between them. Similarly
constraints on sub-units will be imposed by higher level units and the
larger and more complex the organization, the greater these constraints
will be.

The view is strongly put forward that human constraints have the greatest influence, that technology has not and never will entirely eliminate them. Human needs and their satisfaction or deprivation will affect the level of attainment reached as compared with that required by the task-efficiency system. Different tasks will present different opportunities for satisfaction or the lack of it and individuals will differ in their ideas of what constitutes satisfaction and deprivation. The three factors involved in this satisfaction–deprivation syndrome are inter-personal and internal group relationships, intergroup relationships and the nature of the task itself. By arranging for task boundaries to coincide with sentient boundaries organization can provide satisfaction along the dimensions of all three factors. But such arrangements may be harmful in the long run if they inhibit the acceptance of necessary change.

Organizational model building

Setting down the basic ideas from which Miller and Rice develop their theory seems to have taken a long time but it is necessary because those ideas are in many respects quite different from those derived from the American culture. We can now turn to their development of a theory. In order to do this, they start by constructing organizational models.

Ideally the optimum form of organization would be one designed purely to meet the requirements of primary organizational task performance. This is rarely, if ever, possible because of the constraints imposed by the availability of resources and those imposed by political, social and economic conditions. The starting point should be the precise definition of the organization's primary purpose and the use of this to identify the import, conversion and export activities required and the resources needed to carry them out. (As an aside it is admitted that existing organizations that have grown and developed may not have precise primary tasks.) Having determined the processes and activities needed the next step is to discover the natural boundaries in the system caused by discontinuities in activity systems and orders of differentiation which provide the levels of hierarchy. It is then possible to define the managerial systems needed to control transactions across internal boundaries, to regulate the relationships between systems and between sub-systems and those between the system as a whole and its environment. The key factor in all this is the ability of the human group to devote itself to different activities to meet different tasks. Differing roles and activities are allocated to different individuals and groups but it is not always possible in doing so to predetermine completely the pattern of inter-relationships which will be involved in operation.

In operating, management, as the controlling body, needs four kinds of boundary control:

(i) Regulation of task-system boundaries to regulate the system as a whole and the constituent activity systems.

(ii) Regulation of sentient group boundaries.

(iii) Regulation of organizational (departmental) boundaries.

(iv) Regulation of the relationship between task, sentient and departmental boundaries.

Transactions across boundaries

The whole of Parts II, III and IV of the book is devoted to rather detailed description and analysis of various research projects dealing with boundary situations. For our purposes only relevant conclusions will be extracted.

Export systems involving transactions across the boundary between the enterprise and its external environment are two-way systems and involve the member of the organization responsible for them in the boundary area of the 'customer' organization. Consequently the salesman, for instance, has a sentient group which does not coincide with his task group. Similarly retail shop staff can under certain circumstances align themselves with customers rather than their employing organization.

Where sentient group boundaries enclose and coincide with more than one task boundary the system may function well under stable conditions. But under conditions of change in the tasks conflict and obstruction are likely to arise through strains in the sentient group. Family firms are particularly likely to suffer from conflict between family ties and obligations and necessary business changes.

Temporary and transitional task systems

The problem of the coincidence of task and sentient boundaries inevitably causes difficulty in times of change. With the very rapid growth in technological and other changes now occurring some form of temporary and transitional task system is needed to be able to cope. This, say Miller and Rice, is project organization. The essential features of project organization are that it is built round a particular task having a limited time span and the team that carries it out consists of members drawn from whatever disciplines and departments may be necessary to provide the skills and knowledge required for the project. On completion of the project the team is dissolved and the members return to their normal departments. In this way task boundaries defined by the project do not coincide with sentient boundaries which may be departmental and/or professional.

The elimination of organizational boundaries within enterprises

Further illustrations of project-type organization are given relating to research work and air-line operating. While interesting in themselves they are not really essential to our purpose so we come to Part V which starts with the claim that these examples try 'to establish the basis for a theory of organization applicable to any enterprise',[11] and 'we used both industrial and non-industrial examples to illustrate our proposition that the most general form of organization is what we have called the project type'.[12]

A modification is allowed in that 'temporary' and 'transitional' are relative terms and the key factor is the rate of change within the enterprise. Should this be very slow then 'temporary' and 'transitional' may last for considerable periods of time.

The central core of the argument appears to lie in the three concepts of task groups, sentient groups claiming allegiance, and change. If the rate of change is minimal then task group and sentient group boundaries should coincide to obtain commitment by members to the task. When task and sentient boundaries coincide then management will have to take special steps to introduce innovation when it is necessary. If they do not coincide then management will have the role of controlling the transactions across the task-sentient boundaries. Under conditions of increasing technological and social change stable groups particularly on the task side become less and less likely and project organization will be the answer to the resulting problems. Stable departmental and strictly hierarchical organizational structures would only add to the problems resulting from rapid change.

The discussion is taken a little further to bring automation and computerization in as current forms of major change. The effects of this are shown in a carefully detailed description of the changeover involved in converting a departmentalized steel mill into a high technology, automated, and computer controlled mill. The conclusion, briefly stated, is that a completely new technology such as this cannot be grafted on to an old unsuitable departmental organization. The new technology, the process of change and the new emergent organization required after the change is completed have all to be thought through and worked out together.

Task and sentient systems and their boundary controls

Miller and Rice complain politely that their thesis has had to be developed from such material as they had acquired from consultancy and that they had not been given the opportunity by the firms concerned to test their hypotheses by detailed research and experiment.

Even so, they still maintain that the project-type organization is not only appropriate and necessary for 'temporary' and 'transitional' systems but it 'also provides the best basis for a general organization theory'.[13] It involves precise definition and control of the boundaries of activity systems and of groups. It also '. . . requires the reconciliation of two, often contradictory views of enterprises . . . to ensure efficient task performance . . . to satisfy the needs of those who are employed in it'.[14]

References

(1) Miller, E. J. and Rice, A. K. *Systems of Organization* (London: Tavistock Publications, 1967), p. xi.
(2) Ibid, p. xi.
(3) Ibid, p. xii.
(4) Ibid, p. xiv.
(5) Ibid, p. 15.
(6) Ibid, p. 15.
(7) Ibid, p. 20.
(8) Ibid, p. 20.
(9) Ibid, p. 25.
(10) Ibid, p. 29.
(11) Ibid, p. 225.
(12) Ibid, p. 225.
(13) Ibid, p. 251.
(14) Ibid, p. 251.

Bibliography

BOOK BY E. J. MILLER AND A. K. RICE
Systems of Organization (London: Tavistock, 1967).

P. R. Lawrence and J. W. Lorsch
1967

At first reading it may seem to be repetitive to include Lawrence and Lorsch in this book. Their inclusion is, however, quite deliberate. For one thing their book seems to demonstrate very clearly how, during the latter half of the decade, many starting points and many routes were converging towards the same end – an analysis of management in systems, terms of structure, behaviour, and environment. There seems, too, to be yet another good reason for including their ideas. Instead of separating the Classical and Human Relations Schools as being out of date and largely irrelevant to modern thinking they put forward very persuasively the idea that Classical, Human Relations, and 'Modern' thought are actually pointers along the same necessary continuum of patterns of management. These patterns are, it is suggested, related to the environments in which they have operated. Lawrence and Lorsch state their case as 'A Contingency Theory of Organizations'.

They modestly admit that the factors and the examples of research they have included are insufficient in themselves to provide adequate proof of a confirmed theory but they suggest they could be pointers to an integrated theory of management. They do not at any point make a significant claim to belong to the Systems school but their concept of the firm as an open system interacting with the contingencies of the environment makes the claim for them by implication. The confirmation they seek is surely building up.

Much of the book, like so many others of this time, is a detailed account of empirical research work. The primary purpose in this case is to relate comparative success and failure in different firms to the congruence or lack of it between their organizational patterns and the environments in which they exist. As Bertrand Fox, Director of Research at Harvard, says in his Foreword 'What kind of organization does it take to deal with different environments?'[1]

It is important to understand the bases from which any theory starts. In this case the major concepts are few in number and possess relatively simple relationships. They are:

(i) An organization is an open system with inter-related behaviour patterns on the part of its members.

(ii) Members' behaviour patterns result from interdependency on the formal organization, the task and the personalities of the people involved.

(iii) Members build up frameworks of expectations about others' behaviour.

(iv) Large organizations must be differentiated into parts or subsystems that then have to be integrated if the organization is to survive.

(v) Adaptation by the organization to the requirements of its environment is a major function.

(vi) The differentiation into sub-units is essential so that each can deal with a different aspect of the environment. None but the simplest organizations can deal with the environment as a whole. In addition to division into departments, differentiation includes the differences in attitudes and behaviour that result.

(vii) The differentiation into sub-units makes the opposite process of integration or co-ordination of the sub-units essential in order to achieve the aims of the organization as a whole.

(viii) The states of differentiation and integration and their relation to the environment are central to the Contingency theory.

These concepts are considered to be adequate as a base and to possess the advantage that they are capable of all being comprehended simultaneously. Complexity for complexity's sake is to be avoided.

In a similar way the researches on which the theory rests have been limited to the minimum number of aspects that seemed necessary for the hypotheses. There are only four of these:

(i) The differences between managers in different jobs in their orientation to major and sub-goals.

(ii) The differences in time orientation of managers and its relation to the aspect of the environment with which they are directly concerned.

(iii) The differences in inter-personal orientation to members of the same sub-unit, to equals in other sub-units, to members at other levels, and to other sub-units.

(iv) Variations in the form of organization structure.

Once again it is necessary to be as precise as possible about the meanings attached to the same words in different contexts. As differentiation occurs again and again here is Lawrence and Lorsch's definition of it

– 'the difference in cognitive and emotional orientation among managers in different functional departments'.[2] In this case 'functional' is used to mean major aspects or divisions such as production, marketing, research and not specialization in the Taylorian sense. Similarly integration means 'the quality of the state of collaboration that exists among departments that are required to achieve unity of effort by the demands of the environment'.[3] It is also used to denote the processes and organizational devices used to attain collaboration.

It is interesting to speculate on the use of 'managers' in the first definition and 'departments' in the second. Assuming that the use of the two different words is deliberate it raises intriguing questions about the similarity of the orientation of a manager and of his subordinate managers and/or departmental staff. Another question is the relation of integration to the scope and depth of the manager's sphere of influence. As the research is all at managerial level these questions do not appear to have been answered.

It is claimed that Classical theory assumed that all necessary integration would be achieved rationally and automatically by the issue of orders from the top down the hierarchy. (Author's comment. This misses Fayol's 'gang plank' or 'bridge'.)[4] But the hierarchy is only one of many means of dealing with the conflict which is inherent in differentiation. On the other hand, the Human Relations theory with its emphasis on emotive aspects puts the emphasis on inter-personal skills and ignores the need for differentiation and the inevitability of conflict. Neither is entirely wrong, neither is complete, and the 'one best way to organize' is the alchemist's dream.

Instead a number of questions are posed for answering:

(i) What are the differences in the environmental demands facing various organizations? What is the relation between these differing demands and the internal functioning of organizations?

(ii) Do organizations in stable environments use the hierarchy more to achieve integration? If so, why?

(iii) Is the same degree of differentiation in orientation found in organizations in different environments?

(iv) If different industries need different degrees of differentiation does this affect the problems and methods of achieving integration?

If effective answers to these questions can be found, with the necessary degree of generality, they will dispose once and for all of the practical manager's rooted objection to theory – 'My business is different'. The answer is 'Of course it is and now theory can explain why and, perhaps, provide the tools to do something about it'.

While the main emphasis of this research is on the questions of differentiation and integration Lawrence and Lorsch think there could be a psychological spin-off for managers themselves. Different forms of organization may match or conflict with individual temperaments but in more general terms an organization structure that is properly related to its environment and has the appropriate integrative mechanisms will function effectively. Within a structure such as this managers should find 'powerful sources of social and psychological satisfaction'[5] which will meet their needs for achievement, power, affiliation with others, and a sense of competence.

The research strategy

While the details of the research work will not be given here a brief explanation of the strategy is not out of place. Two stages were involved. The first was a detailed study on a number of firms in one industry having reasonably comparable environments. At this stage the purpose was to find how far the effectiveness of each firm correlated with the match between its internal organization and its external environment. The second stage took as its base recognizably different environments provided by three different industries. In each industry a highly effective firm and a less effective competitor were chosen for detailed study. This time the purpose was to study the effects of different environments on internal organization and to check the relative effectiveness of different patterns of organization. Together the two approaches should provide a generalized pointer to the degree of differentiation and integration required to give effective performance under environments varying from stability to extreme flux and change. They should provide the death knell to any idea that there is one best form of organization.

Organizations in a diverse and dynamic environment

For the first part of the research a section of the plastics industry was chosen because its environment fulfilled particularly well the requirements of diversity and dynamism. Uncertainty was greatest in the scientific knowledge on which the entire industry depended to develop new products and processes. New knowledge could appear at any time and in any place and the feed-back period for getting information on whether new discoveries were required by the market was relatively long. In the marketing area products were tailored to customers' requirements but competition for customers was very keen and customers' needs were extremely varied. This area could be described as moderately uncertain. Production was a continuous process and highly capital intensive. Change in materials could be handled easily and major change in technology was relatively slow. So this area was relatively predictable.

The first conclusions from the comparison of firms in this industry are only claimed to be generalizations. They relate to the three major aspects considered – research, marketing, and production.

(i) The differing degrees of uncertainty mean that the primary tasks of managers in the different aspects are themselves different.

(ii) The formalization of organization structure is in inverse ratio to the amount of uncertainty (cf. Burns and Stalker).

(iii) The personal styles of management are task-orientated in extremely certain and uncertain environments and personal relationship-orientated in moderately uncertain environments.

(iv) The time-orientation of a manager is directly related to the feedback time from his environment.

(v) The goal-orientation of managers, generally but not always, was towards his sub-unit goals of research, marketing, or production.

(vi) These generalizations show evidence for and reasons why departments are organized differently.

Actually research was sub-divided into fundamental research and applied research. Fundamental research possessed the greatest uncertainty and showed characteristics at one extreme. Applied research, getting a new idea to production stage, was somewhat less uncertain and generally fell between fundamental research and marketing in its characteristics.

Two or three points need emphasis here. Lawrence and Lorsch are particularly concerned with managerial behaviour and everything outside the manager is considered to be environment. The generalizations are no more than averages and individual managers could and did vary from the average. The question of success or failure is not under consideration at this stage. In more general terms the fact that departments differ in their organization patterns has been known for as long as organization has existed. Lawrence and Lorsch have drawn attention to a reason which had not been explicitly recognized but there can be a number of other reasons for the differences apart from uncertainty in the environment.

Turning to the degree of differentiation in organizations and its correlation with performance Lawrence and Lorsch seem to move beyond personal management styles into areas of unit and sub-unit performance. Their conclusions are:

(i) Firms with higher performance levels have organization structures that differ significantly less from the needs of the environment than those of firms with medium or lower performance levels.

(ii) The ability of a firm to cope with its environment is related to achieving a degree of differentiation which is consistent with its environment.

(iii) Departments will be more effective if their members have attitudes and interests based on departmental goals, have time horizons consistent with their tasks, and have suitable modes of behaviour towards each other.

(iv) The degree of control or latitude exercized in the organization will improve performance if it is correctly related to the nature of the task to be performed.

Differentiation alone is obviously not enough. The greater the degree of differentiation the more difficult it becomes to get successful integration but the most successful firms achieve high differentiation *and* the highest integration. Moderately successful firms do not achieve both effectively and the least successful firms most lacked integration.

Differentiation also presents problems on another dimension. By implication it involves differences between departments in outlook, objectives and time-span. Consequently it leads to conflict and the greater the conflict the more difficult integration becomes. It is a short step from that to the realization that effective resolution of conflict is essential for effective performance. The conditions given for success are not by any means entirely new but they will stand repetition as they are so often ignored.

(i) Problem solving between departments must take place at the level at which the required knowledge exists. In stable environments this will tend towards the higher levels of management, in unstable ones it will tend towards lower levels.

(ii) Special structures or individuals may have to be built into the organization structure to cope with differences where the amount of uncertainty is such that higher levels will not have sufficient information.

(iii) Such integrative mechanisms must have a point of view in between those of the departments to be integrated in terms of goals, time-spans and orientations.

(iv) In disputes the integrators must have, and must be accepted by both departments as having, the most important voice in achieving settlement. This means that they must have the technical and integrative competence to justify their position.

(v) Integrators must be assessed and rewarded by higher management in terms of long-range effectiveness not short-term results.

(vi) Of all the possible methods of joint decision-making or conflict resolution the open problem-solving approach, called confrontation by Lawrence and Lorsch, is the one most likely to be successful with high differentiation and high integration. In the open problem-solving approach all parties involved are able to state their point of view and have it considered in reaching the decision. The total influence exerted is high.

In concluding this section which is drawn entirely from the review of different firms in the one industry Lawrence and Lorsch make two reservations. One is that no theory exists to evaluate the relative importance of all the conclusions so far. The second is that their researches relate only to one type of environment common to one industry. Other environments could make quite different demands on other industries.

Environmental demands and organizational states
The research then expanded into the second stage where high and low performance firms operating in quite different environments were compared. The specific purposes were to try to discover what differences in organization structure were required by different environments and whether the requirements for success were similar or not under different conditions.

One generalization drawn from this stage is that where one of the three aspects of the environment greatly over-rides the other two in importance, it tends to influence the goals in all departments and so leads to a lessening of the degree of differentiation. Only the same three major aspects were considered as before, that is: research and development; marketing; and production. On the other hand in spite of wide differences in environment roughly the same degree of integration is required for success but its nature tends to change to match environmental differences.

The more detailed conclusions are:
(i) In effective organizations the states of differentiation and integration will vary depending on the environment facing them. There is no one single pattern for success.
(ii) The more diverse and dynamic the environment is the more the effective organization will be differentiated and the more highly integrated it will be.
(iii) Less differentiation will be required for success in less diverse and more stable environments but a high degree of integration is still required.
(iv) The problems in achieving a high degree of integration are increased by greater differentiation in the organization and by greater uncertainty in the environment.

(v) Differences in environments will require different means of achieving integration.

Further aspects of resolving inter-departmental conflict

A number of important sidelights on conflict come from this second stage of the research. Under conditions of a more certain and predictable environment the knowledge required to resolve inter-departmental conflict existed generally at the higher levels of the hierarchy. Where major aspects of the environment tended towards uncertainty the knowledge really required for the most important decisions existed at the middle and even lower levels of management.

So effective management under relatively stable conditions tends towards the Classical hierarchical pattern. But for it to be effective, the higher managers have to be technically competent, must have the necessary knowledge and these must be combined with widespread acceptance of and confidence in higher management by the middle and lower levels. High level decision-making tends to be by the use of confrontation (Lawrence and Lorsch's term) with smoothing-over or compromise as the back-up method when confrontation cannot be used. Integration in these circumstances will be more effective and lead to greater success if the departments concerned feel that their opinions are given reasonable weight and that those exercizing influence have sufficient knowledge of the required kind.

Under conditions of medium uncertainty special integrating departments and individuals and direct contact between middle unit managers are the pattern for success provided certain essential conditions are fulfilled. The integrators must have well-balanced orientations towards the main functions of the firm and towards the different time perspectives. Again through their ability and knowledge they must be 'seen' to have more influence than individual unit managers. The total amount of influence exercized must be greater and more widely spread for success. Finally in the most successful firms decisions are made by the manager or integrator with the greatest amount of appropriate knowledge in the particular situation.

To be honest all this looks so obvious that it should not need recording let alone emphasizing. To be more honest there can be few middle and lower managers who have not on many occasions ranted and raved about decisions, taken by 'them', that have little, if any, relation to the real facts of the situation.

As general conclusions to this section Lawrence and Lorsch put forward three:

(i) High performance, successful organizations have methods and practices of handling disagreement which are consistent with their environments.

(ii) In order to achieve the required states of differentiation and integration, more effective methods of handling conflict are essential and they must be appropriate to the type of problem met.

(iii) An effective organization must at least approach closely to the states of differentiation and integration required to match its own particular environment.

Lawrence and Lorsch say that this is a highly abstract and over-simplified answer. This sounds over-modest. Admittedly the research on which it is based is limited in scope and variety. But successful and unsuccessful practices, good and bad management and widely differing environments have been investigated, analysed and compared. The result is a generalized theory at a level of abstraction which makes it immediately applicable for more empirical testing under other conditions. It may well prove to be a major step forward.

A contingency theory of organizations
For our purposes this will be set out as a series of relatively simple propositions:

(i) The differences in the internal states and processes must be linked to relevant differences in the environment.

(ii) Variables in the organization are in a state of complex relationship with each other and with the environment.

(iii) Effectiveness in the organization depends on having a proper match between the internal states of differentiation, integration and problem solving on the one hand and the external states of diversity, uncertainty and strategic issues in the environment on the other.

(iv) Internal differentiation must match external diversity.

(v) Internal integration must match the external demand for interdependence.

(vi) Differentiation and integration are inversely related.

(vii) Success depends on integrating devices which are consistent with the diversity in the environment.

(viii) Successful conflict resolution depends on good integrating devices operating at the level(s) in the hierarchy at which the appropriate knowledge and skills exist.

(ix) The more unpredictable the environment the lower the level of the organization involved.

(x) The relative strength of departmental influence on decisions should not be fixed but the greater influence at any one time must be given to the department most directly connected with the dominant, strategic aspect of the environment related to the decision involved.

(xi) Factors internal to the organization which contribute to success are:

(*a*) confrontation in conflict situations;

(*b*) influence based on competence and expertise rather than formal status;

(*c*) balanced orientations among integrators;

(*d*) rewards based on effectively unified efforts by all.

(xii) An organization that successfully reaches these requirements will be effective and will reach the required states of differentiation and integration.

Implications

Despite the admitted hazards in drawing conclusions from a generalized theory, such as omitting to consider other relevant but unrecognized factors and using value judgements in determining what is or is not effective, Lawrence and Lorsch use the last chapter of their book to speculate on the possible implications of their theory. A few of them really seem to be no more than the propositions already given and these have been omitted.

They start with the suggestion that managers who are specifically aware of and able to handle the appropriate degree of differentiation will make better decisions on organization structure. In taking such decisions, that will involve simultaneous differentiation and integration, they must be able to make diagnostic analyses of the organization and the environment and actually make and use them.

Considerable training of managers at all levels will be required in at least the following aspects – improving their competence in dealing with each other, with subordinates, and with superiors, improving their methods of problem solving, improving their ability to de-personalize differences of opinion, of points of view, and of solutions to problems. It might just be that the most important implication of all is omitted here – convincing middle and especially top management that they need such training!

It will be necessary to determine very carefully the criteria on which to base the degree of differentiation required in a given organization. These criteria will give a frame of reference for determining what conflict is about when it arises, what causes lie behind differences in judgement, and what relevant knowledge is required for a solution.

Finally conflict within an organization is and must be accepted as a normal, continuing problem to be used as a means of progress not as something to be avoided. Progress will result if effective methods and devices are used to deal with it.

To round off the book Lawrence and Lorsch project their view of the viable organization of the future. In brief they accept the trends of the last twenty years or so as continuing but with much greater understanding and knowledge. The behavioural sciences of individual and group psychology and sociology will be widely applied by organizational development departments staffed with behavioural and administrative science specialists. These departments and top management will have the primary task of correctly linking the differentiation and integration levels within the organization with the diversity and needs of the environment.

Work itself will undergo vast changes. There will be a great increase in the variety of purely 'human' work as distinct from 'human involved with machine' work. Much of the 'human' work will consist of eliminating entirely the 'human involved with machine' work and converting it into 'all-machine' work, i.e. complete automation.

The assumption of an ever-increasing rate of change in the environment will mean that only organizations which can evolve the required degree of differentiation and integration will survive. They will succeed, will grow, and growth (on the right lines) will lead to further success. Organizations which cannot do this will not survive and their disappearance will increase the scope for the successful. Vertical and horizontal combination and merger will both be used for growth. The result will be massive organizations which will be able to work across public and private sectors, across nations, across industries. They will provide a wider variety of challenging and worthwhile jobs to meet people's increasing aspirations and fewer and fewer dull routine jobs to suppress and kill them.

Perhaps the most vital aspect of the future is left till last. These massive, well-adapted, well-integrated organizations will not run themselves however good their design. At the last analysis human leadership will be needed on a larger and more effective scale than ever before to revitalize and keep these enormous organizations in existence. It will be needed at local level to cope with diversity and integration, at organizational design level to deal with structure, and at top level to formulate the framework of purpose for the organization as a whole.

References

(1) Lawrence, P. R. and Lorsch, J. W. *Organization and Environment* (Boston: Harvard University, 1967), p. vi.

(2) Ibid, p. 11.

(3) Ibid, p. 11.

(4) Fayol, H. *General and Industrial Administration* (London: Pitman, 1963)

and Pollard, H. R. *Developments in Management Thought* (London: Heinemann, 1974), pp. 91–2.

(5) Lawrence, P. R. and Lorsch, J. W., op. cit., p. 17.

Bibliography

BOOK BY P. R. LAWRENCE AND J. W. LORSCH
Organization and Environment (Boston: Harvard University, 1967).

7

J. D. Thompson — I
1967

In Part I of his book *Organizations in Action* Thompson[1] sets himself and succeeds in an enormous task. In his Preface he comments that useful theories can neither assume that everything is unique nor that everything is alike. A mature science explains patterned differences around universal elements. The task he sets himself is 'to identify a framework which might link at important points several of the now independent approaches to the understanding of complex organizations',[1] to identify concepts and to develop from them potentially significant propositions.

The result is a book of concepts, propositions and illustrations which should be compulsory reading for every Managing Director, President, and manager – present and future. It is a comprehensive theory of organization at a higher level of abstraction that gives it a universal application.

The Introduction sets the stage. Organizations act. The question is what makes them act. What impersonal forces generate and guide organizational behaviour? How far do the concepts of rationality and uncertainty influence the situation and in what ways? Is it true that similar technologies and environments produce similar patterns of organization and organizational action?

Strategies and systems
Two models of systems that involve different strategies form the basis of Thompson's theory. The first, the rational model, consists of a 'closed' system. This is a collection of inter-related and interacting parts that in some way or other is isolated from interaction with its environment, or, at most, is only affected from outside by predictable forces. In a 'closed' system provided its present state and the forces operating within it are known the next future state is determined and predictable. This may involve some simplification of reality because the variables and relationships must be few enough to be capable of being comprehended altogether and their interaction worked out mentally.

In incorporating 'closed' systems into his theory Thompson has turned his back on the revolt against Classical theory. The Scientific Management of Taylor, Urwick, Fayol, Weber and others was built around an early concept of 'closed' systems. Their closure was obtained by assuming that organizational goals, repetitive tasks, uniform resources, effective planning, and known, or at least predictable, markets could be taken for granted as given. With a 'closed' system, such as this, efficiency was the criterion of success. But by doing so they threw out the baby with the bath water. The whole point of Thompson's approach is that he retains a 'closed' system and rationality for that part of organization to which it is applicable and at the same time accepts the opposite 'open' system for the remainder of the organization where 'closed' systems are unsuitable.

The 'open' system or natural system model differs from a 'closed' one in that in addition to having its own internal structure, interactions, and inter-relationships it is affected by and must react to outside influences and events in the larger environment over which it has no control although it may be able to exercize some mutual influence over them. It is, by implication, too complex with too many variables to be comprehended at any one time as a whole; subject to unpredictable and uncontrollable forces; concerned primarily with survival rather than efficiency; and arises through evolution and adaptation rather than deliberate planning. An 'open' system is assumed to be self-controlling by bringing in the concept of homeostasis. Actually a homeostat is a 'mechanism' (e.g. a thermostat) for ensuring that when outside conditions change and prevent the system from operating as required the operation is automatically adjusted to return to the required result. Thompson takes this idea a little further by assuming that the 'homeostat' in an 'open' system of organization will be a process which ensures that the organization adapts to a changing environment in such a way as to ensure the survival of the organization. The process is adaptive behaviour by the people comprising the part of the organization concerned in response to problematical situations.

To sum up at this stage, the organization as a whole is divided into two broad groups which operate under fundamentally different conditions. There is a predictable 'closed' system which is rationally controlled with efficiency as its criterion and there is an 'open' system operating under conditions of varying uncertainty where the control is adaptive behaviour and the criterion survival. Both exist side by side; both are necessary to explain reality.

Having reconciled or, at least, brought together the old and the new, Thompson goes on to the other concepts on which he bases his theory of action in organizations. First to come into the net is the idea adopted from

Simon, and March and Cyert that organizations are mechanisms for facing and solving problems, for choosing courses of action in the light of alternatives. But, because of inherent limitations on the organization's power to gather and process information and to predict from it, the problem solving or decision-making process is based on 'bounded rationality' instead of the 'complete rationality' assumed by Classical management theorists. From the same source comes the idea of satisficing as the objective instead of optimization.

The third base is taken from Talcott Parsons. It is the suggestion that the phenomena related to 'closed' and 'open' systems do not occur at random throughout a complex organization but are specifically related to separate levels in the organization. The phenomena divide into three distinct groups – technical, managerial, and institutional. Technical phenomena relate to the task, to materials, to co-operation of people and belong to the 'closed' system aspects of the organization. Institutional phenomena relate to the organization as a whole and its relationship with its outside environment. These belong generally to the upper end of the 'open' system. Managerial phenomena arise from the interaction between and the reconciliation of the needs and demands on each other of the 'closed' technical system and the 'open' environment boundary system.

Thompson accepts Parson's view that these three are not a continuum shading gradually from one to the other but are distinct and discrete areas which are quite different in their nature. But there must be an interaction between them, institutional to management and management to technical. Any one of them can hinder the work of the others by withholding or modifying the contribution which it should make. The job of management is to remove by some means or other uncertainty from the technical system so that it can operate as a 'closed' system. At the other end the institutional level operates under the greatest uncertainty in relating the organization as a whole to its environment.

Finally Thompson draws, again from Parsons, on the idea that between organizations there will be differences in technology which cause differences in organization not only at the technical level but also at managerial and institutional levels because of the interaction of the three.

Rationality in organizations

Within the 'closed' system of the organization action is presumed to be based on technical rationality. This depends on systems of belief about what outcome is desired and the cause/effect relationships which exist. Assuming that a given outcome or result is required, the state of knowledge about the present state of affairs and about the effects of alternative courses of action or use of resources determines what should be done. There are two criteria of performance in this type of rational behaviour – instrumental, meaning that the desired result is produced, and economic, meaning that the result is produced with the least necessary resources and effort. Thompson considers that insufficient attention has been given to instrumental criteria, to considering fully what outcomes are desired and the extent to which they are achieved.

The nature of the instrumental criteria is largely determined by the technology within which the firm works. Woodward's classification is rejected as not being general enough to deal with all existing variations so Thompson develops his own.

The first group consists of 'long-linked technology'. Typical of this group is the long mass-production line, but the essential feature is a long series of operations which must follow each other in sequence so any one operation is dependent on the previous one if it is to perform correctly. Ideally it is based on a single technology, technical requirements are specific and well understood, work is repetitive, suitable for work-study procedures and gives time for errors in methods to be found and corrected.

The second group is described as 'mediating technology' in which the essential is service to customers or clients who wish to remain independent and outside the organization. Banking is quoted as an example. Complexity here arises from using standardized operations to meet many needs spread over time and space. The typical organizational form is bureaucracy.

The third group is 'intensive technology'. The characteristic here is that effort is put into modifying some specific object(s) and, most important, that feed-back is received from the object itself during operations.

At first impression Thompson's three categories are much wider than Woodward's, so wide and so different that they seem almost to leave large gaps uncovered. The key to this paradox is that Thompson's classification is based on the characteristic types of relationship and cause and effect related to the technology used rather than on differences in the technologies themselves. As it is the *effects* on organization structure with which Thompson is concerned, his classification is valid and meets his needs.

Two final words need to be said before turning to the propositions which are the core of the theory. Complete technical rationality, which includes both instrumental and economic varieties, is a theoretical abstraction towards which 'closed' systems are assumed to be always striving. Secondly rational operations assume that power exists within the system in order to control the use of resources.

We can now turn to the first of the propositions which together form the theory. Throughout the rest of the book they are set out in the most careful logical detail. For our purposes they will be summarized, hopefully without doing too much damage to their meaning. Throughout Thompson prefaces his propositions with 'Under norms of rationality'. This will be taken as understood and remembered.

In order to exist, an organization depends on input processes to provide resources and technical processes which use the resources – these are the 'core' technology which forms the base of the organization, and on output processes to dispose of the results of operations to the environment. Input and output processes being linked directly to the environment need to be 'open' systems. The core technology rationally needs to be sealed off from the uncertainty of the environment so that it can operate as a 'closed' system. Input and output processes perform their function by acting as buffers and themselves absorbing the uncertainty. These absorption activities involve extra costs and at some point management rationality requires a decision on the balance between extra costs and allowing some uncertainty to get through to the core activity.

In addition to absorbing uncertainty the 'open' system input and output processes seek to smooth out variations by levelling activities (e.g. sales drives in slack periods) and to anticipate them by forecasting so converting them into constraints which can be handled by the logic of the 'closed' system core technology.

When these three methods all fail to reduce uncertainty sufficiently, the organization turns to rationing to adapt outside demands to internal possibilities. (Author's comment. Thompson gives the impression of this as a one-way process, i.e. rationing customers when demand unexpectedly exceeds capacity. It would seem equally rational to employ rationing the other way, e.g. a sudden and unexpected breakthrough in technology might increase the demand for capital and other resources. In order to meet this demand and remain viable, in the absence of further funds and resources, rationing of resources to previously rational activities would be demanded.)

Domains of organized action
One method of reducing uncertainty that has not been mentioned so far is the integration of aspects of the environment into the organization itself usually by merger or takeover. For example a firm dependent on another firm for a vital component can by taking over the second firm ensure that at least it does not sell to somebody else and so remove one uncertainty from its environment. But, however far this process of integration is taken, there must come a point where it is not worthwhile to take it further and the uncertainty of the environment takes over.

This area over which the organization gets control is called the organization's 'domain'. Large or small the 'domain' consists of the pattern of points at which the organization has boundary transactions with and meets the uncertainties of the environment. The extension of the area of the domain involves introducing more core technologies.

At the points of contact between the 'domain' and the environment exchanges of one sort or another take place, e.g. a sale of the product, a purchase of raw material, taking on a new employee, arranging a bank loan, etc. Such exchanges can only occur if there is agreement or consensus between the organization and the part of the environment concerned. More or less constant interaction at these boundary points sets up a set of expectations about what each point will and will not do for both the organization and the part of the environment concerned. This set of expectations guides the organization into some sorts of activity and away from others so formalized goals and goal-setting by the organization need not be assumed. They arise from the interaction of members of the organization with the task-environment, that is, that portion of the total environment that is relevant to the organization's tasks and surrounds its domain.

As the different aspects of the task-environment are themselves interrelated with and have transactions with yet other parts of the total environment they are not irrevocably tied to any one organization and every organization can be said to be dependent on its task-environment. This creates uncertainty so rational management will try to manage this dependency. Thompson quotes Emerson (1962) for the idea that the dependence of an organization depends directly on the extent of its need for a particular resource and inversely on the number of available sources of supply in the environment, and for the statement that dependency is the opposite of power. This concept of power disposes of several difficult points in previous theory such as the concept of power as a generalized attribute of organizations in general, the need to link power with assumptions about intention and use, and the idea that the total sum of power was limited and a gain by one party meant a loss to another.

In order to reduce or eliminate dependency organizations will seek to maintain alternative sources of supply, to increase their prestige so making the task-environment more favourable to them, to increase their power relative to the aspects of the task-environment on which they are most dependent. Organizations can increase their power in relation to other units by reducing the latter's degree of dependency. Dependency may be met by agreed contracts, by co-opting members from the dominant organization, by coalescing or merger.

If an organization is to remain in existence for long it must solve 'political' problems to create and maintain a viable domain. The problems relate to the institutional (top) level of the organization because they involve determining the most worthwhile position on balance with overlapping and conflicting interests; they involve compromise; they involve relating to a continually changing environment; they involve the optimum reconciliation of interdependence with the environment and norms of rationality.

Organizational design

Given a certain domain, technology, and task environment, and that manoeuvring and compromise to maintain the domain is costly, it can be expected that rational organizations will design themselves to minimize these costs. In order to do this, organizations tend to include within their boundaries activities which would be crucial to their existence if left outside in the environment. In long-linked technologies this tends to be by vertical integration at the ends of the input and output processes. In mediating technologies the tendency is to increase the population served and in intensive technologies the object worked on tends to be incorporated.

Any action leading to incorporation and so removing contingencies increases the number of components and probably the technologies of the organization and therefore increases the problem of maintaining a balance between the components especially when one or some of the components can only be acquired in large quantities at a time. Assuming some large quantity of some particularly needed component has been acquired then the rest of the organization will seek to grow until that component is fully occupied. This may not be so easy if the task-environment cannot or will not take the resulting increased output. The alternative to growth along the same lines, if that is blocked by the task-environment, is to extend the domain by, for example, diversification through merger.

As it is a recognizable fact that many concerns have not expanded and diversified in this way there must be good reasons for exceptions. These may be legal restraint or direct intervention by the Government, the lack of certainty of the availability on reasonable terms of a crucial resource, the lack of power to achieve the desired state, the subordination of the norm of rationality to some other norm, or the possibility that the desired state is only recognizable with hindsight so it cannot be envisaged as an aim to be reached.

Technology and structure

Structure here has the dual meaning of departmentalization of the components in the organization and the relationships between them. Also in this section only the technical core, the 'closed' system is under consideration. Such a structure is a socio-technical system and is made up of human beings and non-human resources. While the non-human, technical aspects provide the orientation or background it is the social, human structure that is mainly considered.

Structure is needed for both instrumental and economic rationality. Given a need to be met and uncommitted resources to meet it an *ad hoc* synthetic organization will tend to arise spontaneously to relate available resources to a known need. This will tend to be instrumentally effective but not economically efficient. In cases like this there is only time to get on with the job nearest at hand and none available to review or revise operations. This sort of situation arises at times of natural disaster, say a flood or an earthquake where there is not only uncertainty but, even further, uncertainty as to where uncertainty exists.

On the other hand when there is time to develop a structure on the base of bounded rationality this structure provides boundaries for members actions and, therefore, a basis for economic rationality and also the source of interdependence between sub-units. Thompson postulates three types of interdependence. Pooled interdependence arises when unless each part of the organization performs its own task adequately the whole organization is in jeopardy. Sequential interdependence relates to operations which follow each other in sequence each being dependent on the performance of the previous one for its own ability to perform effectively. Reciprocal interdependence arises when two units of the organization mutually affect each other. These forms of interdependence become more common and the effort of co-ordination to cope with them becomes greater as the organization becomes more complex.

Co-ordination is required to achieve concerted action and organizations try to achieve it in various ways such as standardization of rules and practices, pre-planning of activities, feed-back of information and mutual adjustment. Whatever form co-ordination takes, it involves activity in communication and decision-making.

The bases for sub-dividing organizations into departments and positions in the structure are common purpose or common contribution to major organizational purpose, common processes, 'customers' in common in the widest sense of the word, geographical area. As sub-units are now recognized as being multi-dimensional so that it is impossible to subdivide on one criterion alone the problem changes to deciding the relative importance of the different criteria in each case.

This leads to a number of propositions on structuring organization. The overall aim is to minimize the cost of co-ordination. To do this, interdependent positions are organized in a common group that is localized and, within prescribed limits, autonomous. Within such a group co-ordination must be by mutual adjustment so the group is kept as small as possible. Where units are inter-related in sequence, they are placed in a common group again localized, with limited autonomy and as small as possible. Where neither type of inter-relation exists groups are created which can be co-ordinated by standardized rules and regulations.

The creation of these three sets of groups makes it possible to handle inter-relation and interdependence within each group, that is first-level co-ordination. But as co-ordination between the different groups is also required, higher level groups combining the first level groups into larger, second-order ones is necessary. In large complex organizations third, fourth, fifth and even higher-order groups are required to carry through all the co-ordination needed. This creates the hierarchy or multi-level structure of the organization. At each higher level the co-ordinating or over-arching group should only link together sub-groups which are inter-related and again the principles of the smallest possible, localization, and conditional autonomy should apply. In this way Thompson implies by 'hierarchy' a steadily more inclusive clustering of sub-groups to handle problems of co-ordination that are incapable of being solved by the sub-groups themselves.

Finally the use of standardization that must cut across multiple groupings involves the use of liaison positions between groups and rule-makers. Co-ordination that cannot be achieved by sequential grouping is achieved by representative committees. Problems of reciprocal interdependence which cannot be met by grouping are met by task-forces or project groups.

It might, perhaps, be advisable to put in a reminder that throughout all this the assumption is one of 'under norms of rationality'. The principles are what would happen if everyone were in possession of all the facts, completely rational, without emotion, and prepared to take decisions and act in this way.

Organizational rationality and structure
So far in considering the principles of organization structure Thompson has assumed the rational logic of the technical core of the firm which is presumed to operate as a 'closed' system cut off from the task-environment by preceding and following processes. Now it is the turn of these processes to be considered. While they are an integral part of the total organization they have contact and relations with the task-environment. Thompson aptly calls them 'boundary-spanning structures', influenced both by internal organizational restraints and by conditions in the task-

environment in which they operate. The real problem here is adjustment to external variables rather than co-ordination.

The external variables are regarded as constraints and various possible descriptions are given such as homogeneous or heterogeneous, stable or shifting, unified or segmented. They may also be divided into geographical space/time and social consisting of individuals and groups including other organizations. The nature and amount of external variety with which an organization has to deal is reflected in the number, variety, specialization and complexity of its boundary-spanning units.

The principles for coping with such variety are that a heterogeneous environment will be divided into homogeneous sections and structural units set up to deal with each section; these structural units will be subdivided to match their ability to function with a corresponding portion of the environment. If the task-environment is stable the organization unit facing it will rely on rules and bureaucratic structure to cope with it, and if the range of variation in the task-environment is known again rules and bureaucracy will be used. The other variable in the task-environment is unpredictability. In order to deal with this, the appropriate unit or sub-unit of the organization will monitor the environment for present and possible change and will plan responses to meet the change.

Obviously the two sets of alternatives, heterogeneous/homogeneous and stable/dynamic are not mutually exclusive so there can be heterogeneous and stable, homogeneous and stable, heterogeneous and dynamic, homogeneous and dynamic combinations. More heterogeneous task-environments place greater constraints on the organization. Greater dynamism presents more contingencies. The organization arranges its boundaries so as to produce boundary-spanning units facing a limited range of contingencies within a limited range of constraints. Again, a reminder that rationality is assumed.

To summarize, organization outside the stable core technology is built up from grass roots sub-units into complex structures as a result of solving problems of change in task-environment, in technology, in domain. Size by itself does not necessarily involve complexity, e.g. a simple technology and a simple task-environment will produce a simple organization. Complexity in organization arises when co-ordination and adaptation present major problems and the core technology is well separated away from the boundary-spanning units. This separation leads to a centralized over-arching level composed of functional divisions that will be responsible for master planning which translates the varied, disconnected, irrational restraints and information coming through the boundary-spanning units into logical premises on which the core-technology can act and decide rationally. Within the master planning heterogeneity and dynamism will make for decentralized decision-making based on surveillance possibilities. In extremely large complex structures with several core-technologies and much interdependence with boundary-spanning units the organization will be split into separate domains, each with its core-technology and its own related boundary-spanning units. A common form of this can be recognized in product-division organization. The greater the complexity of organization structure the greater the interdependence of units and the greater the number of types of co-ordination used. Decisions from different sources are more likely to clash and ends are more likely to be displaced by means.

The assessment of organizations

Thompson suggests that the crucial problems in assessment are how an organization knows when it has maximized achievement and how it assesses its fitness for the future. Assessment obviously involves some standard with which to compare the actual but no single measure is available. To be realistic standards must be accepted as varying 'from *crystallized to ambiguous*'.[2] Similarly cause-and-effect relationships vary from known and quantifiable in 'closed' systems, through varieties of multiple causes and/or multiple effects to complete impossibility of finding out any relationship. Additionally there can be variations between true cause-and-effect and believed cause-and-effect, usually on the lines of oversimplification. Efficiency tests should measure performance against crystallized desirability under conditions of complete, perfect knowledge. Below are instrumental tests where achievement of the end is the test but knowledge is incomplete so there is always the possibility of an unknown better way. Finally when the desirability of the end is uncertain whether the available knowledge is complete or not, only vague social standards can be used for comparison.

At the top institutional level the main criterion must be fitness to survive into the future. Here Simon's satisficing concept rather than maximization must be used. Past history, other organizations and improvement in particular aspects are used as bases for comparison related to the task-environment.

Assessment can and must be measured along different scales. The basis of organization is such another. Where interdependence is controlled by rules, conformity or lack of it is the measure. When control is by scheduling or planning, achieving quotas is the measure. When mutual adjustment is the control method, the confidence of one unit in another is used. Conditionally autonomous groups must be assessed by external judgement.

The different types of measure are usually not equally important so individual weighting has to be given to each type according to the unit being considered. Problems of assessment, if they are to be handled correctly, tend to be extremely complex.

References

(1) Thompson, J. D. *Organizations in Action* (New York: McGraw-Hill, 1967), p. viii.

(2) Ibid, p. 85.

Bibliography

BOOKS BY J. D. THOMPSON
Organizations in Action (New York: McGraw Hill, 1967).

8

D. Silverman
1970

Whatever hopes there may have been during the decade at which we have been looking that management thought might at last start to move towards some consensus on a generalized theory, are challenged one by one by Silverman. No less than the first five of the ten chapters of his book have as their objective the criticism of the main streams of thought during the previous twenty years.

Silverman is in no doubt at all about the position. Very early on he says, 'Perhaps to a greater extent than is true in many other areas, the study of organizations has been of interest to members of a wide range of disciplines with rather different perspectives,'[1] and 'It is, therefore, unfortunate but hardly surprising that the present state of the field should bear little resemblance to an ordered collection of knowledge.'[2]

Equally he is no doubt as to what he intends to do about it – 'to bring to this situation a reasoned argument deriving from a self-consciously sociological perspective'.[3] He supports his intention with four propositions which can be summarized in this way. There is a certain pattern in the development of the study of organizations, but one of the directions of that pattern, the Systems Approach, is seriously limited. Another approach based on an emerging sociological frame of reference will be more useful than attempting to find another synthesis. His basis is an 'Action Frame of Reference'.

Criticisms of current theories
Before turning to Silverman's own theory a brief look at his first five chapters will be useful for two reasons. It will provide some comment on the work of other authors in this book and it will demonstrate the lines of thought along which his theory develops.

A great deal of work has been done from many angles to pin down the nature and definition of organization, formal, informal, and social. Much of it has been in the direction of linking organization and goals. Silverman maintains that while formal organization cannot be uniquely described it

70

is a useful general concept. Some boundary is needed between formal and other forms of social organization in order to relate to the differences in the orientation of people towards formal organizations and towards other social organizations.

This seems to mean that an organization, formal or otherwise, is what it is because of the way the people involved think about it and act towards and within it. So far as formal organizations are concerned they are said to possess certain distinguishing features:

(i) They appear at definable points in time and are consciously created structures set up to achieve certain purposes defined by the founders.

(ii) The original purpose has only limited value over time in explaining the behaviour of members at a later date but it has great value as a symbol to which lip-service is paid to justify action.

(iii) Within the organization the majority of members will take its structure and pattern of relationships for granted but members in the upper echelons will be much less inclined to do so.

(iv) Changes in the patterns of relationships and 'rules of the game' will only take place after much discussion and a great deal of attention to their implementation.

These features certainly emphasize the idea that the formal organization is the creation of its members.

The systems approach of environment, input, throughput, and output seems to come under attack from two directions. In the first place great difficulty is attributed to determining what the actual outputs are and secondly equally large problems arise in dealing with effectiveness and efficiency. Silverman notes with approval the inducements – contribution theory developed by Barnard (1938), Simon (1957), and Goffman (1968) as a satisfactory explanation of human behaviour in terms of the sets of meanings attributed to social contexts.

Three separate 'systems' approaches are mentioned and found wanting. The 'closed system' approach arguing from universal psychological and sociological laws fails to take into account the fact that the meanings given to situations by individuals and their consequent actions are affected by factors both within and outside the organization. It cannot be a 'closed system'. The next step, the 'partially-open system', takes the environment into account up to a point. Its view, however, is still wrong because it regards the factors within the organization as the determinants and the conditions in the environment as limiting controls. Consequently it fails completely to show the inter-relationship of internal and external factors. 'Open-system' theory, too, fails to meet with approval because, while it links structure and needs as determining behaviour, it does not go behind needs to determine the meanings attached by individuals and groups to situations. The meanings attached are the real source of action. Also, while it purports to show the function of the environment in providing goals, resources, and primary task and the survival of the organization as a form of homeostasis, it does not explain why organizations react at different rates to their environment. Silverman's view is that the differences are caused by the human inputs to the system of individual and group dispositions, and differing views of reality. (Author's comment. It seems important to point out that this separation of the human input element from the rest of the system seems to be the essential base of Silverman's 'Action theory'. In my view, and it may be Silverman's also although he does not to my mind make this clear, he is not producing a substitute for 'Open Systems' theory but is analysing in greater detail one of the many different inputs into an 'open system'. The really important question then becomes, 'Does he integrate his "Action theory" into the total "Open System" theory and show the inter-relationships with other inputs, or does he treat it as something distinct?')

He does possibly go some way towards answering the question himself a little further on. He discusses briefly a theory put forward by Krupp in 1961.[4] This maintained that 'Systems' theory like the goal approach puts all the emphasis on the management viewpoint instead of on purposive human conduct that could have intended and unintended results. Analysis should be based on the different aims and purposes of all members of the organization and their ability or lack of it in terms of power and authority to impose their will on other members. At this point he retires gracefully to a position astride the fence and admits that both approaches are not as limited as they appear. 'The real debate . . . is concerned with the relative insights that may be derived from analysing organizations from the transcendental view of the problems of the system as a whole, with human action being regarded as a reflection of system needs, or from the view of interaction that arises as actors attach meanings to their actions and to the actions of others.'[5] This is not quite as convincing as it might be. It is still posed as an either/or situation. But there could be a hint that 'the problems of the situation as a *whole*' (my italics) could include the meanings attached by members and their interactions.

The next 'victim' is the Structural–Functional approach of Merton,[6] Selznik,[7] Parsons,[8] and Katz and Kahn.[9] Once again Silverman considers the approach has some value but his purpose is to show its deficiencies to demonstrate the need for his own alternative approach. Structural–Functionalists are said to argue that the relation of the parts to the whole of an organization may explain deviations in conduct as social phenomena related to some outside wider purpose of society. They consider the causes and consequences of social equilibrium, and problems of conflict and change are regarded as subsidiary.

Here Silverman seems to assume some congruence between Structural–Functionalist and Systems approaches, as indeed there is. It is, however, a little disconcerting to find suddenly that the Systems approach is valuable to sociology because of its insistence on mutual multi-dependence of all factors in the situation and on misunderstanding and unintended consequences. But he insists that the Systems approach involves moving away from and discounting the actor's definition of the situation and of the choices available to him. It is primarily interested in the consequences of action instead of the causes, i.e. human motivation.

Back to pure Structural–Functionalism with Selznik as its originator. Silverman's view of its basic concepts is that they consist of the paramount needs of the organization, continuity, homogeneous outlook, consent and participation, and recalcitrance or resistance from members arising from the fact that they have needs that are not met in the organizational situation. To Silverman this involves the reification of the organization, in other words the organization develops an existence and a personality of its own distinct from that of its members. Basic needs of an organization can only exist in a stable system which is largely independent of its environment and even then only their consequences, not their causes, can be usefully discussed. Selznik does not and cannot get round to causes.

Parsons' version of the social system is regarded as unsatisfactory because of its one-sidedness which Parsons himself is said to admit. Where change is concerned it focuses on consequences not causes.

Katz and Kahn (see Chapter 14) are the last to be dealt with in this section. Although their book is called *The Social Psychology of Organizations* they are described as representing the movement away from psychology to functionalism. They are supposed not to deal adequately with conflicts of interests, of values, and of norms, with the causes of change, with the definition of systems, with the source of organizational goals, and with organizational effectiveness.

Having dealt with formal organization, systems, and structural–functionalism, Silverman turns to the Human Relations School and its successors. The Human Relations School, based on the Hawthorne investigations, fails because it ignores the effects of the environment in which the organization exists and because its assumption that there need be no real conflict between worker and employer is unrealistic. It looked for easy solutions rather than structural causes.

The post-Human Relations theories or, rather, some of them are found in Part II of this book, so they will not be repeated here. Silverman attacks the very roots of the approach. How valid is the concept of personality needs? Are they real or 'pegs' created by psychologists? Are they independent variables and do they explain behaviour? Must they be satisfied within the context of work or can they be satisfied outside? He questions whether the methods proposed by, say, Argyris and Likert would be either efficient or even practical. Schein's attempt (see Chapter 17) to link psychology and systems fails to recognize the limitations of systems.

Finally, and briefly, the concepts of socio-technical systems come in for criticism. The influence of technology on ideas, motivation and behaviour is by no means as general as supporters of these ideas would have us believe. In whole areas of commerce, service industries and even much manufacturing industry technology is not the essential dominating factor it is supposed to be. This school of thought, says Silverman, is entirely British. It is based on abstracted empiricism rather than general theory. It emphasizes the problems of systems, deals with 'how' but not 'why' questions. It does not recognize that fundamental distinction between what is (fact) and what ought to be (value judgement). Finally it pays too little attention to sociology!

Comment

Hopefully this has been a fair, if abbreviated, account of Silverman's first five chapters. His purpose in writing them seems obvious. He has picked up from here, there, and everywhere the weak points which he feels will be met by his theory that is still to come. While it may not be possible to agree with all his criticisms it must be admitted that the full, definitive theory has still to appear. Silverman's 'ordered collection of knowledge' in some ways seems further off than ever. From his point of view attack may well be the best form of defence and the shortcomings of other theories the base on which to build his own. It is a logical approach.

The logic of including it here is more problematical, especially as many, if not all, of those criticized would probably hotly dispute Silverman's comments. First and foremost it is included for Silverman's own reason, as a lead-in to his theory. There is, however, another reason. While it is hoped that this book does represent accurately the 'essence' of the books analysed, it is not implied that any one of them has yet got the one and only, the complete, perfect answer. The reader will get more from the book if, at all times, he has at the back of his mind two questions. 'Does this fit my experience?' 'Does it explain the what and the why of the things going on around me?' Silverman has specifically put these questions in more detailed form.

The action frame of reference

The old question of which came first, the chicken or the egg, is given a new slant in the Action Frame of Reference. The behaviour of the individual can be viewed, as theorists in the first part of *A Theory of Organizations* maintain, as a reflection of the organizational structure and its problems. Silverman turns this round and suggests it is equally valid to look at the organization as the result of the interaction of people trying to solve their own problems. He takes this further by suggesting that the environment outside the organization can be regarded as a source of the meanings which individuals use in defining their own actions and in making sense of other people's actions.

Seven propositions are set down as the base from which to work:

(i) Social sciences and natural sciences deal with entirely different orders of subject matter which have different perspectives.

(ii) Sociology is concerned with understanding action rather than observing behaviour. Action arises out of the meanings that people use to define social reality.

(iii) Meanings are given to men by their society. Shared meanings on a large enough scale become institutionalized and are experienced by later generations as social facts.

(iv) While society defines man, man defines society. Particular collections of meanings are only sustained by continual reaffirmation in everyday facts.

(v) Through their interaction men also modify, change and transform social meanings.

(vi) Explanations of human actions must take account of the meanings which those concerned ascribe to their acts; the manner in which the everyday world is socially constructed yet perceived as real and routine becomes a crucial concern of sociological analysis.

(vii) Positivistic explanations, which assert that action is determined by external and constraining social or non-social forces, are inadmissible.

Matter reacting in a physical, natural system does not understand its own behaviour. It is purely an objective fore-ordained reaction to a given stimulus with no trace of subjective overtones. Detailed observation of the process itself provides understanding of its logic and complete predictability.

Man acts in, and in so doing defines and creates, a social world or system in order to attain his own ends. A social system has an internal logic of its own. The sociologist has to try to achieve a subjective understanding of the actions of individuals in a given situation, and this is extremely difficult to do. His generalizations are limited to statements of probability that individuals will act in terms of certain typical motives or intentions. Even then if he concentrates too much on actual behaviour he may miss its real significance to the people involved and so be unable to predict accurately the reaction of the people at whom the behaviour is directed. In brief, behaviour depends on an internal logic although sparked off by a stimulus that may be an external occurrence or an internal realization that outside circumstances are not satisfactory.

Action arises as a process of selection from alternatives of the one course most likely to assure an outcome satisfactory to the actor. His choice will be influenced by a pattern of expectations derived from past experience and of perceptions of probable reactions from other people. (Author's comment. It seems that this explanation can only apply to rational conduct or at most to habitual conduct based on earlier rational assumptions that still hold good. Irrational and non-rational behaviour is outside its scope. It also must, it seems, assume a scale of preferences for the actor that will be either/or for simple choice and a graduated scale for multiple-choice situations. It appears to ignore the possibility of multiple, concurrent or conflicting goals for the individual.)

The water gets deeper as Silverman goes on to say 'Meanings are given to men by their society and the past societies that preceeded it'.[10] But only a few paragraphs ago the internal logic of the social system was that people assign meanings to situations and that different people could assign different meanings to the same situation. It would seem that both processes can and do occur but not simultaneously in the same individual. Either he accepts the current society interpretation or he invents his own. But it must follow that the greater the influence assigned to society in determining for the individual the meanings, attitudes, perceptions, goals which he accepts the more deterministic the whole situation becomes, at least in the short run.

Silverman follows Durkheim in assuming that society is an inter-related series of institutions each of which consists of an hierarchy of positions having status, rights and duties. The hierarchy persists in spite of changes among the people comprising it. Within the institution and the hierarchy a pattern of accepted meanings and of expectations regarding the behaviour of others in the organization is built up over time. People follow the expectations required of them partly because of their upbringing that generally tends towards conformity and partly because they come to accept and believe in these expectations. The stock of shared social knowledge among the members of an organization is a series of accepted assumptions about appropriate behaviour in different contexts. But the roles and structure that form a major part of these accepted assumptions only provide the framework for action. They do not determine it. There remains an element of choice. Social norms need not necessarily be expressed in behaviour. There may be conflicts between social values.

Social order is, therefore, problematic and requires further analysis in terms of motivation towards conformity on the one hand and the possibilities of coercion on the other. There is also the problem that social norms, values and expectations may, and probably will, change over a period of time. These changes may be due to a reaction to long-term changes in the work environment or in the more general aspects of society as a whole.

To remove this from the area of theory to everyday knowledge may not be out of place in view of its importance and its particular relevance to the last half of the twentieth century. No one who worked either as manager or operative before and after the Second World War or even heard their parents reminiscing about the 1920s and 30s can fail to recognize the enormous differences in attitudes to work before and after. It would be foolish to suggest that there was only one cause. The changes in social security, in full employment, in education, in the development of radio and television, in technology, in the size of large firms must all have contributed to changes in expectations, in social norms, in acceptable forms of behaviour.

We must return to Silverman. He is unhappy about analysing organizations in terms of systems. Social order is neither tidy nor deterministic enough. He accepts Weber's thesis that people interacting with each other within an organization may attach different meanings to their interaction and even to the values that they share. Social relationships can operate on a minimum shared fund of knowledge that enables people to predict with reasonable certainty what others will do. But action without shared values is more likely to be the result of the use of power by one party and, in the terms of Mary Follett, of 'power-over' rather than 'power-with'. From yet another point of view, systems presume order. Social order is not ordered enough. Human action is continually producing new situations and creating new problems for which there are no routine, ordered solutions.

Turning more directly to the Systems Approach this is said to look on human behaviour as being constrained and determined by a social system of impersonal processes. This impersonality is in direct contrast to the Action theory or frame of reference which emphasizes that actions by people result from the meanings that they personally attach to their own and to other people's actions and that people are constrained by their own personally constructed view of outside reality. On the face of it these two views appear to be contradictory and mutually exclusive but they are followed immediately by Cohen's (1968)[11] suggestion that they are complementary. People and society make each other by their interaction and man has special biological characteristics that make it possible for him to choose whether to act in accordance with an outside system or his own personal views.

Another suggestion is that the Systems Approach deals with the large-scale macro-level of organization and the Action Approach with the individual micro-level. Yet another is that the Action Approach examines the sense in which society does *make* the man and by doing so the Action Approach provides an explanation of social systems which makes the Systems Approach unnecessary.

However, in the end Silverman seems to draw back. The argument as to whether the two are complementary or contradictory is merely marginal. His real purpose is to show that 'the action frame of reference can be a useful source of propositions in organizational analysis'.[12]

Action analysis of organizations

There have been many studies that have tried to relate the behaviour of individuals in an organization with observable aspects of the organization itself, and especially with the rewards offered or withheld. More recently the emphasis has shifted to bring in the relation between actual and expected rewards as a vital factor. But expectations only have a meaning in terms of the individual's orientation, his social position, and the situation facing him. It needs the action frame of reference to explain what is, in fact, a very complex situation.

The explanation must start by distinguishing between different orientations and discovering the reasons for the differences. People may have different aims and different expectations due to their previous individual experiences from birth, to differences in the standards they have come to accept, and to differences in their experiences in the organization. These have affected their expectations and aims in one direction or another and, indeed, may have created new ones.

The resulting differences in orientation will give differing degrees of feelings of involvement in the organization that may vary from the highest moral involvement through indifference to alienation that is just not quite strong enough to cause the individual to leave the organization. Involvement may express itself in different ways and will also be affected by the way in which authority is exercized.

All members of the organization will tend to use strategies of action which are likely to preserve or extend their sphere of discretion about their own conduct. Against this the role system of the organization will indicate the actions expected from individuals. Only a thorough knowledge of all these factors can provide a valid base for understanding expectations and action.

Organizational change

Silverman thinks that much of the theorizing about change has been oversimplified. It has tended to assume that the causes of change lie outside the organization and that the latter has a built-in tendency to adapt its internal structure towards a new state of equilibrium that matches the new conditions. In reality, he claims, change may be in the rules of the game or in the attitudes of members towards them. It may be due to external causes or it may come from the interaction of the people with the organization. Adaptation to it will never be automatic or impersonal but will depend on the definitions of the situation supplied and used by the people concerned. In these terms the action frame of reference explains how changes result from the interaction of the people concerned. Whatever the cause it may confirm some expectations, destroy others, make the attainment of some aims easier, others more difficult or impossible. In some or many ways it makes people alter their definition of the situation, leads them to new forms of interaction and amends the institutional stock of knowledge. On top of this the results of change are not entirely determinable because any action may have unforeseen and unintended consequences and prediction is usually, if not always, based on incomplete knowledge.

The logical Action Approach must look at change in six areas and in the following logical sequence:

(i) The present role-system, its interaction patterns, its historical development, and the resultant pattern of shared values.

(ii) The typical level of involvement among members and the factors that have led to it.

(iii) The present definitions of the situation and expectations of typical members and groups.

(iv) Typical actions of members and the meanings that they attach to them.

(v) Nature and sources of intended and unintended consequences of action.

(vi) Resulting changes in involvement, aims, interaction amongst members, and in the institutional stock of knowledge.

The contribution of the Action Approach

Specific contributions towards understanding organizations which are claimed for the Action Approach are:

(i) Its equal relevance to analysing the orientation of members and the role-system which emerges from interaction.

(ii) It explains different reactions to apparently identical situations.

(iii) The relationships between members of an organization may arise from the needs of the system or as a generally unintended consequence of the motivated social actions of individuals and groups.

(iv) The pattern of organizational structure may differ even when similar groups are pursuing similar ends if other related groups are pursuing different ends or when the power of groups to impose their will on others varies.

(v) The degree of consensus among individuals and among groups is more important for action than shared values.

(vi) The lack of consensus does not necessarily imply open conflict; toleration of differences is possible.

(vii) People may share the same expectations although their reasons for them may vary.

(viii) The Action Approach can explain change that occurs from within the individual, group or organization. It is not necessary to postulate direct outside causes.

(ix) Only the Action Approach enables full and complete reasons for behaviour to be given which do not leave exceptions to be 'explained' by extra-organizational factors.

The comparative study of different organizations

Silverman considers that most comparative studies which have been done have tended to be limited in scope because of the researcher's own approach from some more or less narrow specialist base. An Action Approach comparison by getting behind appearances and face values to real meanings would obviate the narrow approach and enable meaningful comparisons to be made. In particular it would investigate in each organization:

(i) The predominant structures of meanings given to situations, the role systems and the extent of reliance on coercion or consent.

(ii) The characteristic patterns of involvement, attachment to rules and definitions of situations.

(iii) The typical strategies used to obtain ends and goals.

(iv) The relative abilities of groups to impose their view of situations on other groups.

(v) The origins and history of the development of meaning structures.

D. Silverman

Support for the Action Approach

The whole of Chapters 8 and 9 in Silverman's book is devoted to culling aspects and ideas from other authors' writings which Silverman claims support his views. He is careful to point out that the authors concerned are not limited to just the topics he has picked out. It is a long and impressive collection even when any due allowance is made for over-enthusiasm in seeking support. Space does not allow it to be given detailed attention here but it covers the main topics of attachment and commitment to organizations, wants and expectations, factors in orientation, strategy and tactics in actions, power structures, patterns of interaction, rationality and decision systems in relation to meanings structures. It seems he has found support for every aspect of his new approach.

Conclusions

Silverman argues that the social world in which organizations exist and of which they form a large part is in a continuous process of definition and re-definition through the motivated actions of people. These actions depend on experience, orientation, and accepted meanings that are continually being changed. The current institutionalized, accepted views lead to the accepted rules of the game but neither the rules nor their acceptance remain certain and static. Dynamic change is the only possible description of the situation. The present position is a point in a process that has been pre-defined by what has gone before but which is always leading on to new emergent definitions of reality. The starting point for breaking into and understanding this process lies in discovering the differences in subjective perspectives and meanings. These are the foundation stones on which all else rests.

References

(1) Silverman, D. *A Theory of Organizations* (London: Heinemann Educational Books, 1970), p. 1.

(2) Ibid, p. 1.

(3) Ibid, p. 1.

(4) Krupp, S. *Pattern in Organizational Analysis* (Philadelphia: Chilton, 1960).

(5) Silverman, D. op. cit., p. 41.

(6) Merton, R. K. *Social Theory and Social Structure* (Glencoe. Ill: Free Press, 1949).

(7) Selznik, P. *T.V.A. and the Grass Roots* (Berkeley: California University Press, 1949).

(8) Parsons, T. *The Social System* (Glencoe, Ill: Free Press, 1964).

(9) Katz, D. and Kahn, R. L. *The Social Psychology of Organizations* (New York: Wiley, 1966).

(10) Silverman, D. op. cit., p. 130.

(11) Cohen, P. S. *Modern Social Theory* (London: Heinemann, 1968).
(12) Silverman, D. op. cit., p. 143.

Bibliography

BOOK BY D. SILVERMAN
   The Theory of Organizations: A Sociological Framework (London: Heinemann, 1970).

PART II

Further Psycho-sociology

9

An Overview

Well before 1960 the Human Relations School with its over-emphasis in the individual and the 'one big happy family' at work had run its course to extremes. It had been applied in practice, in America at least, and had been found wanting. New, but insufficiently tested, theories were being put forward by people like McGregor, Argyris, Likert and Herzberg.

These new insights needed extensive testing by empirical research and experiment before they could be said to be proved and acceptable. Such proof, if available, would in itself be a big step forward and fully justify the title 'further developments'. The proof became available and seems sufficient justification for the inclusion in this Part of the book of three names, Argyris, Likert and Herzberg, that have already appeared in the earlier volume, *Developments in Management Thought*. These three authors not only produce what appears to be considerable empirical evidence to support their earlier theories but, in each case, they expand their ideas into broader fields.

A. K. Rice wrote his book just before 1960 and it appears to bring together into a logical whole many ideas which had developed from projects previously carried out by members of the Tavistock Institute of Human Relations. In concept and ideas it belongs to the 1960s rather than the 1950s. Essentially it developed the idea of the 'socio-technical' system in which the technical requirements of the work ceased to be the sole dominant determining factor. Management, by using methods which showed genuine concern for and consideration of the workers' psychological and sociological needs, could in consultation with the workers devise methods and systems which met *both* the needs of technology and of the workers to the advantage of all.

The theory of the lack of congruence between the work situation and the workers' psychological needs that had been developed by Argyris to account for immature behaviour and conflict was extended by him into the wider concept of mental health. This brought in greater realism by making it possible to explain the tolerance of immaturity and by introducing realistic concepts of self-concept, self-awareness and self-esteem. A further and very useful idea introduced by Argyris was that of psychological energy. Important, too, and worthy of more attention than it appears to have received, is his account of managerial training and the implications involved. Argyris's contributions cover the period 1960–4.

Progress along any one direction is seldom uniform and continuous and, indeed, it is questionable whether it should be for best results. The 'doubting Thomas' has an important function to play in raising questions which might be overlooked in an excess of enthusiasm. Strauss (1963), playing the role of an outsider looking in, raises two fundamental issues which cannot be ignored and which could challenge almost the whole of the rest of Part II. Should we not accept that under present conditions dull routine work for the majority matched by viable, psychologically satisfying forms of non-work pursuits is, on balance, the best that industrial civilization can do? Should we not put our efforts, not into improving work, but into automating and abolishing it to the point where it becomes a minor aspect of life in which the satisfactory pursuit of leisure becomes the real purpose? Twenty-first-century hedonism versus a nineteenth-century Victorian ethic modified by inappropriate twentieth-century intellectual, middle-class values. It is a point of view, a challenge which could not be left out.

Blake and Mouton in 1964 added a new and significant dimension to management thought. In a way they are the odd ones out in that they are both practising management consultants and not academics. It is, however, this very fact which gives their contribution its significance.

As consultants their prime purpose would be to improve the managerial performance of their client companies. But to do this they needed a solid theoretical base on which to work. This seems to have been provided by Likert's concepts of 'job-centred supervision' and 'employee-centred supervision'. They expanded these to cover the whole field of management practice and converted them into the 'Managerial Grid'. For the five main positions on the Grid, the four corners and the centre, representing five styles of management they developed five groups of behaviour, the conditions which favoured each and the action necessary to move from one style to another.

Their original book *The Managerial Grid* sets out the theory in detail. A later book *Corporate Excellence through Grid Organization Development* shows that what, at first, might have seemed just another gimmick was, in fact, a very important development.

True to their heritage from the Michigan Institute for Social Research Katz and Kahn (1966) progressed steadily on the lines of massive empirical research adding further insights and greater realism on their way. Two major issues on which they shed more light were the functions of the 'role' concept as distinct from the individual and the functions of communication within the organization.

Likert has been included because in 1967 he supplied so much empirical evidence to support the basic theory developed earlier in *New Patterns of Management*. In doing so he also provided a further expansion of detail.

But at one point it does seem as if he may have let a very significant cat out of the bag. One sentence leads to the suspicion that most, if not all, the empirical work on which his theories were based was done in medium-sized firms employing hundreds rather than thousands. If this was really the case then it throws up a question and a challenge as big as the one raised by Strauss. It is a question of cause-and-effect. Are the results claimed by Likert due solely to the forms of managerial behaviour and organizational structure which he postulates or are they due to those patterns *being used in medium-sized firms*? With the very large majority of managers and workers being employed in a relatively small number of very large organizations the real significance of the question is there for all to see.

Of all the writers of the 1950s Herzberg was, perhaps, the one most open to the charge of imputing middle-class values to the shop-floor operative. His hygiene/motivator theory was originally based on a study of engineers and accountants and it is doubtful whether one could get more middle-class than that. By 1968 he felt he and others had produced enough evidence to meet the criticism and to establish a base for his theory across all levels from Managing Directors and Presidents to floor-sweepers. But there is another good reason for giving Herzberg a second hearing. In 1968 he was prepared to develop his theory into a specific and detailed plan of action. Theory alone was not enough. He who develops a theory must be prepared to demonstrate how to put it into practice. Herzberg does.

And so to 1970, the end of Part II of this book and to Schein. As in the rest of the book each author dealt with has largely been left to stand on his own two feet. Schein is one, perhaps of several or even many, who was prepared to try at the end of the decade to draw the many threads together and to weld the different approaches into a common pattern. Perhaps the best idea of the 'state of the game' is shown by the fact that he was compelled to replace 'economic man' *and* 'social man' by *'complex man'*.

10

A. K. Rice
1958

Almost a decade before Miller and Rice's book, *Systems of Organization*, drew together the threads of thought being developed at the Tavistock Institute for Human Relations, A. K. Rice had written *Productivity and Social Organization*.[1] This book gives a very full account of the development of a new management system and of new organizational and social structures at the Ahmedabad Calico Mills over the period 1953–6. Additionally, and from our point of view, more importantly, it sets out the theoretical base on which the Ahmedabad Experiment was founded and the conclusions to which it led.

The experiments here and the earlier ones in British coal-mines are significant from two points of view. In the first place they were far and away ahead of most thinking in Britain at that time. Ultimately the second significant point, which relates more directly to the Ahmedabad Experiment, may be the more important. It is this. The general culture and atmosphere, the social conditions, the managerial climate, in fact the whole environment of Ahmedabad was so essentially different from that of Britain or America that it might seem inevitable that the theories and practices of Western industry would not prove applicable or suitable. There are differences, of course, but on the whole Rice's conclusions about Ahmedabad resemble so closely those of the mainstream of American thought that it is tempting to believe that universal laws and concepts are beginning to appear. Certainly the parallels are too close to be pure accident.

The descriptive details of the background and even of much of the experiment itself must be omitted here, interesting though they are. The assumptions, the concepts, the results and the conclusions will fill the bulk of this chapter.

The post-war industrialization of India was, according to Rice, causing a breakdown in the traditional social structure especially in the towns. The old composite family group of three or even four generations was being replaced by a new social system of small groups. Rice uses this idea to support the validity of the sociological concept of small 'natural' groups. But Likert comes to much the same idea of small 'natural' groups in the independence–competitive culture of America, and the problems of long-wall mining operation in British coal-mines produced the same conclusion. This must raise the fundamental question of whether a 'natural group' culture is a general human characteristic rather than the result of a particular social culture.

Still at the very start of his story Rice makes a vital point which should not be forgotten. The management of the Calico Works, although primitive by Western standards at the beginning, was in the mood to question all its preconceived ideas and practices, was fully prepared to co-operate in and to initiate experiments at all levels including its own, and was able to keep its nerve and persist in the face of all doubts and setbacks.

The main concept underlying the whole experiment is the interaction of social and technological change, the assumption that change in either the social system or the technology of an organization cannot be effectively dealt with in isolation. Changes in technology are bound to have repercussions on the social structure and organization and the interaction between the two cannot be left to chance if the best results are to be obtained. As a corollary such changes must involve corresponding changes in the management system. This socio-technical approach assumes that technology puts demands on the work organization and the social and psychological needs of people impose demands on the social organization. The assumption of Classical theory that technology is pre-eminent and that, at best, the human beings will adapt or that, at worst, they are simply appendages to machines is roundly condemned as wholly inadequate. Results show that when the technological and social organizations are properly matched and meet the real needs of both systems, the gains in efficiency and effectiveness are outstanding.

The initial cause of the experiment was the realization by top management that the potentially great improvement in productivity which should have followed the installation of automatic looms did not occur whatever management did. The relationship between the researchers and the Company was that of consultant to client. All experiments and changes were fully discussed with management, trade unions, and, as far as possible, with workers although with them the language barrier presented large problems. Implementation of decisions was almost entirely in the hands of the local management as the consultant researchers could only be with the Company for limited periods of time. Rice openly admits that the data available on results is only 'industrial data' (presumably largely Likert's end-result variables) and that as a complex variety of simultaneous change processes were going on at the same time the direct correlation of cause-and-effect proved extremely difficult. While at times the effects of events and processes other than the ones being analysed may have been ignored or not realized, it seems fair comment to suggest that the general conclusions are still valid and have been sufficiently supported elsewhere.

Basic concepts and assumptions

Right at the very beginning Rice was compelled to state his (largely) implicit assumptions in explicit written form in order to communicate effectively with a management to whom they were largely new. This is fortunate in a way because so often implicit assumptions are taken for granted and the failure to spell them out leads to confusion. At the stage of 'present development', presumably 1953 when the experiment started, they can be summarized as follows.

Any production system (Rice uses this term to mean the whole firm, sales, buying, research, and finance as well as production) performs many tasks at the same time. The tasks, their content, and their distribution between departments and units vary from firm to firm and over periods of time for the same firm. Manufacture, selling, employment, profits and dividends are given as the prime tasks or objectives at the conscious level. At conscious and sub-conscious level the system provides more or less adequate mechanisms for meeting the needs of the social system – social and psychological needs and defences against anxiety.

Each system or sub-system has, at any one time, one primary task – the one it was set up to perform. In making judgements about organizations the two essential questions are: 'What is its primary task?' and 'How well is it being performed?' (Author's comment. In the last paragraph each system or sub-system was said to be performing 'many tasks at the same time'. It seems that Rice must now be assuming that these tasks can be put in some order of priority or, at least, that one can be selected as 'primary'. This is by no means as easy as it sounds and it seems to ignore completely the question of conflict between tasks and goals.)

Powerful psychological and social forces ensure a considerable capacity for co-operation among members of the organization in working to achieve the primary task. This is a group phenomenon over-riding the possibility that individual and group attitudes may differ. It will exercize influence over members for as long as they remain in the organization. But Rice either quotes or uses the same approach as Argyris. This concept of co-operation towards a primary task depends on adult, reality-based behaviour.

Expanding on this theme, the effective performance of a primary task is psychologically satisfying in itself; difficulties in the way of performing satisfactorily may cause a group to close ranks and achieve higher co-operation. People generally have a manifest or latent need to get on with the job and a management that makes this possible gains respect while one that does not, creates frustration and demoralization, dissatisfaction and apathy.

Following these generalized assumptions there are more detailed ones.

(i) People engaged in a task should experience, as far as practicable, the satisfaction of completing a whole task. Extreme sub-division of tasks causes dissatisfaction.

(ii) Tasks should, as far as possible, allow for self-control by the worker or group.

(iii) Where different tasks are related in some way the organization must allow satisfactory relationships between the individuals or groups concerned.

(iv) Efficient organization implies that neither fewer nor more people are employed on a 'whole' task than can perform it efficiently. At the same time the group employed on the 'whole' task must be capable of satisfying the social and psychological needs of members.

(v) Two people comprise the smallest possible satisfactory group. Six to twelve, with a mode of eight, is the next most satisfactory size.

(vi) The range of skills required within the group should, for stability, be such that they can be understood by all members of the group. If some skills are too high for this then they make for difficulties of communication within the group.

(vii) Group stability and internal leadership are also helped if there are fewer differences in prestige and status between individuals in the group.

Two further assumptions were made specifically for the conditions in India although it is difficult to see why they should not be of much wider application.

(viii) Differentiation of tasks within a group should be on the basis of skill required and equipment used. This differentiation should include an hierarchical element so that more highly skilled jobs have a higher position and status. At the same time there must be provisions for rising to higher status jobs and for interchange between jobs on the same level.

(ix) If for social reasons members of small workgroups can no longer work satisfactorily with the group to which they belong, they should be able to change to another group on a similar task.

Apart from being an explicit guide to the management of the Calico Mills this list has much wider interest as a guide to the fundamentals of a socio-technical system of management.

Operating and managing systems

An early attempt is made here to incorporate into the general theory a few aspects of elementary systems theory. Any industrial system (firm) can be likened to an open system. Within the total system there are two main systems – the operating system and the managing system.

An operating system can be defined in terms of what is imported into it, processed, and exported from it. Complex organizations can have more than one system of each kind, e.g. parallel product divisions or home and export marketing divisions, and any system may be sub-divided into second, third, fourth, etc. order sub-systems.

Such division into systems and sub-systems implies that the management cannot be all contained in any one operating system, so that, while each system or sub-system will have its own internal management, there must also be an external management system to control and service the operating systems.

This systems aspect can be looked at from both ends. It can start with the total system, the firm, and sub-divide into first, second, third, and so on sub-systems until it comes to the primary production group with a primary function which is self-contained in terms of management, control and service. Or it is possible to work the other way and start with non-differentiated primary groups and build up to differentiated larger groups as a management system is introduced to control and service combinations of smaller groups.

The first experiment

This took place in one section of the automatic loom shed production system and in the management system. Despite the fact that only one of the assumptions set out above was being met, morale in the shed appeared to be good, workers and supervisors got on well together and had a reputation for competence and hard work. Working conditions were as good as possible. On the face of it, in Classical terms, the system should have worked well, but both the quantity and quality of production were well below that which they should have been under the new technology of automatic looms.

In terms of Rice's socio-technical assumptions with only one of them being met the system should almost have ground to a halt. The fact that it did not could only be explained in terms of high individual tolerances of uncertainty, of an inefficient managing system, of lack of group structure, and of concealed, sub-conscious dissatisfaction.

As a limited experiment top management opted for a partial reorganization on socio-technical lines rather than the Classical 'cure' of adding more supervision, more external controls, and tighter inspection. Internal control systems were to be built into the operating system and the production system was to be reorganized to provide for stable small-group structure in the work force.

Results

Both the shop supervisors and the workers adopted the new scheme with tremendous enthusiasm. They had been consulted about it in advance and were encouraged to participate by selecting and forming their own workgroups. They insisted on having the new jobs called A–E to signify clearly the grading and status, something which normal job titles would not have done.

The most obvious result was the tremendous enthusiasm and the determination of the workers to make 'their scheme' work. Participative methods solved problems of work allocation and variations in cloth, made provision for absenteeism due to the fact that about one day in five seems to be a religious festival day for one sect or another, and determined the relations between the small-groups leaders and the official supervisors.

Rice emphasizes the language difficulties involved in full participation methods where any collection of a dozen workers, almost entirely illiterate, might speak four or five languages or dialects. But he claims that the wholesale and enthusiastic acceptance of the new methods infers an intuitive recognition that the new small group organization would satisfy needs of which they, the workers, were consciously unaware. 'Such intuitive acceptance brooked no argument. Nor did it require any reasoned questioning.'[1]

Another point that Rice makes very strongly was the attitude of management. Contrary to all the expectations of the workers and, indeed, the natural impulses of managers who, previously, had been very involved with the shop floor, management left the workers to form their own groups. Later, when excessive enthusiasm led to a vast decrease in quality, management again stood on one side and left the workers to find their own solutions. He concludes that this display by management of an expectation that workers could cope and could behave rationally produced the very behaviour patterns for which management hoped despite the fact that such patterns had previously been non-existent. With the much lower educational standards of Indian workers, greater dependence on management might well have been expected rather than the mature, rational independence which occurred. This is strong support for McGregor's theory Y.[2]

Some 7–8 months after the first experiment considerable difficulties were arising and production and quality had both dropped down to pre-experiment levels. By this time the whole automatic shop was working the new system and under-manning, insufficient training and a trade depression had all contributed to the problem. Again participative methods of problem-solving were used with a high level of frankness and mature behaviour on both sides. Changes in practice and in the management system all worked out by agreement eventually brought the situation back to the new normal standard but it took some 2–3 years to work through.

Interpretation and conclusions

Rice repeats his conclusion that acceptance of the scheme was intuitive rather than reasoned. But the adoption of it as 'our system' by supervisors and workers ensured that it was made to work through the period of early teething troubles and that when major problems and regressive behaviour broke out later they were at first largely ignored.

When after 8 months the scheme virtually broke down over the whole shed, management's first reaction was to put the blame everywhere except on themselves. But joint investigation procedures and the resulting acceptance by management of the workers' point of view, which, in fact, was the correct one, restored the mutual confidence between workers and management. Corrective measures eventually got the operations back to the high standards achieved by the experimental group.

A number of interesting inferences are drawn at this stage:

(i) Effective performance of a primary task is an important source of satisfaction at *all* levels of work.

(ii) Although it may be latent and need drawing out, there exists a much larger capacity for voluntary co-operation to achieve effective performance than Classical theory or many practising managers are prepared to admit.

(iii) The experiment supports both the natural group of about eight hypothesis and the whole task hypothesis.

(iv) There is a correlation between personal relationships and work effectiveness.

(v) Unnecessary interference by supervision when group autonomy has been established leads to regressive behaviour.

(vi) Workers prefer clear-cut, easily understood divisions and symbols of status.

A. K. Rice

The non-automatic shed

Rice quotes Lewin's thesis that situations and attitudes become 'frozen' over long periods without much change and that some major event or effort is necessary to unfreeze the situation before significant effective change can occur. In the experiment already described the unfreezing agent was the introduction of automatic looms.

The introduction of automatic looms into the non-automatic sheds was prevented by Government action. To 'unfreeze' a very 'frozen' situation in these sheds an experimental unit to try out new methods of organizing work was set up. It was away from the non-automatic sheds and manned by volunteers. The 'unfreezing' agent was the decision by management to allow non-automatic workers *at any time* to stop their own work, to visit the experimental unit, to talk to the volunteers, and even to stay to help them. This was communication 'by sight and contact'. Under any circumstances it would have been dramatic. With five languages and illiteracy in the sheds it was not only dramatic it was, in fact, the only possible way.

If anything, the management system and the social conditions in these sheds were even worse than in the automatic sheds. The original planning for the experimental unit was done by top management and the consultant, as participation at this stage was regarded as impracticable. The supervisor selected to run the unit came from the automatic shed and had been through all the experiments there. He was allowed to pick his own team from a large number of volunteers. As the team became established and developed the capacity to do so, they were brought into consultation on all changes.

Although management over the whole period so far had obviously gone some way towards generating mutual confidence and trust, there was still a credibility gap. For instance, none of the workers really believed, until it happened, that the new higher rates of pay would be paid or that all work could be stopped for full consultation on difficulties when they arose. But, as management did and continued to do these things and showed that it would take serious notice of what the workers said, mutual trust developed. With this improvement workers began to make constructive suggestions and supervisors began to experiment on their own without reference to higher authority. Patterns of behaviour such as these became self-reinforcing as time went on.

Despite an absolutely disastrous start to the experiment when hordes of workers came from the sheds not only to watch but to stay and 'help' the experimental unit finally settled down very successfully and gradually the new system was extended to all or parts of the other sheds.

95

Interpretation and conclusions

Because the non-automatic system had virtually remained unchanged since it had been imported from Lancashire seventy-five years earlier, more difficulties were expected and met than in the automatic shed. The changeover did, of course, take much longer.

The parallels with the earlier experiment were quite striking. As workers became involved in the changeover the same attitudes of a determination to make 'our system' work, group loyalty, and spontaneous reaction became apparent although they did take longer to work through. There appeared to be the same unrecognized social and psychological needs and problems which led to intuitive acceptance of the new methods.

New managing systems

So far we have concentrated on changes in working methods. Occasional references to changing management attitudes and systems have not been spelt out. Now Rice turns specifically to these.

In brief the system existing at the start was traditional and primitive. The Managing Agent (Director) was all-powerful with the minimum non-specialized management team below him and immediately below them the supervisory staff. Managers, including the Managing Agent, paid frequent visits to the shop floor by-passing supervision. Authority and responsibility patterns were in a state of chaos.

During the post-war period massive external changes had been taking place. Trade unions, political change, increasing competition, and new technologies combined to convince the Managing Agent that the ability to bring about change within the firm was essential but that his existing management structure was unable to do so. He also fully realized that the need for change *started with himself*.

The account of the changes in the managing systems seems the least satisfactory part of the book. Briefly they seem to have been:

    (i) Creation of a recognized top level management to support the Managing Agent.

    (ii) Creation of three Second Order Operating Divisions and three Second Order Control and Service Divisions.

    (iii) New Fourth and Fifth Order Operating systems were created in operating divisions.

    (iv) By-passing by higher management was stopped.

    (v) Proper promotion and discipline policies and practices were set up.

Although it is not part of the managing system as such it is obvious that an extremely important change was that of the attitudes and practices of the managers themselves. Existing managers were retained, promotions were largely from within and each divisional manager was fully involved in major re-organizations in his own division. Again Rice says that it is impossible to relate particular effects to particular causes, but that the new management succeeded better than the old had done.

Social and technical change

Rice devotes the last part of his book to a wider survey of the problems involved in socio-technical systems using as his base other work done through the Tavistock Institute up to 1957.

Tasks and their organization

Primary tasks, especially the primary task of the whole organization, become much more difficult to define and to reach agreement on as technological and managerial systems become more and more complex. There is an increasing probability that decisions related to the primary task of one unit will, at least, seem inconsistent with those of other units.

Over a period of time a group set up to perform a primary task may redefine it to suit their own particular ends and eventually it can become contrary to or subversive of the main primary aims. Even within the small group it is possible for implicit and unrecognized differences of interpretation to arise which militate against effective performance. Changes are most likely to succeed when they are seen by all involved as furthering a primary task which they recognize and accept.

Small primary task groups of around eight have been confirmed by the Ahmedabad experiments but variation may be necessary to take into account individual personalities, the structure and culture of the society, and the cultural patterns of leadership.

The organization of systems

Operating and management systems are used by Rice and others to illustrate the change from the informal one-boss situation of the one-man firm to the large scale, impersonal management of the large firm. The separation is needed because one managerial system may control several operating systems. But the managerial system has its own input–conversion–output processes and may itself be divided into sub-systems.

Within the management system Rice differentiates between the control and service functions. But he also adds another form of control, that which one operating system imposes on another or others by virtue of its behaviour as shown in quantity and quality of output and other actions. These two forms of control are obviously quite distinct.

How far operating systems are prepared to accept the control and service functions of the management systems depends on the aspect of the control or service *vis-à-vis* the operating system, the way the functions are performed, and the status of the relevant part of the management system.

General management
Where sufficient differentiation, specialization, and delegation have occurred top or general management becomes solely the management of managers. Frequently for one reason or another, e.g. personal preference or unequal development, one or more aspects may not have been differentiated and may still be wholly or partly held in general management hands. Rice claims that this is frequently a source of difficulty and more attention is given to some aspects at the expense of others. At the same time he admits that due to different rates of growth and personal problems, differentiation is, in fact, seldom complete and delegation is often imperfect. In consequence the operation of the pair-relationships between the top manager and his immediate subordinates becomes vital to effective performance.

The management of mechanization and change
The evolution of a machine technology has led to resultant changes in the organization of work and in the social structure. These changes, with their emphasis on the machine at the expense of human needs, have led to a lop-sided development. In the long run this neglect of human needs has resulted in full effectiveness not being reached.

At the same time mechanization is unlikely to occur at the same rate in all inter-related aspects of production. Rice quotes Trist's view that efficiency will be reduced when all sub-systems have not reached the same degree of mechanization.

On the human side the growth of machine technology has increased the skill demanded in designing, maintaining and supervising machines but it has drastically reduced the skill required in operating and minding them. At the same time machine technology demands more stable and reliable operation. The result has been improved (usually tighter) supervision, more programming and better maintenance. Rice also suggests reduced labour mobility although this seems somewhat dubious as machine minding demands less and less skill.

There is a suggestion that while mechanization of production has gone ahead the related systems of marketing, personnel and the parallel management system have not moved ahead in the same way. There is a double difficulty here. The failure of these systems to progress is holding down the benefit that could be obtained from more sophisticated production and, perhaps even more damaging, existing management systems have themselves resisted the need for improvement by differentiation and specialization.

In a direct approach to the management of change itself Rice sees a number of related problems that require attention. With mechanization the new operational and management systems must transcend individual task organization, and the control system consequently must be more differentiated and more complex. Greater complexity in the systems involves a correspondingly greater increase in integration to maintain co-ordination while at the same time it increases the risks of poor communication and control. Science-based industry, as most of it is now, involves a virtually continuous assimilation of change.

Technology in prescribing both equipment and methods sets limits to the flexibility permissible in the organization of systems. But technology must not be taken as the only factor. Within the limits set there must be room for manoeuvre and the most satisfactory system will be the one that uses these limits to the utmost to provide opportunity for the greatest satisfaction of social and psychological needs. At the same time basic cultural and social norms provide limits to the range of mechanization which can be used.

Rice concludes with the view that the almost universal demands for higher standards of living involve an increase in mechanization which has not only already occurred but must also be projected into the future. Such change has not, up to now, been consistent with the social and cultural background and especially with traditional views. His hope is that planned, controlled change is more likely to achieve the synthesis of technological and human needs than is haphazard, piecemeal change. Only in this way can we avoid the sacrifice of the human being on the altar of technology and 'progress'.

References

(1) Rice, A. K. *Productivity and Social Organization* (London: Tavistock Publications, 1958), p. 81.

(2) McGregor, D. *The Human Side of Enterprise* (New York: McGraw-Hill, 1960), ch. 4.

and Pollard, H. R. *Developments in Management Thought* (London: Heinemann, 1974), pp. 226–32.

Bibliography

BOOK BY A. K. RICE
Productivity and Social Organization (London: Tavistock, 1958).

II

C. Argyris
1960, 1962 and 1964

If there is one significant difference in emphasis between this book and its predecessor *Developments in Management Thought*[1] it is that all the theories summarized in this one are explicitly based on field research in live, ongoing organizations.

Argyris's book *Personality and the Organization*[2] was analysed in *Developments in Management Thought*. The three which followed it in 1960, 1962 and 1964 are dealt with here. The first two are, in effect, accounts of experiments and research conducted to test and advance the theory put forward in 1957. The third develops a refined theory based on further empirical research.

The first, *Understanding Organizational Behaviour*[3] was described by Argyris as being primarily written for himself as an attempt to describe more definitively how research in industry was conducted and what was required from researchers. He added the hope that it might show to managers the ways in which research might help them.

Neither this book nor the second one warrant a full analysis here, that treatment is reserved for the much more important 1964 work, but they are significant enough for a summary of their main findings.

The specific focus of the project was to obtain an understanding of human behaviour in organizations starting from two variables, the formal organization and the individual, and to go on from there to an attempt to predict behaviour and to derive viable methods of controlling it. Two fundamental assumptions (much abbreviated here) underlie the whole approach. One is the view of organizations as equivalent to living organisms in which, while much that happens is unique, only chaos can result from treating all phenomena as separate events. All organization of living matter is relative to reaching some end or goal. The second is that, in studying complex organizations, the traditional scientific method of breaking down complex wholes into separate parts that can be studied separately and then synthesized back into the complex whole breaks down completely. The main ingredient in the complexity of organizations is the inter-relatedness and interaction of the parts. In trying to study the parts separately this essential ingredient gets completely lost. So in studying complex systems and organizations the complexity itself must be accepted as an essential part of the study.

The theory in *Personality and the Organization* was summarized in eight propositions. Slight modifications of these are introduced here, e.g. the occurrence of conflict, apathy and disturbance can be predicted but cannot be quantified; organizations with psychologically immature employees can avoid conflict and regressive behaviour by providing conditions which meet the needs of immature people; the individual and the organization are not separable, consequences are the resultant of their interaction.

From this Argyris builds a 'framework' that gives him a tentative conceptual definition to use in studying the first firm – Plant X. An organization is

   (i) a plurality of parts that
   (ii) maintain themselves through their inter-relatedness and
   (iii) through achieving specific objectives
   (iv) while accomplishing (ii) and (iii) adapt to the external environment
   (v) and thereby maintain their inter-related state of parts.

The research into and the analysis of data from Plant X produced the following conclusions:

   (i) Plant X had developed a hiring system that tended to bring into the organization only such people as were predisposed to accept the norms and culture of the organization.
   (ii) Management was satisfied with the results of the hiring system so it became self-confirming.
   (iii) The most important predispositions among employees were wages, job-security, non-involvement beyond own job, some control over own job (e.g. speed of work, kitty), feelings of 'togetherness'. These needs 'fitted' the requirements of both the skilled and semi-skilled departments of Plant X.
   (iv) The technological requirements of the skilled and semi-skilled departments differed. They were high quality work, variety, generalist skills and aloneness, passivity, routineness respectively.
   (v) The work may have influenced employees' dispositions somewhat after they had joined by encouraging some aspects and discouraging others.
   (vi) Management was satisfied with and prepared to reinforce the

norms of the employee culture. This reinforced the employees' tendency to behave in accordance with them.

(vii) Foremen had all been appointed from the ranks and presumably had already accepted the norms of employee culture. Instructions from management to obtain high production, low labour turnover, low grievance rates led to passive leadership which left men alone except to ensure they got fair rates of pay. Foremen tended to push decisions up to management.

(viii) Management were dissatisfied with the foremen so they tended to put pressure on them and to by-pass them by frequent visits to the shop floor.

(ix) Foremen felt their jobs were unimportant, menial and contained little challenge or responsibility. Their low status increased their dependence and inhibited them from initiating changes to improve their position.

(x) Except for the foremen the organization was functioning effectively in terms of output, labour turnover, grievances and morale due to the psychological contract of employment, and the employee culture.

From this analysis Argyris predicted that with regard to a proposed change in working conditions workers would not object to it so long as their wages and job security were not affected; would not want to be involved in decisions on its implementation; and that any feelings of annoyance that arose initially would die down as workers re-established their control over their immediate environment. All these predictions were confirmed by the workers' actual reactions to a change in work methods in the skilled departments.

Further hypotheses were advanced about managers' reactions to feedback about the results of the research. Information that the foremen felt under pressure and complained of their low status was, as expected, accepted by management. A further hypothesis was that because managers were satisfied with the workers they would be surprised by the findings about the workers' predispositions to non-involvement, to control of own immediate environment and to being left alone. This hypothesis was confirmed. A further prediction that management would be primarily concerned with effecting changes in the foremen and their culture by suggesting increases in their pay and raising standards for their performance was also confirmed.

A further change in budget procedure which was meant to increase managerial control also produced a number of predictions. Among these, three were perhaps of most significance. The specialists in the controller's office were predicted as assuming that their job was to increase the pressure on workers and foremen by raising production goals, cutting down the freedom for error, tightening piece-rates, and eliminating the 'kitty'. In line with this it was predicted that management's response would be to increase their interaction with and their pressure on the foremen. This, it was predicted, would put the foremen in a different situation. They could not openly resist the management and, understanding the psychological contract with the workers, they could not pass the pressure on to the workers. Their reaction would be to complain that the scheme was too complex and unworkable.

Unfortunately time and opportunity to confirm these predictions in Plant X were not available. The alternative, which fortunately was possible, was to find another similar plant, with similar conditions where similar changes had taken place some time earlier and to check whether the actual results there agreed with or differed from the predictions made for Plant X. This was called Plant Y.

Before the research was conducted in Plant Y Argyris developed fifteen hypotheses which were put away in a sealed envelope until the conclusions had been drawn from a year's research in Plant Y. Of the fifteen predictions all but one were definitely confirmed, mostly by direct evidence but in a few cases by inference drawn from indirect evidence. The remaining one prediction was neither confirmed nor disproved.

Argyris is careful to point out that this work merely outlines the method and theory of one approach to the study of organizational behaviour. He describes the approach as immature and as leading to more unresolved questions. These are:

(i) What are the criteria by which a researcher can decide that he has discovered a valid pattern of the relevant variables in the situation or has created an adequate model of them?

(ii) What specific operational definitions will show that a model represents the organization as a whole adequately?

(iii) How can the behavioural contents of different 'parts' of the model be defined?

(iv) How do major dispositions become an informal employee culture?

(v) The assumption that an organization is self-maintaining implies a degree of tolerance within and between 'parts'. How can the behaviour mechanisms that set up and operate these tolerance levels be described and explained?

(vi) How can isolated studies of organizations be developed into valid generalizations?

After setting out a considerable number of practical questions on the methodology and concepts involved in research into organizations Argyris comes round to a question that has hung over the whole account of the work since the first introductory paragraphs. It will be remembered that there he was insisting on the need to study complexity as a whole and on the impossibility of studying parts in isolation. But this is just what he has been doing – analysing behaviour in terms only of psychology. He says, 'The questions above focus on the organization as a whole. Very little is said about its environment. The omission of the environment does not imply that organizations are relatively closed systems unaffected by their environments. Nothing could be further from the truth . . . it is acknowledged, however, that a complete organizational theory will require that the organizational and environmental studies be integrated'.[4]

For 1960 this was a far-sighted view (and a correct one as later events showed) but it did not prevent Argyris from claiming that such research, limited though it would be, would have very real advantages for practising managers.

Two years later in *Interpersonal Competence and Organizational Effectiveness*[5] Argyris sets out the description of and his conclusions about an experiment in training managers. The President of a large corporation, who had heard of Argyris's theory on inter-personal competence, asked him to move into one of the divisions of the corporation and to assess the performance of its managers. If thought necessary, Argyris was to develop and run a training programme.

The book starts with a discussion of the nature of modern organization and the meaning of inter-personal competence and its relationship to organizational effectiveness. This is followed by a detailed description of the analysis and diagnosis of the management and the feed-back of the findings to the managers themselves. The outcome was that it was decided that a training programme was needed and, equally importantly, that the managers were capable of going through and accepting such a programme. The programme took the form of 'laboratory' training for the top dozen or so managers in which by open, unfettered discussion they would be brought to understand their attitudes towards each other and the results that followed. These attitudes were essentially based on suspicion of each other and a general lack of confidence in each other. Generally these were not recognized for what they were but they caused much deviousness in behaviour and lowered considerably the level of managerial performance.

A detailed and very interesting account is given of the conduct of the training programme itself. Its immediate results were a very marked decrease in suspicion and mistrust between the managers involved, a marked increase in the openness of approach between them, and greater effectiveness at their level.

But the effect on overall performance was decidedly limited. The immediate subordinates of the managers had not been involved in the training and themselves became suspicious of their 'new' managers and found the new attitudes and practices difficult to accept. At lower levels the very same problems of suspicion, lack of confidence and poor inter-personal relations continued to exist and hampered the effectiveness of improved performance at the top level.

Somewhat ruefully Argyris concludes that limited training activities of this kind can have good results for the people directly concerned but, because they are limited and do not effect changes in other inter-related areas of the organization, their effect on total organizational effectiveness is likely to be small. Improving effectiveness by training must be a long-term business with appropriate training applied simultaneously at all levels.

It is time now to turn to what is probably Argyris's major work *Integrating the Individual and the Organization*.[6] He describes it as presenting an up-to-date version of *Personality and the Organization* incorporating changes due to further research and, more optimistically, a preliminary theory on how to redesign organization in order to take full advantage of the energy and competence of the individual. The aim is to show how, by each side giving a little to meet the needs of the other, it should be possible to achieve a better result than minimal satisficing. At the same time the ideal of optimizing is admitted to be unrealistic.

Basic concepts
But what is to be more than minimally satisficed? Three earlier criteria are rejected out of hand – maximum profit, the one happy family, and manipulation of the work-force by management. The accepted criterion is effectiveness measured along a number of different scales such as fully functioning individuals showing competence, commitment, and self-responsibility on the one hand and active, viable, vital organizations on the other. The emphasis has shifted from the clash between mature personality and required immature conduct to the more positive one of mental health.

Mental health itself is demonstrated to be a complex, many-sided phenomenon. It involves work, tension, some frustration, realistic aspiration levels, realistic challenges, striving, competence, effective dealings with the environment, freedom to be more (not less) responsible, and a meaning to life. This does not mean that everyone should aspire to being an Einstein or a Michelangelo. What is a satisfactory level of achievement of these aspects will vary from one individual to another. The important thing is that each satisfices in relation to his own capacities.

Reviewing briefly a wide selection of writing, Argyris makes two points which require particular emphasis. One is that the informal organization is not simply a defensive mechanism used by individuals to protect their mental health against disruption by the formal organization. It can itself have a negative effect on mental health. His other point is that, while the separation of the formal from the informal organization may be challenged from the point of view of the operation of the organization as a whole, from the point of view of studying the parts they can be separated. In reality, however, the operation of the organization is the interaction of the two organizations.

Extreme complexity is a fundamental attribute of large organizations and, while this fact must be accepted, some simplification relative to the theory developed is essential. Argyris's scheme is meant to show the changes required in organization (and the individual) to obtain the most possible human energy for productive effort. The relevant factors involved are:

(i) Individual needs, attitudes, values and feelings.
(ii) Group attractiveness, goals, processes and norms.
(iii) Organizational activities and policies.
(iv) Informal activities.

This list is not necessarily complete. Other factors may be found to be involved.

Traditional concepts about organization are inadequate and new ones are needed which will make it possible to see the organization as one integrated behavioural system made up of multidimensional parts. Two authors are quoted, apparently with approval, who regard organizations as 'open' systems embedded in and interacting fully with their environment. But it does seem that Argyris has a somewhat ambivalent attitude towards the full open systems theory. He uses the phrase 'one integrated behavioural system'. If this is to be taken literally then it seems that significant aspects of the firm such as technology, working conditions, finance, policy, become part of the environment in which the behavioural system exists. The conversion to a 'systems man' seems far from complete.

The relation between the personality of the individual and the organization is that they are 'discrete units with their own laws, which make them amenable to study as separate units'.[7] Personality factors can cause, create and maintain an organization, can operate to ignore its coerciveness, and can even go so far as to destroy it. A relation that can have such opposite effects must obviously be complex with many inter-related factors at work. It is the boundary at which this inter-relationship exists that is the centre of Argyris's work.

While it is admitted that there are great differences between formal organizations in apparently similar circumstances and great similarities between others in different situations, to develop a general theory these differences must be ignored. At a later stage more detailed models can be added to account for them.

The ambivalence about 'systems' theory is confirmed by the admission of an 'arbitrary boundary' placed around the organization. Everything within the boundary is part of the study. Much of that which is outside is to be ignored for the present and left for others to study. One important exception is the influence of the social and cultural environment on that which goes on inside the organization. Eventually a complete theory that includes the individual, the organization, and the environment must be developed, but the time has not yet arrived.

The input
In line with his aim of dealing with the behavioural system Argyris limits himself largely to the analysis of human inputs while taking account of the fact that many other inputs into the total system will influence his particular approach.

Human inputs are all energy in one form or another. The visually obvious one is physiological energy in the form of physical movements. Although the point is not clearly brought out, it seems obvious that mental work and energy are regarded here as a form of physiological energy. Behind manual and mental energy lies the much more important concept of psychological energy. The two forms, physiological and psychological, are inter-related but from the behavioural theory point of view the vital one is the psychological. It is obvious that with all people there is a limit to the physiological energy that can be used over a limited period. Sooner or later sheer fatigue and exhaustion take care of that. But it is a very elastic limit. The man who is too tired to do any more work will, half an hour later, spend far more energy in a round of golf or in digging the garden than he would ever have done working for the same length of time! The determining factor for most of the time is psychological energy. Argyris admits that psychology still has many theories and many disagreements and that he is only going to put forward those ideas that will help in understanding his ideas.

Psychological energy can only be *assumed* to exist as a plausible explanation of everyday conduct. With no bodily change, which can be explained in terms of physiology, people are able to increase or lose the amount of physical and mental energy they can produce. In everyday language it can be summed up as 'I feel like it or I don't' or even 'It's all in the mind'.

The explanation is not, of course, as simple as everyday language. Psychological energy is assumed to exist when a person's needs are 'in tension' in relation to some objective or some outside circumstance. The need for action to reach some more or less specified goal is felt. This supplies the internal stimulus to carry out the activity required to reach the goal. The tension is released and psychological energy ceases to operate when the goal is achieved. There are, of course, other ways of releasing psychological tension but, for the moment at least, we are not concerned with them here. This concept of psychological energy must inevitably lead in to a consideration of 'self' and personality.

The self

A good deal of this section is dealt with more fully in *Personality and the Organization* so the following is a brief refresher and new approaches. The individual is a collection of needs, values and abilities which originate from his inherited characteristics and interaction with previous experience. Personality is the integration of these into an organized pattern that has meaning and consistency for the individual. It has conscious and unconscious aspects. Self-concept is the view that the individual has of himself and is based on the conscious aspects of his personality. The ideal self-concept will always include aspirations for needs and values not yet attained.

It is assumed that all people have a need to experience a sense of competence in dealing with life. What is considered an adequate sense of competence will be a matter for the individual. Increasing recognition of problems and successful solving of them so that they stay solved with the minimum necessary energy are all assumed to increase an individual's sense of competence. Problems will involve competence at two levels. One is the intellectual level where competence in analysis, logic and original thinking is required. The other is inter-personal competence, the ability to deal effectively with other people. Inter-personal competence leads directly to two other aspects of the self.

Self-awareness is rather more than the self-concept. It involves evaluation of the self-concept and its relation to the environment, and understanding of whether or not the two are congruent. Where the self-concept and the environment do not match, the situation will be seen as a threat to the self. The self may be deliberately adapted to match the environment (integration) or the threat may be ignored, rejected, or distorted. Acceptable feed-back from other individuals will increase self-awareness provided it is not regarded as threatening.

Self-esteem comes from a sensible analysis of one's self-concept, self-awareness and competence which results in a value judgement that is satisfactory according to one's own standards. Argyris maintains that self-esteem is increased as:

(i) The individual is able to define his own goals.

(ii) The goals are related to the individual's central needs and values.

(iii) The individual is able to define his own paths to his goals.

(iv) The goals are realistically related to his aspirations and abilities. If they are too high or too low they will reduce his self-esteem.

The concept of mental health, which is the main plank in the new approach, involves self-concept, self-awareness, and self-esteem. But it goes further and requires psychological success. Here the significance of the environment of the individual becomes paramount. It must provide in amounts that match the individual's personality:

(i) A significant degree of self-responsibility and self-control.

(ii) A significant commitment to goals.

(iii) Significant productiveness and work.

(iv) An opportunity to the individual to use his more important abilities.

In case this all sounds too much like perfection in a perfect world Argyris leads on to one qualification. The individual can only 'see' and assess the world in terms of his own self-concept. Whoever he may be he soon learns from experience that what he 'sees' may be wrong. This leads inevitably to feelings of doubt and uncertainty which can only be coped with if he gets confirmation from 'outside' that his perceptions are accurate. If he gets this confirmation it raises his self-esteem, his ability to cope, and his competence in dealing with other people.

The argument has now gone full circle back to psychological energy. Potential, psychological energy is a direct function of the state of self-esteem. Actual energy is a function of the degree of experiencing psychological success. Psychological success, self-esteem, self-awareness and self-concept are essential ingredients of the 'proper state of mind' – mental health.

(Author's comment. Before going further it seems that there are two points that are worth making here. Argyris implies them but does not explicitly make them. The first is that self-concept through to psychological success must be relative to a particular individual. Because of inevitable differences in personality, background and situation what would be high self-esteem and psychological success to one individual could be regarded as utter failure by another. This does not invalidate the theory, in fact it makes it more realistic by clearly removing any possible aura of the 'ivory tower'.

The other is the connection between experiencing psychological success and actual energy. Until the action is successfully completed and the goal attained psychological success cannot really be experienced, so it cannot influence the output of actual energy. It appears rather that the important factor is the *expectation* of success. This will increase as the action shows signs of achieving the goal and the expected probability of a successful outcome will be increased in proportion to the ratio of previous successes to failures.)

Back to Argyris. The individual is not a self-contained island. His state of mind, needs, abilities, experiences, and probability of success are all influenced by the state and norms of the society in which he exists. For present purposes the work environment is the most important aspect of society. In particular this environment may condition what needs the individual develops, the probability of his attaining them, and his concept of the meaning of success and failure.

Finally competence is not the same as efficiency in its narrow sense of minimum costs. It is minimum output of energy to achieve psychological success and self-esteem for all according to their needs. Neither is psychological success the abolition of problems. It is their successful solution.

The organizational dilemma

The dilemma arises because organizations start with a structure usually based on the ideas of Scientific Management and designed by the founders of the organization. This structure will have unintended consequences and in order to meet these, individuals will add an unintended (by the founder's) structure of their own. While this unintended structure will be antagonistic to the initial structure it will, in fact, work with the initial structure to guarantee the latter's existence and maintenance. (Author's comment. While this seems to be a much oversimplified picture of organizational growth we must accept it for the moment to develop Argyris's thesis.)

Additionally the informal activities and structure will have three consequences. They will make the real organization much more complex than the formal (founder's) version. They will help the organization to function more effectively despite 'red-tape' and unplanned-for exigencies. They will enable individuals to perform the required activities in ways that will increase their psychological returns from the activity.

The common argument that the majority of workers do not aspire to psychological success is met on two grounds. It is admitted that what constitutes psychological success varies very much between one individual and another (this picks up the point made on pp. 105–6) and that, while the background upbringing and experience of most workers does not lead them to expect it, this does not mean that they cannot do so given the right conditions. The concept of aspiration to psychological success is central to Argyris's argument because by its use he can 'derive and predict certain informal or unintended consequences of organizations which are supported by existing studies and independent theorizing'.[8]

From this point there follows a restatement of the arguments in *Personality and the Organization* about dependence, submissiveness, lack of self-control and self-responsibility. The more recent argument that interdependence exists both ways between management and workers is dismissed as a special case.

Argyris does admit that there are cases where the conditions are such that they could be expected to lead to dependency, frustration, and immaturity but they do not. In summary the two main reasons for this are where priority needs such as physiological and security ones are not met so that 'higher' psychological needs do not become operative, and where cultural norms of various kinds make for acceptance of the conditions.

The basic dilemma of the organization then is the lack of congruence between the needs of the individual aspiring to self-esteem and an appropriate (to him) level of psychological success on the one hand and the requirements of the pyramid structure of the organization on the other.

The nature of the system at the lower levels

Individuals are by nature adaptive organisms, but they can adapt to the organization in different ways, e.g. conforming by psychological processes that reduce mental health or by modifying their working conditions and patterns away from those required by the organization so as to reduce pressure and frustration. The first form of adaptation lowers performance and the probability of reaching organizational goals. The second, while antagonistic to the system, will, in fact, enable it to work better. They are necessary to help employees make the system work.

At the lower levels where the prospects for self-actualization and satisfying psychological rewards are likely to be less, the pressure for more pay and concern with differentials are likely to be more marked. This tendency is confirmed by early indoctrination from the previous generation that work is simply a question of the pay packet at the end of the week.

But this hypothesis is not as universal as it once was. There can be exceptions. Not all organizations are so designed as to suppress self-expression and the achievement of psychological success. Not all individuals desire psychological success or can be led to want it. Frustration and lack of mental health can occur in precisely opposite circumstances where the individual does not want psychological success and the problems and challenges that go with it, while the organization requires him to do so.

Lack of congruence between the needs of the individual and of the organization is the key factor leading to unintended actions and consequences. Congruence between them does not do so whether it is based either on self-actualization or on submissiveness and immature behaviour.

Finally at this level Argyris turns to the question of whether aspirations, self-esteem, psychological success are 'middle-class' values that sociologists and psychologists, themselves assumed to be 'middle-class', are imputing incorrectly to working-class people. He suggests that the working-classes live in an environment that values apathy, indifference, resignation and fatalism and that the more highly skilled workers tend to be lower–middle or middle-class in their orientation. He goes on to suggest that the lower the skill involved in the work the less the satisfaction derived from it. The crucial variables are control over one's own work and the chance to use one's personal abilities. By implication this shifts the argument from class to control and skill which must surely be safer ground when social barriers are being increasingly eroded.

On balance the argument seems to come out as something of a compromise. The relatively impoverished world of the lower-class, both psychological and material, tends to produce cultural norms that value apathy, indifference and, as these mirror the realities of life as it is, the individual accepts them in order to retain some semblance of sanity. From the immediate point of view this is perhaps just as well because if all workers at all levels suddenly demanded psychological success the greater part of modern organization would be completely unable to cope and would collapse in chaos. But although this may be the reality Argyris remains convinced that all people are capable of aspiring to and achieving their appropriate degree of psychological success if only the repressions and distortions could be removed. Only very convincing empirical research which has yet to be done to disprove his thesis will convince him otherwise.

The nature of the system – managerial levels
It is at the lowest level of management, the supervisor, that the greatest problems and conflicts exist. Only in the rare cases where the aims, norms and attitudes of both management and workers are congruent can the

supervisor have a satisfying job. Under any other circumstances as the man in the middle he is bound to suffer some, if not all, of the following – conflict of loyalties, conflict of aims and purpose, feelings of ambivalence as to which side he belongs, unjustifiable demands on him from either or both sides, and lack of essential information to carry out his job. How he will react will depend on his relations with and concern for his workers, his view of his job as prescribed by his superiors, and his own internal view of himself. Trade unions, increased tendencies towards mechanization and automation, and specialized planning departments are all tending to diminish the role and increase the frustration at supervisory levels.

Higher up the managerial hierarchy these conflicts tend to disappear as the two cultures of the workers and of management begin to overlap less and less. Argyris thinks that the more important factors for effectiveness in management are the objectives as defined for each job and the level of inter-personal competence.

The idea of inter-personal competence is developed much further than in *Interpersonal Competence and Organizational Effectiveness* mentioned earlier in this chapter. We must, therefore, give it a little more attention.

Argyris maintains that at managerial level there is a strong tendency to conceal feelings and emotions and to emphasize rationality because rational behaviour towards organizational objectives is seen as good, whereas emotive behaviour is seen as bad. All problems will be brought up as rational, intellectual and technical ones although, in fact, management would be much more effective if emotive problems could be brought out into the open as such and dealt with adequately. Despite the professed rationality of this behaviour the resulting failure in dealing competently with each other will decrease the rationality and predictability of managers' behaviour which is essential for organizational effectiveness. Managers begin to feel confused and to experience failure but, to maintain their own self-esteem, they project this failure on to the actions of others. This leads to a vicious circle of greater emphasis on the rational and technical leading to greater confusion and more defensive action. The existence of power implicit in the managerial hierarchy through the superior's right to assess and grant or withhold promotion to subordinate managers makes the latter 'play it safe'. They conform to the expectations of the superior as they see them, and develop behaviour patterns which show dependence on the superior – the traditional 'yes-man'. This dependence is further increased by competition between managers and departments, internal 'politics', and feelings of mistrust of others. As a result the superior in his attitude to his subordinates becomes convinced of his superiority and that he is indispensable, and increases his control over them. Again a vicious circle. 'It is not long before the seeds have been planted for conformity, decreasing self-esteem, dependence and psychological failure.'[9] The manager's feelings of commitment to the organization, such as they are, will be external to himself and will come from dependence on the power, ability to grant or withhold rewards, and influence possessed by his superiors. It will not be generated from within himself by personal acceptance of and involvement in the real objectives of the organization. This gloomy picture is developed as a hypothesis from assumptions about organization and psychology which are taken as given but it is given considerable confirmation in Whyte's *The Organization Man*.[10]

Before proceeding further Argyris summarizes what he has said so far adding a few sidelights which deserve mention. He admits that he is working with an oversimplified picture. (Author's comment. This is important to bear in mind in what follows. Oversimplified situations tend to produce oversimplified solutions that do not work properly in real-life complexity. Argyris himself is fully aware of this but the reader should not forget it.) The behaviour at all levels in the organization that is unproductive, in the sense that it is working against the real objectives of the organization, tends to become an end in itself and to consume much energy in carrying it out and preventing its discovery by the higher levels in the hierarchy. The amount of correct information going through the system tends to decrease. There is a tendency to 'add unnecessary staffs, levels of authority which protect those who fear making decisions'.[11]

Organizational effectiveness and ineffectiveness
Immediately there is a problem. What is effectiveness? Argyris argues that each group within the organization will see effectiveness in terms of its own experience so there may be as many views of it as there are groups and each will feel impelled to defend its own view against all comers. In particular, top management, seeing the organization as a whole, dislikes differences below and to avoid them imposes control which leads to tension. This ultimately becomes accepted as part of life and leads to demands from below for strong leadership and so confirms top management's own view.

We are, therefore, looking at a very difficult aspect of organization and it is as well to start with basic ideas. Organization has five essential characteristics:
 (i) Plurality of parts.
 (ii) Inter-relatedness of parts by which they maintain each other.
 (iii) Specific objectives to be achieved.
 (iv) Adapting to the environment while carrying out (ii) and (iii).
 (v) Maintaining inter-relatedness.

By implication organization has three core activities – achieving objectives, maintaining the internal system, and adapting to the external environment. Setting objectives or goals and problem-solving are assumed to be at a different level of analysis and to cut across all three core activities. The problems of unintended actions and consequences are assumed to exist, at least to some extent, in all organizations. A 'steady-state' is assumed to exist when over a period of time social actions between the members have developed a pattern of reciprocal relationships which maintain the *status quo*. Each part or unit of the organization has a function to perform which, if not carried out over a long period of time will destroy the organization. Survival of the 'whole' depends on the interactions of *all* the parts not just a few master parts. The 'whole' of the organization is different from the sum of its parts, not because it has an existence in its own right, but because it results from the interrelatedness of the parts. Finally the organization is embedded in an environment that influences it and with which it must come to terms for survival.

The difficulty of defining effectiveness is dealt with as follows '. . . as an organization's effectiveness increases it will be able *to accomplish its three core activities at a constant or an increasing level of effectiveness with the same or decreasing increments of inputs of energy*'.[12] Viewed critically this has two apparent defects. In a sense it is tautological – effectiveness . . . (is) an 'increasing level of effectiveness'. 'Increasing rate of output' would surely be better if one could be certain of being able to measure rates of output for each core activity. Secondly it omits the most likely case of increased effectiveness, increased output from core activities for a *less than proportionate increase* in inputs. These criticisms do not invalidate Argyris's argument. Total effectiveness is the sum of the scores for each of the three core activities. Argyris agrees with Likert in assuming that inputs are not completely measured in terms of financial costs and that human costs and hidden costs over short and long periods need to be taken into account.

By contrast organizational ineffectiveness occurs when a system requires increasing inputs for constant or decreasing outputs and this state sets off repetition of the same process. Again the degree of ineffectiveness is assumed to be measurable, but its definition will vary according to the values held by the individual defining it. Organizations are assumed to have a tolerance level of acceptable ineffectiveness and all are assumed to have some degree of it. The level at which it becomes serious will vary from time to time and from one organization to another.

As in individual psychology, stress for the organization is not, of itself, either good or bad. If it presents a challenge which can be and is overcome this is equivalent to psychological success and will increase psychological energy and result in a search for and success in dealing with other challenges. But it is assumed that most forms of organizational stress lead to organizational ineffectiveness.

Organizational discomfort is a state where individuals or groups experience negative feelings towards the organization which they are unable to control and whose real causes are unknown.

Pseudo-effectiveness occurs when no discomfort is reported but deeper analysis shows that long-term ineffectiveness is occurring but is hidden by some compensatory mechanism, frequently short-term measuring devices that ignore hidden costs.

From this analysis Argyris draws three immediate conclusions:

(i) 'The unintended activities with their protective defenses and the resulting employee attitudes towards being productive lead to a situation in which

(a) increasing increments of energy will be used non-productively.

(b) the potential energy input will decrease

(c) the probability of resolving these problems will decrease.'[13]

(ii) 'Participants will tend to experience feelings of uncomfortableness which are beyond their control to correct.'[14]

(iii) 'In order to protect the unintended activities, the participants at all levels feed up to the top information that makes the organization look more effective than it actually is. This will lead to pseudo-effectiveness.'[15]

There is a short-lived note of optimism which suggests that in an organization where members at all levels experience adequate degrees of psychological success an atmosphere will build up that will lead to more and more effectiveness and that will carry new participants along with it. Such an organization need never die. More likely is the fact that different parts of the organization will suffer different levels of stress and/or will have different capacities for handling it. Consequently some parts will wear out and become ineffective before others. As pointed out earlier, organization health and effectiveness depend on adequate performance from *all* parts not just a few key parts.

The difficulties for organizations are increased by the fact that their managers are fully occupied with day-to-day problems and have neither the time nor the inclination to do the necessary analytical and diagnostic work involved in determining the true state of effectiveness. As concepts and techniques for analysis become more and more sophisticated managers will need more diagnostic experts to advise them. But the manager should be able to do 'first-aid' diagnoses so that he can recognize and distinguish between problems for himself and problems for the expert.

So far Argyris has limited his analysis to the question of internal 'steady-states'. This, of course, is an abstraction. Real life involves problems of change and effective problem-solving to maintain organizational health.

Problem solving and organizational effectiveness

Adaptation to internal and external stresses, removing recognized ineffectiveness, and innovation all call for problem-solving processes. They all upset the 'steady-state' that exists or towards which the organization is moving.

Problem-solving is effective when it solves problems in ways that ensure that they remain solved, use minimal energy to provide good solutions, and cause minimal damage to the problem-solving process itself. Problems are solved when the causes of them are eliminated and the system returns to its previous 'steady-state' or reaches a new one. The process is ineffective when it uses increasing increments of energy or reduces the amount of energy potential.

Returning to an earlier point Argyris assumes that managers who make decisions or control decision-making meetings accept the values of objectivity, rationality, suppression of emotions which produce defensive action, conformity, mistrust and distortion or suppression of information. Consequently the very values that they assume will lead to effective decision-making actually produce ineffectiveness.

More effective decision-making should result from behaviour of the kind postulated later for greater organizational effectiveness and from better recognition of the real nature of the problem. Better invention of alternative courses of action and assessment of their probable consequences and better choice between alternatives are also needed to improve decision-making.

The mix model

This rather curious term leads into a series of hypotheses about organizations based on the analysis so far. The initial assumptions are:

(i) Organizational effectiveness implies a system with an improving input-output ratio.

(ii) Increasing effectiveness involves increasing psychological energy available for work.

(iii) The first step is to decrease unproductive organizational activities.

(iv) The second is to increase the probability of psychological success and self-esteem for the individual.

(v) To do all (or any) of these will involve modifying and adding to the strategy of designing organizations.

This does not mean the human-relations approach of completely people-centred organization. Challenge, strain and stress are essential ingredients but they must not be carried to excess so that there is no chance for some let-up. The optimum point is where they stop decreasing unproductive activities and the energy needed for core activities.

Change will be required in both individuals and in organizational structures and patterns of behaviour. How much change for either is not yet known and needs much empirical research.

Certain essential properties of organizations can be derived from their intrinsic nature. They can be set down as opposites the one side tending towards organizational ineffectiveness, the other to effectiveness.

Leading to ineffectiveness	*Leading to effectiveness*
One part or sub-set of parts controls the whole.	The whole is created and controlled through the inter-relationship of the parts.
Awareness only of random plurality of parts.	Awareness of pattern among parts.
Objectives related only or mainly to parts.	Objectives related to the whole.
Inability to influence core activities whether they are internally or externally orientated.	Ability to influence core activities whether they are internally or externally orientated.
Core activities only influenced by the immediate present.	Core activities influenced by past, present and future.

Argyris maintains that these six properties are mutually interdependent, that what is best in any given situation is still to be empirically proved but that generally an organization that approximated more to the right-hand side would present greater opportunities for psychological success and consequently would tend to be more effective.

This is really the end of the hypothesis. It is followed in some detail by an account of empirical research work which, it is claimed, does not prove the hypothesis but does, at least, demonstrate its plausibility.

The third part of the book develops in considerable detail the form that an organization might take to conform with the hypotheses presented earlier. Argyris himself describes it as 'brainstorming'. Lack of space prevents its inclusion here and, to be honest, it is only the restatement of the hypotheses in prescriptive form.

There is, however, a summary of probable future directions for improvement that must be included:

(i) Management's basic values, their implementation and the core activities of maintenance and adaptation.

(ii) The values involved in effective relationships.

(iii) The relation between power/authority concepts and internal commitment.

(iv) New needs and aspirations at lower levels, especially self-esteem, commitment and psychological success.

(v) Enlargement of jobs.

(vi) Organizational policies and practices needed to induce general concern for organizational health.

(vii) Other organizational structures to supplement the pyramid.

(viii) Situation-centred leadership.

(ix) The effect of contraction and undermanning on behavioural settings.

(x) Changes required in control systems as mutual trust and interdependence increase and psychological success becomes an operative factor generally.

It seems almost inevitable that the sword of Damocles hangs more noticeably over Argyris than any other authority. Is he asking for the millennium, the perfect world of perfect people? At the time he wrote this book he argued that recent research on personality and learning, if valid, gave his hypothesis a theoretical base.

References

(1) Pollard, H. R. *Developments in Management Thought* (London: Heinemann, 1974).

(2) Argyris, C. *Personality and the Organization* New York: Harper, 1957).

(3) Argyris, C. *Understanding Organizational Behaviour* (London: Tavistock Publications, 1960)

(4) Ibid, p. 163.

(5) Argyris C. *Interpersonal Competence and Organizational Effectiveness* (London: Tavistock Publications, 1962).

(6) Argyris, C. *Integrating the Individual and the Organization* (New York: J. Wiley, 1964).

(7) Ibid, p. 13.

(8) Ibid, p. 37.

(9) Ibid, p. 105.

(10) Whyte, W. H. Jnr. *The Organization Man* (London: Penguin Books, 1960).

(11) Argyris, C. *Integrating the Individual and the Organization* (New York: J. Wiley, 1964), p. 111.
(12) Ibid, p. 123.
(13) Ibid, p. 123.
(14) Ibid, p. 132.
(15) Ibid, pp. 132–3.

Bibliography

BOOKS BY C. ARGYRIS

Understanding Organizational Behaviour (Homewood: Dorsey Press, 1960).
Interpersonal Competence and Organizational Effectiveness (London: Tavistock, 1962).
Integrating the Individual and the Organization (New York: J. Wiles, 1964).

G. Strauss
1963

In 1962 a seminar on 'The Social Science of Organization' was held at Pittsburgh. Twenty-four social scientists prepared papers in advance for discussion over a period of two weeks by four groups of social scientists. Each group had a 'critical observer' sitting in the whole time. The observer's job after the seminar was to produce a paper giving 'a perspective on organizations that would represent his own initial perspective sharpened and tempered by his two weeks of interaction with persons of other views'.[1] Of the four papers included in Leavitt's book the one entitled 'Some Notes on Power Equalization' by G. Strauss seems to have the most value from our point of view.

Strauss starts with the Human Relations movement of 1940–60. He contends that the main thrust has been towards the equalization of power, the reduction in status differentials between supervisors and workers, and a reaction against the worst characteristics of Taylor's Scientific Management and Classical organization theory as developed between, say, 1910 and 1940. Human Relations approaches generally, and power equalization in particular have been claimed to produce more efficient and productive organizations with more contented and better-adjusted employees.

Under the umbrella of Human Relations there have been four main lines of approach. Herzberg's 'hygienic' supervision is given as the first method although, in fact, it pre-dates Herzberg's theory by anything up to twenty years. This consisted of removing or avoiding factors in the work situation which led to feelings of dissatisfaction. This is a negative, avoidance-of-trouble approach. In itself it does not necessarily involve any power equalization and could quite well be used by a benevolent, autocratic management.

The second method is the delegation of decisions on means and methods to lower levels in the hierarchy, and measurement and assessment by results instead of close, personal supervision. While this may produce some increase in autonomy and creativity it is suggested that it puts the emphasis on the individual rather than the group and on short-term rather than long-term results.

Participation, the third method, is described as permitting [*sic*] subordinates to take part in the decision-making process. (Author's comment. Without being too pedantic it could be questioned whether 'permitting' is quite the right word. It subsumes the equal right of higher management to withdraw permission at will. So any power 'shared' with employees would probably depend on their subscribing to the 'right' decisions as seen by management. This is hardly participation in its true sense.) Strauss suggests it depends on building up the power of groups or Likert's linking-pin concept. He also attacks it as being inconsistent, insincere, ineffective and manipulative.

The final approach consists of inducing changes in the attitudes and behaviour of employees by bringing about changes in the people themselves and in their values instead of changing the environment in which they work. This is regarded as impractical, idealistic, and as an attempt to tackle the problem from the most difficult end. Even if people do obtain greater insight and understanding, this may only increase their frustration.

As an aside it must be stated here that the four approaches quoted by Strauss go well beyond the real Human Relations approach of the 1940s and 50s and their supporters would be more than somewhat insulted by being described as members of that School.

Personality versus Organization Hypothesis

The basis of this hypothesis is given as Maslow's hierarchy of needs as subsequently developed by Maier, Argyris, Herzberg, and McGregor. Psychological needs, concepts of maturity are held to clash with organizational needs and to produce dysfunctional results such as apathy, withdrawal, aggression, psychological immaturity, and a vicious circle of ineffective behaviour, leading to more pressure from management, even more ineffective behaviour, and anti-management norms among groups of workers. It is suggested that management can, by providing high wages, avoiding the main dissatisfiers, providing liberal non-work benefits, and not breathing down people's necks, lead employees to *think* that they are happy. This, however, is a 'phoney war' situation in which both management and workers have settled for low achievement, low aspiration levels, and apathetic, minimal standards.

Having partially stated the psycho-sociological approach rather than the simpler Human Relations approach and criticized it as he has gone along, Strauss really gets down to full-blooded criticism.

Criticism

The psycho-sociological approach is a normative, prescriptive description of how management should behave and not an objective analysis of how real workers (and managers) do behave. Its whole basis is unrealistic as it is founded on value judgements that, by and large, are those of the academic professor safely cocooned in his study and lecture theatre.

Contrary to the professors' views, there are in real life many people who do not share their values, who are perfectly happy to do a routine job that makes minimum demands on them, who obtain their real satisfactions in life outside the factory, and who fit perfectly well into the technology which demands only attendance, obedience to orders and the performance of minimal, machine-paced, monotonous work.

Expressed another way the self-actualization theory over-emphasizes the idea of the personality – organization conflict, the suggestion that self-actualization is a universal need, and the importance of the job as a means of satisfaction. Further the amount of alienation from work has been grossly exaggerated, modern society provides more, not less, scope for skill than earlier ones, and only a limited amount of uncertainty and freedom can be tolerated by most people, beyond that certainty and security are vital needs.

While Strauss condemns the psycho-sociological school, in effect, for building a theory on a projection of their own personal, subjective values he goes on to put forward a value judgement of his own. Would it not be better to forget about job-satisfaction, press on with automation as quickly as possible, reduce the working time to a minimum, and concentrate on making leisure the valuable and meaningful part of life?

Organizational Economics

At this point Strauss's argument, or, to be more precise, his terminology, seems to become a little obscure. On the face of it he is discussing the economics of 'power equalization' but in almost the same breath he refers to the 'personality–organization hypothesis'. While it is extremely doubtful that the two terms are synonymous it can be accepted that both could have more or less similar results in terms of productivity and both visible and hidden costs. Whatever his phrasing it will be assumed that he is referring to the whole field of the psycho-sociological approach.

His main point is that this approach ignores, or at least misapplies, the concept of organizational economics, by which he means the balancing of the *total* gains and costs of this approach. The suggestion is that while there are 'hidden' costs of autocracy (which must surely be too narrow a word) and that supervision on traditional lines can cause people to work less hard than they might under other methods, these costs and losses are frequently over-estimated. At the same time the potential increases in production to be brought about by improved methods of supervision and management are also often over-estimated. The fact that there will be costs incurred in training in new methods and possibly losses of production while people adapt to new ways is also often overlooked. There is some truth in this cold water douche of realism when the over-enthusiasm of some supporters of near-idealistic methods is considered. At the same time excessive pessimism is equally out of place. The real difficulty lies in trying to put figures to the various aspects involved, and in relating them directly to particular changes as effect and cause.

There are other anomalies at the psychological level. Excessive anxiety and aggressive behaviour are admitted to be harmful both to the individual and to the organization. But when do these become excessive? At all times through the recorded and pre-recorded history of man dissatisfaction with what is, anxiety about the future, and properly applied aggression have provided the main spurs to improvement and achievement. Apathy, it is suggested, may be the best answer to work which for reasons of technology cannot be changed into any semblance of being meaningful and satisfying. Argyris is quoted as authority for the suggestion that a matching of routine work under hygienic supervision with immature, dependent, non-aspiring workers can produce a stable situation that satisfies both management and workers. It does not optimize either satisfaction or production but it may be the best possible solution without tremendous changes in society and technology.

In summary, the personality–organization (power–equalization) thesis is not meaningless but for many workers the net gains to be obtained by applying it to their work would not be worthwhile. No one style of supervision and leadership will be appropriate in all cases. The right one in any case must be found in terms of 'organizational economics' or true net gains or losses.

Forms of power allocation
Having disposed of the excessive enthusiasm and brought psycho-sociology down from the heights to the reality of profit and loss Strauss turns his attention to a detailed analysis of the methods of allocating power.

The allocation of power between superior and subordinate in terms of decision-making is assumed to lie along a continuum from absolute dictatorship by the superior on every detail to complete freedom in all respects for the subordinate. There is also the possibility that the superior, who is assumed to have the power to grant or withhold allocation, may change the amount allocated to subordinates from time to time and/or in the light of changing circumstances. Four different forms of allocation are specified: participation, consultation, autonomy, and delegation, although it is stated that these terms have been used without precise definition.

Typical points along the continuum of allocation may be:

(i) Superior decides without considering subordinates.

(ii) Superior decides on what he thinks subordinates want.

(iii) Superior consults subordinates showing that he wants little opposition and decides himself.

(iv) Superior consults subordinates, decides, and leaves subordinates to do as they please.

(v) Joint decision by superior and subordinates but superior lets it be known what decision he wants.

(vi) Joint decision but superior makes little attempt to influence result.

(vii) Normally joint decision but superior retains right to over-ride group when he thinks it necessary.

(viii) Superior uses influence to guide and teach subordinates to reach good decisions but allows them to make mistakes so that they will learn from them.

(ix) Decision delegated to subordinate but subordinate knows general lines along which superior wants him to act.

(x) Subordinate has complete freedom of action.[2]

Participation

As a start Strauss suggests that not enough research has so far (1963) been done on participation, on the variables involved in it or on whether or why it results in higher productivity. In varying degrees from simple consultation to full group decision and delegation it does involve some approach to power equalization and very slight to wide degrees of autonomy for the subordinate. So long as it does not produce excessive feelings of insecurity, autonomy can be satisfying in itself but it has no apparent direct connection with productivity. In the case of participation on decisions involving change for the subordinates a good case can be made out for the change being seen as more acceptable or at least less unacceptable. Participation has the effect of enabling informal leaders in groups to use and consolidate their positions in relation to their groups. It may also improve attitudes through generating feelings about satisfactory exchange between superior and subordinates and individual and group pressures for achievement.

The relation between participation and achievement is seen as not being direct or one way. To feel a sense of achievement an individual must, it is suggested, possess certain skills of which he is aware and which he values as part of his self-image, have a generalized need for achievement, recognize his job as a test of his skills involving reasonable difficulty, and receive feed-back that he is succeeding. This is related by Strauss to productivity in only one way. If the individual has participated in the decision as to what is to be done he will put forth greater effort to do it successfully because his skill in coming to a correct decision is at stake. But where the individual does not value the skills involved or feels that he does not possess them participation will have no effect on achievement. Work-centred and more highly skilled workers are more likely to respond to participation methods.

Participation in decision-making by the group instead of the individual brings other factors into play. Group norms and group pressures are involved and the latter can be more powerful than the pressure exerted by a superior. Participation in group decision-making may increase identification with the group, increase some individuals' status (and lower others!) and make the group more cohesive. It also makes the individual more sensitive to group norms.

At the end Strauss is still unconvinced; it is still a matter of pros and cons. If participation reduces resistance to and resentment against management, if it provides a form of catharsis, if it sets up an exchange relationship, if it increases group cohesiveness *and* group norms match management objectives, then it may increase productivity. For unskilled and semi-skilled workers it is more likely to be a hygiene factor reducing dissatisfaction rather than a positive motivator.

On the other hand people whose ideas are rejected in the processes of participation may become alienated. The greater cohesion of the group may be anti-management. It may lead to expectations that cannot be fulfilled so causing frustration. It does involve costs of time, possible frustration in working through to solutions that may be nothing more than lowest common denominator compromises.

Delegation
As a form of power allocation delegation is universal in all except the one-man business with no employees. (Author's note. Strauss uses the wording 'widest used form of power equalization'. It is assumed that 'equalization' is an unintended slip. Delegation allocates power between ranks in the hierarchy but no one would seriously suggest that a foreman has power equal to that of his managing director.) The feasibility of delegation depends on:

    (i) The likelihood of subordinates being able to make adequate decisions.

(ii) The need to conform to common patterns of behaviour and decision.

(iii) The possibility of the superior having indirect means of making sure subordinates do make right decisions.

The freedom allowed to subordinates to make delegated decisions cannot be absolute. Rules and standard procedures, goals and objectives as generalized guidelines, indoctrination, and technology all act in one way or another to restrict freedom of decision. Where considerable risks are involved or consistent decisions are essential, delegation is likely to be more restricted while routine conditions and parallel specialization make it more likely.

Adequate decision-making by subordinates involves their motivation to take the risks involved, clear and well understood objectives, adequate information and channels of communication, and a technology which allows it.

Optimum degree of power equalization

There is, according to Strauss, no simple answer. It depends on the extent to which power equalization increases motivation which, in turn, leads to higher productivity. Much technology demands only adequate performance and opportunities to increase it by increasing motivation are either minimal or non-existent. Against the possible gains there are the costs; costs of re-designing jobs, costs of training, costs of time spent in consultation or participation, and costs of possibly lower quality decisions.

We have come full circle, back to organizational economics and balancing hidden, visible and unknown costs and losses against possible, and maybe unquantifiable, gains. Strauss hopes that further research will lead to a better specification of the variables involved.

References

(1) Leavitt H. J. (Ed.) *Social Science of Organizations* (New York: Prentice Hall, 1963), p. iii.

(2) Ibid, adapted from Table on p. 59.

13

R. R. Blake and J. S. Mouton
1964

Introduction

There can be few books on management that have a greater impact on their readers than Blake and Mouton's *The Managerial Grid*. They have brought together their experience and knowledge gained as management consultants and an important development in the theory of management. In doing so they have produced a work which has enabled managers who thought that improvement in managerial performance might be possible to advance stage by stage to achieve it. If sales volume for the book is an indication of their contribution to the improvement of management practice, that contribution must rank very high by any standards.

In brief Blake and Mouton divide the styles of management into five basic groups along the two dimensions of concern for work and concern for people. Basic descriptions of each group are given covering aspects of behaviour, attitude, reactions, causes, and results. These descriptions are very heavily documented by references to relevant books and research work. They constitute the main part of the work. Other chapters deal with façades, 'mixtures' of groups, self-analysis for readers and an approach to implementing the improvement of managerial performance.

A much fuller account of the stages involved in improving performance is given in *Corporate Excellence through Grid Organization Development*. This includes numerous anonymous case histories where the authors and their staff have been involved in implementing improvement programmes. It is not, however, dealt with in this chapter.

It is said that a picture is worth a thousand words and Blake and Mouton are well aware of this. Their starting point is the graph shown on the opposite page which provides the title 'Managerial Grid'. The vertical axis represents degrees of 'concern for people' on a low to high scale graduated 1–9. The horizontal axis represents degrees of 'concern for production', again low to high and 1–9. Five basic combinations of degrees along both scales are used to illustrate the five groups of management styles. 1,1 management represents a low degree of concern for both

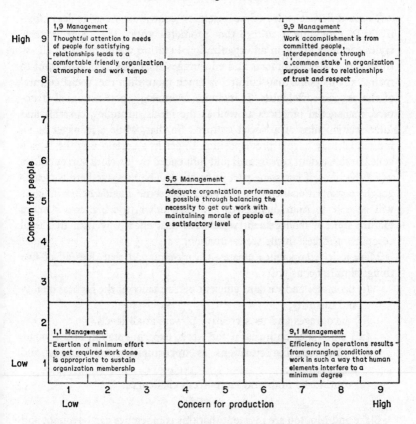

Figure 1. The managerial grid (reproduced by permission of Gulf Publishing, Houston).

production and people; 1,9 management is highly concerned about people at the expense of concern about production; 9,1 management on the other hand puts maximum emphasis on production and is only minimally concerned with people and then only in a negative way to ensure that they do not obstruct production. 5,5 management shows concern for both production and people but shows this by balancing the needs of one against the other and reaching compromise solutions. 9,9 management is the ideal where management methods achieve maximum production/profit by involving and obtaining full commitment from all the people involved. It optimizes by setting up a situation where the real needs of people are fully met in contributing towards organizational needs.

These different styles of management contribute more or less effectively to providing a culture that promotes work. The more effective styles can only occur in an organizational culture which not only allows them but actively promotes and encourages their use. It is important to realize at this point that 'culture' is much more than the 'social culture' of the psycho-sociologists. It includes technology, organizational structure, managerial practices as well as the ideals, attitudes, customs and inter-relationships of a 'social culture'. So that, while a manager as an individual may have a predisposition to act in a certain way, he is to a considerable extent constrained and influenced by his work surroundings which he himself has some part in creating. The message here is clear – get the organizational culture right and with some outside help managers will be able to train themselves and each other to a higher and more mature style of management which can deal effectively with the 'total complex of forces' in the work situation.

Managerial competence creates a work situation that does all of five things simultaneously. It:

(i) promotes and sustains efficient performance of the highest quality and quantity,

(ii) encourages and uses creative powers at all levels,

(iii) stimulates enthusiasm for work, experimentation and change,

(iv) uses ongoing situations as opportunities for learning and improvement,

(v) continually finds and meets fresh challenges.

Blake and Mouton are insistent that this competence can be taught and learned and that this has been demonstrated in practice. But what is best in detail depends on the actual circumstances of each case.

The managerial dilemma

The organizational system within which managers operate has certain fundamental characteristics. The first of these is purpose or a collection of purposes. Without this any organization ceases to exist but it is not always clearly defined or recognized by or acceptable to the people who comprise the organization. Also it may not be reconcilable with the individual objectives of members. Secondly an organization must consist of people. Thirdly it must have an hierarchy based on positions having rank, authority, and responsibility. Finally these and other aspects not specifically mentioned will mesh together to form the 'organizational culture'.

The dilemma for the manager seems to arise in two ways. On a more general level there are various different sets of assumptions that can be made about these fundamental characteristics; competitiveness, co-operation, conflict, people versus production, business ethics, to name but a few. At a more specific level the dilemma is still more often seen as how to reconcile the conflicting aims of the organization and the personal aims of the people being managed.

The five different Grid positions represent the basic sets of assumptions on which managers base their managerial behaviour. At any one time and for an individual manager the set in use will result from his own personal characteristics, the immediate situation with which he is faced and the traditions and established practices (the organizational culture) of the organization in which he is working. But there are two important qualifications to this concept of basic assumptions. No single set of assumptions will by itself provide sufficient guidance to meet every possible eventuality, so each manager is assumed to have an alternative 'back-up' set to use when his main set fails. Additionally sets of assumptions are not fixed and immutable for all time. Education, training, experience, and changes in the surrounding organizational culture are all capable of leading a manager to change some or all of his assumptions and, in consequence, to change his behaviour.

9,1 Managerial style
Each of the five basic managerial styles is given its own chapter in the book. While they vary considerably in length the pattern of treatment is the same in each case. A condensed version such as this is bound to emphasize the repetitiveness and I ask for the reader's indulgence.

Managerial behaviour in this style will centre around the twin assumptions that there is a contradiction between the needs of the organization and those of the individuals and, that the needs of the organization for production/profit are paramount.

In line with these assumptions the manager:
(i) arranges work and conditions to prevent human attitudes and feelings interfering with production;
(ii) behaves as a task-master with the emphasis on hierarchy, position, authority, and obedience;
(iii) regards it as his job to plan, direct, and control work in detail;
(iv) punishes for mistakes and violations of permitted conduct;
(v) does little or nothing to encourage creativity and commitment;
(vi) establishes uniformity of action through policy, rules and procedures;
(vii) sets quotas and targets to maximize production;
(viii) regards production and profit as his sole aim and criterion.

Relationships under this style are on a boss–subordinate, 1:1 basis. One to many (boss–group) patterns are avoided and interaction between equals is discouraged as being anti-productive. The formal hierarchy of the traditional organization chart is the basis. Superiors regard meetings with subordinates simply as formal means of getting information and passing on decisions.

Formal communication generally follows the hierarchical pattern but senior managers may frequently by-pass their subordinates to get information from 'lower-down'.

Conflict is a never-ending chore of fire-fighting. Where it is based on the interpretation of fact the manager should be able to resolve it rationally. Where it stems from emotional tension and disturbance it will interfere with production and must be brought under control. The usual method is the use of authority to suppress it. While this can prevent the open expression of disagreement, it does not get down to root causes so the disaffection smoulders on and soon breaks out in some other form.

Creativity and change present interesting aspects under 9,1 management. In order to maintain their standing for 'getting results' middle managers are often highly creative in designing plans and procedures for production. These they then try to impose on their subordinates who will tend to react in one of two ways. They may be as highly creative as the manager, but in the opposite direction, by devising schemes and methods to disrupt, neutralize or defeat the manager's plans, to 'defeat the system'. Alternatively they may withdraw into extreme passivity, doing the barest minimum to get by. 9,1 management has not yet solved, if indeed it ever will, the problem of forcing through change against the united resistance of large bodies of workers.

Selection and induction procedures under each of the five styles of management are given as ways which follow logically from meeting the requirements of each style. A similar procedure is adopted in describing the personal behaviour of a manager operating under and following the given style. As they are essentially derived from and largely repetitive of the description of the style they will generally be omitted from this brief summary.

In what would seem to be the weakest link in the chain of the argument this description of personal behaviour is traced back to 'childhood origins' which are described in detail. When we consider all the infinitely varied and multi-dimensional forces that must have operated to result in a particular individual manager at the age of 30, 40 or 50 it must be a gross oversimplification to relate the end product directly to what happened to him before he was 10 years old. So these sections, too, are going to be omitted.

Finally, the conditions likely to lead to the adoption or, more probably development of 9,1 management style and its likely consequences are set out in some detail.

The conditions and circumstances for 9,1 management are:

(i) the attitudes and culture arising from earlier slavery and serfdom patterns';

(ii) the precedents and attitudes left over from the Industrial Revolution and, in particular, the 'boss–worker' relationship and the power which went with the personal ownership of capital – the 'Captains of Industry';

(iii) the self-fulfilling nature of 9,1 assumptions once they are adopted (cf. the argument put forward by Argyris);

(iv) the fact, which must be admitted, that at least in the short run, 9,1 tough management can and does often result in high production;

(v) until fairly recently, at any rate, the much lower educational standards of workers have made the imposition of 9,1 management feasible;

(vi) the technical needs of mass production industry.

The long-term results of 9,1 management are given as:

(i) the vast growth of trade unions;

(ii) a failure to make use of the available and increasing skills of the lower levels of management and of workers;

(iii) a tendency for most lower ranks to shift towards apathy and a minimal involvement in the work situation.

1,9 Managerial style

This is a group comprising the logical extreme of what was known in the 1950s as the Human Relations School. Its basic assumptions are first the importance of people as individuals not solely as means of production and second that output/profit will be maximized by leading instead of driving and by arranging conditions of work to provide the worker with comfort, ease and security. It represents the complete swing of the pendulum from the extremes of Taylor's Scientific Management[2] to the extreme over-statement of Elton Mayo's 'social problems'.[3]

Working from these assumptions the 1,9 manager tends to:

(i) avoid pressurizing subordinates and so creating resistance;

(ii) lead rather than drive, persuade rather than order;

(iii) try to find out what workers want and, as far as possible, plan work and arrange conditions to meet those wants;

(iv) personally help his subordinates in difficulties;

(v) de-emphasize discipline;

(vi) pass on orders from above without accepting personal responsibility especially when they run counter to subordinates' wishes;
(vii) involve subordinates in forms of goal-setting which produce
lowest common denominator targets which are often not related to
production.

The fundamental basis for personal relationships is 'togetherness' or
'the one big happy family'. Subordinates are important to the manager as
people and he must be concerned with anything which upsets them.
Sharing thoughts and getting views occur in group meetings. But the
emphasis on 'togetherness' leads to conformity with the group and real
disagreement is avoided by not bringing it out into the open. In his relations upwards the 1,9 manager is responsive, looks always to get support
and understanding from his boss and so suppresses 'bad news' that might
lead to disapproval.

Communication tends to put the emphasis on informal channels rather
than formal ones. Inevitably with the emphasis on people, social and
personal matters take precedence over production.

With the basic assumptions of the 1,9 style conflict is, and must be,
regarded as harmful and to be avoided at all costs. The manager deals
with it first by appeals to reason and to emotion. If these fail his paramount need for acceptance by his group will lead him to try to smooth it
over, if possible, or to surrender to appeasement. Always the emphasis is
on harmony and agreement so direct issues which are avoided or glossed
over leave the underlying tensions unresolved. One common method of
avoiding involving the line manager in conflict is to set up Personnel
Departments and counsellors to take over 'problems' and so remove them
from the group situation.

Managers tend to avoid creativity and new methods because of the
possibility of arousing resistance and running counter to current thinking
and climate. If subordinates suggest new ideas to them they will 'pass
them up' so that they can take the credit if they are approved and avoid
responsibility for having to reject them.

Feelings of commitment are high on the social level leading to high
morale and, generally, low productivity. Conformity is the norm and
tends towards the lowest common level.

1,9 management, it is suggested, can only arise and survive under
feather-bedding conditions such as cost-plus operating, very high demand
resulting in unavoidable high profits and little need for efficiency, and
situations of quasi-monopoly. (As an interesting aside would Blake and
Mouton have included nationalization if they had been British and not
American?)

The long-term results of the 1,9 style are equally predictable.
(i) Harmonious human relations (but see (iii)).
(ii) Low output due to lack of creative thinking on improvement.
(iii) In the longer term human relations may suffer due to the avoidance of essential conflict situations which are left unresolved.
(iv) The eventual collapse of the 1,9 firm in the face of efficient competition if that exists.

1,1 Managerial style

It would be fair comment that the 1,1 style is one of 'non-management' particularly if Drucker's idea of management as the creative, driving force is accepted. Nevertheless it does occur sufficiently often to justify examination and the hypothesis that the continued growth into ever larger forms of organization may lead to more and more 1,1 management has at least some air of respectability.

The one basic assumption behind this style is defeatism. The 1,1 manager has learnt from experience that he cannot win and that in order to achieve his real aim of personal survival he will withdraw as far as possible and contribute no more than the minimum necessary to ensure that he can remain a member of the organization until he gets his gold watch and retirement pension. Blake and Mouton suggest that it occurs most frequently in large organizations whose operations are very largely routine.

Predictably, the 1,1 manager:
(i) puts people to work and leaves them to get on with it;
(ii) carefully follows the rules himself and ensures that his subordinates know the rules so that any failure is their responsibility, not his;
(iii) accepts only a superficial, non-committed responsibility;
(iv) avoids exposing himself and getting into the limelight;
(v) acts only as a message carrier between levels above and below him;
(vi) ignores all mistakes and violations unless they are such that he cannot avoid personal responsibility;
(vii) 'passes the buck' whenever possible.

The only goals known to such a manager are those of personal survival. Personal contacts up or down are avoided as much as possible. Subordinates are left alone to create their own social conditions and standards of morale. Communication in all directions is limited to the absolute minimum.

The 1,1 manager has a wide range of behaviour for avoiding conflict.

Actual physical withdrawal from the scene, delay and 'forgetting', impersonal neutrality, double-talk, gobbledygook, and passing problems upstairs are his main methods.

At first sight creativity might appear to be the lowest attribute of this manager. Actually it is probably his highest. Tremendous ingenuity is needed to keep up appearances and to ensure survival while actually doing as little as possible. Any creativity at levels below him will either be stifled at birth or must by-pass him to get anywhere at all.

It should be obvious by now that the 1,1 manager is committed only to self-preservation and that his subordinates, being left alone, can develop whatever commitment they wish so long as it does not threaten the boss's security.

The conditions that lead to 1,1 management are equally obvious.

(i) For the individual, feelings of constant failure leading to the loss or suppression of aspirations and to psychologically regressive behaviour.

(ii) Extreme sub-division of work to meaningless tasks.

(iii) Complete absence of competition for the organization.

(iv) 9,1 managers who have been forced against their will into 1,9 management (e.g. by Union pressure) may give up and retire to 1,1.

Against competition it is obvious that the 1,1 firm could not survive for long so, even more than 1,9, it needs a monopoly situation. Equally inevitably it will result in inefficiency, high costs and low productivity. The real danger possibly lies in the fact that in large and very large organizations 1,1 sections and departments can exist unnoticed for long periods of time and be a constant drain on overall efficiency.

5,5 Managerial style

5,5 management could well be described in the three words – moderation in everything. More specifically it is based on what can be called common-sense assumptions that owe far more to past experience than to present knowledge. Briefly these are that conflict is assumed between the needs of work and those of people but that satisfactory solutions can be found through compromise. These will ensure an acceptable level of production and profit without unduly upsetting people. Workers and managers are assumed to be prepared to put a reasonable amount of effort into work provided they are not pushed too far and some allowance is made for their feelings and attitudes.

With this set of assumptions managers will:

(i) place some emphasis on achieving production;

(ii) give some deliberate consideration to people's needs;

(iii) accept responsibility for planning, co-ordination, and control;

(iv) communicate with workers and seek for understanding and suggestions;

(v) carry on a continuous process of adjustment to try to reach and maintain a balance in the situation;

(vi) lead and motivate rather than direct and order;

(vii) use both 'carrot' and 'stick' methods as each seems to be more appropriate to the current situation;

(viii) try to deal fairly with errors while trying to eliminate them by making sure people know what is expected;

(ix) rely heavily on precedents, tradition, rules, and established procedures in day-by-day working.

Of necessity goals tend to be ambivalent under 5,5 management. They attempt to combine and balance primary goals of production/profit with secondary goals of security and satisfaction for those employed. Production goals are set as targets with the implicit assumptions that minor variations either way do not matter and unexpected objections or resistance and changes in circumstances will lead to changes in the targets. Such goals tend to emphasize mediocrity and to generate greater feelings of long-term security.

The general tendency in personal relationships is towards a one-to-one basis with give and take on both sides. However, group sessions and committees will be used for consultation without giving away authority, to get suggestions and ideas and to avoid personal responsibility for decisions that are likely to be unpopular. In the last case the group or committee will not take the decision but will be used to provide the 'evidence' which makes the decision inevitable. As far as is humanly possible personal contacts are used to maintain good relations all round and to reduce friction to a minimum.

Morale is important because if it drops production will fall off. Maintaining it with the inevitable conflict between people and production is management's responsibility.

Communication tends to be multi-directional and to use both the formal hierarchical channels and the informal network. Management 'uses' the informal network to get information that will indicate the levels of morale and acceptance and to 'feed-in' suggestions so as to get reactions. Necessary information which would not be acceptable through formal channels will be 'leaked' into the grapevine.

The 5,5 attitude to conflict can be easily stated. It is compromise. However, achieving compromise is often not so simple. It means avoiding the head-on confrontation whenever possible, giving situations time to cool, finding out how far each side will give, finding solutions which are at least minimally acceptable to both sides. Its two worst aspects must be the inevitable overstatement of cases and needs by both sides to allow room for manoeuvre and the almost equal certainty that both sides will be dissatisfied to some extent with the outcome and be waiting to resume the conflict at some future date. 'Divide and rule' is a motto of 5,5 management.

Creativity leading to innovation and change is far from easy because of the general reliance on tradition and custom. Inevitably it involves a tentative approach which starts by testing opinions to find out how much is acceptable. Even then initiating change will involve much hard work in explaining and persuading and usually large 'carrots' to ensure acceptance.

Commitment by managers is towards the organization and towards men. Acceptable results without disruption is the goal, the method is being 'a good organization man'. Subordinates and workers will be loyal to a firm which provides rewards and satisfactions just higher than average but will have no strong sense of contributing to the organization's objectives.

Blake and Mouton are probably thinking particularly of American conditions when they describe the conditions leading to 5,5 management as being the use of 9,1 management (Taylor's Scientific Management) followed by an overswing to 1,9 (Human Relations movements in the 1950s) followed by a reaction to a mid-point between the two. American socio-political values are also included as causes. In Britain the temptation to ascribe it to the British dislike of logical extremes and the preference for compromise is very strong indeed, but it cannot be the whole answer.

Its consequences are summed up in 'safe' mediocrity although the validity of its safety under the rapidly changing conditions of the last quarter of the twentieth century must at least be questionable!

9,9 Managerial style

At last we have worked our way through to the top right-hand corner of the Grid, to corporate and managerial excellence. The assumptions behind this style are a combination of those reached by the different exponents of modern (1964) psycho-sociology. A high concern for production can be coupled with a high concern for people – the two are not necessarily in conflict, rather they are complementary to each other. The psychological and sociological drives of people can, under the right circumstances, be used to meet organizational ends while at the same time satisfying individual needs. Concerted team effort can provide the condi-

tions for integrating creativity, high productivity, and high morale at all
levels in the organization. Optimum solutions to problems can be found
and implemented.

With the wide gulf that separates these assumptions from those of the
other four styles it is not surprising that the manager views his job in a
different light and acts differently. The 9,9 manager:

(i) sees his responsibility to be that of ensuring that *those most
involved* in the outcome carry out the planning, direction, and
control irrespective of their level in the hierarchy;

(ii) sees that sound decisions are taken by the people with the relevant knowledge;

(iii) provides conditions where:

(a) people can understand the problems, have responsibility for
the outcome, and can contribute to it;

(b) people will want actively to support organizational ends,
support effective leadership, and genuinely participate;

(c) sound solutions can be found by the combined efforts of all
involved.

(iv) provides all facts, figures, and information which are available
to him and appropriate to the level concerned;

(v) encourages and fosters self-direction, self-control, and maximum
self-development by those responsible to him;

(vi) provides the basis for joint feelings at all levels of personal
responsibility for and commitment to a total effort towards agreed
and accepted objectives;

(vii) uses tradition and established practice provided they are critically examined and shown to be still valid as the best solution;

(viii) builds a committed unit of organization which is greater than
the sum of its individual parts;

(ix) uses mistakes and errors as opportunities for learning and
guidance.

It follows logically that correct goals are the key to 9,9 management.
They must be such that they combine organizational and personal goals
in such a way that they mutually support each other and that the achievement of one will necessarily involve the achievement of the other. They
are accepted by all and by their acceptance they provide the motivation
for their achievement.

Personal relationships of all kinds are involved in this style. One-to-
one, one–many, many–one, groups, project-teams, committees are all
used on the basis of what is best for the matter in hand and the circumstances in which it occurs. The basis of all relationships is that of full

personal responsibility for joint effort towards the total job. The manager is the key figure in the team with the multiple role of provider and collector of information, adviser, consultant, coach, helper, and provider of resources and opportunity.

Morale in the 9,9 organization is high because personal involvement at all levels creates the conditions of mutual support, trust and respect and the sense of achievement which are necessary.

Communication is multi-directional passing information to where it is needed and drawing on relevant knowledge wherever it may be found. The essential features are that it is open, honest two-way communication with no colouring, filtering or holding back and no refusal to accept information whether good or bad.

Conflict, from whatever cause, is regarded as inevitable and, indeed, often valuable. There are bound to be differences of opinion, different solutions to problems and even, at times, purely personal antagonism. Under 9,9 management the essential thing is to get all conflict out into the open so that it can be dealt with rationally, the causes removed, and permanent satisfactory solutions can be reached. One of the main tasks of a 9,9 manager is to educate himself and his subordinates to the point where they can all accept and welcome this approach.

Creativity at all levels from the top man to the shop floor reaches its highest pitch under this style. Everyone feels free to submit or contribute their ideas secure in the fact that they will be respected as potentially valuable contributions which will be analysed, judged fairly, and adopted if they contribute to the common cause. If they are not the originator will be given satisfactory reasons why not.

Blake and Mouton make the predictable claim that only 9,9 management produces in all members of the organization a true, whole-hearted commitment to the organization and its goals.

The conditions given as helping in movement towards 9,9 management are:

(i) the possibility of getting a competitive edge through better management;

(ii) the growing understanding of the application of the behavioural sciences;

(iii) the rising standards of general education;

(iv) the need in these days for ever higher levels of creativity to meet organizational problems.

It could be suggested that the authors take the one absolutely essential condition so much for granted that they have missed it. Surely it must be that the top man in the organization or, at least, someone very near the top not only genuinely believes that 9,9 management can be a practicable aim but also has the burning zeal and the ability to educate and carry the others with him in bringing it about.

The long-term consequences of 9,9 management are given as

(i) improved profitability;
(ii) improved inter-group relationships;
(iii) better team action;
(iv) reduced inter-personal friction;
(v) better understanding;
(vi) a higher degree of self-actualization by all members.

The fact was mentioned early on that Blake and Mouton support their argument with ample references. The case for 9,9 management is backed up by no less than 131 references to other sources.

Managerial façades

The five styles of management so far described are, it is suggested, authentic because they are genuinely and honestly based on logical (if misguided in four cases) sets of assumptions. It is a fact, however, that managers can, and sometimes do, put on a front or 'façade' to cover their real intentions and motivation. Generally this will happen through one of two causes – a strong desire for power or a feeling of inadequacy. To display either openly would obviously be damaging to the manager concerned so he acts to build up a reputation which cloaks the real situation. It is possible that a manager may not be consciously aware that he is doing this.

Mixed grid theories

Blake and Mouton avoid the trap of trying to describe all real-life management in terms of only five styles in two ways. Very early in their book they take the nine points along each axis of their grid and from that deduce eighty-one possible combinations. This approach is not developed.

Now they mention briefly six other 'styles' which they regard as mixtures of the five 'authentic styles'. The first is paternalism which is a combination of 9,1 pressure for production backed up by care for people in ways which are not directly related to the work and output.

Wide-arc pendulum management alternates between 9,1 and 1,9. The emphasis is put on increasing production until increasing stress and disturbance cause it to start falling. Then the pressure is taken off and there follows a period of 'human relations' to restore confidence in management's goodwill. Once this is achieved the pressure for production returns.

The third 'style' is counter-balancing or using 9,1 *and* 1,9 simultaneously but in different areas. The direct work situation is controlled by line management on a 9,1 basis. A parallel personnel, human relations function is set up to deal in a 1,9 fashion with the problems created by a tough line management.

Two-hat management is described briefly as the manager who deals with production problems in isolation on Monday and people's problems, again in isolation, on Wednesday. Never does he allow them to become tangled with each other.

Finally there is the 9,1–1,1 cycle. 9,1 pressure for production eventually produces the 1,1 state of apathy which is met by further doses of 9,1 pressure leading to even worse states of apathy.

Organization development

By now it seems that the case for development towards 9,9 style management is the only worthwhile goal. Individual managers can and will improve their own performance as they learn and understand better what is involved and how to use it. A chapter of self-examination questions and another chapter of interpretation are provided to help the individual to see where he stands.

But full development depends on more than individual or even team effort. It depends on 'organization development'. The purposes of organization development are:

(i) to replace common-sense assumptions about management with systematic psycho-sociological concepts;

(ii) to replace unproductive thought patterns with mental attitudes that solve problems;

(iii) to replace inter-personal and inter-group blockages with open and candid communication;

(iv) to replace out of date traditions and practices with standards promoting excellence and innovation;

(v) to define unresolved problems, find, and implement sound solutions.

To bring about this revolution involves entirely new educational methods. It cannot be 'imported' from outside by buying consultancy services. The entire organization, which means all the people who comprise it, must study themselves, their attitudes, their practices and, in doing so, must identify the real problems, the forms of behaviour that need changing and the new goals to be achieved. They must then develop the ways and means for achieving them and monitor progress.

Consultants can be used to provide guidance on suitable strategies and tactics and to train and educate a few 'key' management personnel to set the ball rolling. From these 'key' personnel the process must snowball throughout the entire organization. By administering the process themselves and finding their own solutions managers will provide their own motivation and overcome their own resistance.

But it will not be achieved overnight. Blake and Mouton give a case history of an organization that has been moving to 9,9 for five years and still has some way to go. But the advantages so far have, it is claimed, been infinitely more than worth the effort.

References

(1) Blake, R. R. and Mouton, J. S. *The Managerial Grid* (Houston: Gulf Publishing Company 1964), p. 10.

(2) Taylor, F. W. *Scientific Management* (New York: Harper and Bros. 1947– London: Harper and Bros. 1964).

(3) Mayo, E. *The Social Problems of an Industrial Civilization* (Boston: Division of Research, Harvard Business School 1945– London: Routledge and Kegan Paul 1949).

Bibliography

BOOK BY R. R. BLAKE AND J. S. MOUTON
The Managerial Grid (Houston: Gulf Publishing, 1964).

14

D. Katz and R. L. Kahn
1966

In *The Social Psychology of Organizations*[1] Katz and Kahn give as their starting point the view that neither the psychologist who studies the individual nor the sociologist who considers the group or collectivity of people can give an adequate explanation of the institution known as organization. As the title of their book suggests they consider that only a combination of both linked to an open-ended systems theory of organization can provide useful answers. Such coming together of different disciplines may well provide the basic core of future studies of management and Katz and Kahn seem to provide a good start.

At this stage the open-ended systems theory is described fairly simply. It is a system consisting of inputs, processing, and outputs. The continued existence of the system or organization depends on holding at bay the concept of entropy, that is the natural tendency of all systems to run down ultimately to a random distribution of their elements with no purpose and no organization. Maintaining or expanding the organization depends on a continuous input of human energy and on the capacity and willingness of the environment to absorb the output of the organization. The first job is to describe the organization adequately in systems terms.

Organizations and the systems concept
The valid description of an organization is claimed to be a statement of *what is* in generalized terms and concepts that are at a level of abstraction which makes them widely applicable.

Summarized, the description is as follows. An organization is an open-ended system in which input–process–output transactions occur in a repeated and relatively enduring manner over space and time. The output consists of transactions with the surrounding environment which provide the resources for further inputs to maintain the system. It is a social system in which the process activity consists largely of the patterned activities of the individuals making up the organization, such activities being largely directed to some common output of the system.

The identification of the organization or system and its functions come from tracing the pattern of energy exchange or activities producing the output and the translation of outputs by boundary transactions into fresh inputs that maintain the system, and reactivate the pattern. At this level of generalization goals and objectives are the outcomes that provide the energy input to maintain the same type of output rather than the conscious wishes of individuals. Looked at in this way the organization is an overall cycle or cycles of repeated events which will probably be divided into sub-cycles. These sub-cycles may be integral parts of larger cycles or may be tangential to each other or to a larger system. Sub-cycles involve differentiation and specialization by the people who carry them out.

Other essential aspects of open systems which need to be borne in mind are that they can reach the same end by different routes so there is no one ideal way; that they are essentially dependent on their environment for their continued existence; that the inflow of inputs is not constant; and that adequate feed-back of information from the environment is essential.

Social organizations

Katz and Kahn differ from many 'systems' theorists by insisting that the comparison of social and purely physical systems is misleading. One is not the complete analogue of the other. For instance social systems are not limited by their physical and physiological characteristics. The social system is a structuring of repetitive events which, although it takes place in a collection of human beings, machines, money, and other resources, can continue to exist although the individual resources may change. Using the word 'structure' in a slightly different sense a social structure is a contrived means or tool created by men, consisting of patterns of relationships based on attitudes, perceptions, beliefs, motivations, habits, and expectations. It is through this tool that the inputs operate to create the events that make up the real system. As well as productive inputs to be used in carrying out the basic process, social organizations require other forms of input to maintain them in existence.

With the social organization centred primarily on a collection of human beings which is not automatically predictable or impelled to function in the right direction, control of variability is essential to survival.

The control mechanisms within the organization are called values, norms, and roles. Although these concepts are common to all social organizations their actual form and content will be unique to each social structure. There may also be variability as to what extent they are consciously recognized. These three concepts form an hierarchy from generality to possibly minute detail. At the top are the values, often ideological and inadequately defined, that are the foundation and basis for judgement on the organization's existence and what it is all about. For instance is a railway system a social service or an economic enterprise? Confusion at this level can only have dire consequences. At the second level are norms or generally accepted ideas of what constitutes admissible forms of general behaviour within the organization. The idea of a role is, perhaps, the most difficult to convey properly. A social organization by definition implies specialization and division of labour between its members. In general terms this is done by prescribing the content of each job. In a sense each job then defines a role or pattern of behaviour that is expected from the holder of the job but this does not go far enough. A single job may well contain several different roles of which any one may be appropriate at some time in certain circumstances. For instance, the Managing Director in one morning may exercise the roles of decision-maker, adviser, arbitrator, confidante, or judge.

So a role is more precisely the behaviour expected of an individual under certain more or less defined circumstances. It is narrower and more specific than the behaviour required by norms, is related to a person in a particular job or position *vis-à-vis* his associates at the appropriate time, and many members of the organization will exercise more than one role.

Values, norms and roles are inter-related and interdependent but obviously they operate at different levels. Roles tend to be formalized into systems or mutual patterns that include only the bare essential elements and consequently frequently do not require either the recognition or the use of the individual's whole personality and ability. Norms and values, being concepts applying to the whole organization, should produce a pattern of shared beliefs and ideals which is a guide to all actions. However, sub-division of the organization, specialization, and sub-goals may well result in general beliefs and ideals being ignored and replaced by sub-group values and norms. Where this does happen some effectiveness, at least, of the whole organization will be lost, assuming that the organization values and norms are correct. But both effectiveness and correctness are value judgements and therefore subjective.

For the individual, norms are psychologically useful and inhibiting at the same time. The degree of each will depend on the individual's make-up and predispositions. On the one hand providing he feels able to conform to them they will help towards meeting his needs for security, self-justification, and belonging. On the other hand they will, to some extent, limit his freedom of action to attain his own goals and will create real conflict if he cannot conform to them without violating his own principles. The key factor is his level of tolerance for ambiguity.

One other aspect of social organizations requires attention in this background study of their nature. It is the inevitable tendency of more complex organizations to sub-divide and specialize. In most there will be at least six forms of sub-division. They are:

(i) Production sub-systems – concerned with the basic process of converting the inputs into outputs.

(ii) Supportive sub-systems – concerned with the transactions across the boundary with the environment, obtaining inputs, and disposing of outputs.

(iii) Maintenance sub-systems – dealing with human behaviour within the organization both at the level of required patterns of behaviour and the level of interdependence between different patterns.

(iv) Reward and sanctions sub-systems – related to individual behaviour.

(v) Adaptive sub-systems – concerned with coping with external change.

(vi) Managerial sub-systems – concerned with directing, co-ordinating, and controlling all the other sub-systems.

No organization can exist in a vacuum. At the very least it must be embedded in an environment that will supply its inputs and accept its outputs. Without this it ceases to exist. Katz and Kahn prefer the widest possible view. In order to study an organization, the field must be extended to start with the relation between the super-system, or part of the environment, with which the organization is concerned. Only then can the attention be turned to the system and its sub-systems and the relationships between them.

Finally there are a few subsidiary concepts about social organizations which need to be made clear. Within any set of systems there will normally be one or more leading systems which, because of their status or position, exercise the greatest influence on the inputs of other systems.

Organizational space is a useful concept in that it summarizes a great deal into a couple of words. It is more than mere physical space although that is one aspect of it. It includes the separation of function involved in specialization and division of labour, and the differences in status and in power related to different jobs. All these aspects work together to affect communication, the amount of strain and conflict, and the subgroup or group loyalty within the organization.

Almost equally important is that which is called the 'organization culture and climate'. This can be sensed rather than defined but there can be no doubt about its influence within an organization. Another word for it might be atmosphere and one does not have to be in an organization for long to be able to say that the atmosphere is, say, friendly and co-operative or 'dog-eat-dog' and 'the devil take the hindmost'.

System dynamic is another concept and, fortunately, is more easily explained. It is the ability of the system to modify and adapt its own nature and behaviour to meet change.

Development of organizational structure

Almost inevitably Katz and Kahn start with a brief description of the various Classical models of organization. Equally inevitably they criticize them all, mainly on account of their incompleteness, and say categorically that the only real answer is to abandon the closed-system approach and turn to open-system theory to provide worthwhile answers.

In three giant leaps this approach describes the development of organization. In primitive societies there were people with common needs, a common environmental problem and some form of task that had to be accomplished to satisfy the needs and solve the problem. The answer was co-operative task behaviour, some simple production structure such as a small group with one leader.

The second leap was to a stable form of structure. The new set-up became one of common needs and problems of an enduring nature (e.g. producing food to meet continuous demand) requiring reliable performance to produce the end-product effectively. In order to meet this a managerial structure developed on a more permanent basis which provided an authority structure and set up a tighter, more rigid, and more effective production structure *and* a maintenance system to ensure the required supply of people to man it, to develop rules, and to reward or punish. The maintenance system generally was such that it did not meet the personal needs of the people concerned so informal systems grew up to mitigate this conflict. At this stage, it is argued, the maintenance system met the three required aspects of organization, shared values, task requirements, and rule creation and enforcement.

The third leap does not look so large but is, in fact, probably the biggest of them all. As organizations grew larger and more complex and their contacts and transactions with the expanding environment grew more numerous, vast changes in the organization became essential. It had to develop completely new, highly specialized functions to relate primarily with different aspects of the environment, to look outwards from the organization rather than inwards. Apart from the obvious ones of obtaining the necessary resources of men, money, materials, and machines, and of disposing of the output of the organization, there were less obvious ones of acting as channels of communication, of scanning the environment for information and change, digesting this information, filtering it, and supplying the result to the appropriate internal section of the organization.

In three abstract leaps we have moved from a score of men cutting a track through near-primeval forest to today's massive, monolithic corporation. But there is one other aspect of organizational growth which is essential. In addition to horizontal growth and specialization there was vertical growth in division into layers or an hierarchy of management. This vertical division produced variations of power, privilege, prestige, and rewards. In addition it produced two or more 'classes' of people whose motivation to work was, it is claimed, determined by their work and their position in the hierarchy.

Once a complex social structure has come into being pressures are brought to bear on it for its survival. The obvious ones are the environment and the personal needs of its members. But at the same time the sub-division brought about by complexity causes the specialized sub-units not only to develop their particular function and mechanisms for carrying it out but also to develop their own individual dynamic forces for maintaining the whole structure. For example, the production sub-unit will develop proficiency as its dynamic, maintenance sub-units a steady-state, managerial systems control, integration, survival, and so on. While sub-systems should contribute to the main purpose and to survival their effects are not always wholly beneficial. Attaining efficiency in one sub-system may cause increased costs and inefficiency, both of which may be hidden, in other sub-systems. Sub-systems often tend to rigidity and maintaining the *status quo* to protect themselves against the threat (to them) of change that is in the interests of the organization or structure as a whole. Only too frequently the managerial sub-system tends to compromise and/or to work on a short-term basis to minimize the friction between other sub-systems. Or it may itself be too orientated towards one or two of the other sub-systems so leading to lack of the balance and the overall view which are required.

In general terms a complex social structure or organization does not function with the perfection and regularity of a well-designed machine. Its own complexity, the specialization, the dynamic situation both internal and external, and the fact that it must operate through imperfect human beings all ensure friction, conflict, and the impossibility of perfection.

So far the emphasis has been largely on the maintenance and stability of the organization which do not in themselves provide for growth. Certainly before and for a decade after Katz and Kahn's book this was the sacred cow of organization theory. Bigger must be better! (Author's comment: At the time of writing, early 1976, the first public challenge has just been made as to whether big is better.)

One more aspect remains to be mentioned. The combined approach of structure and function emphasizes creating and maintaining a stable system. But this is not the same as a static system. The emphasis on dynamic change must somehow be integrated into structure and function. One key to this is the assumption that the structure is always moving towards but never reaching an ideal state which itself is always changing. The second key is that the actual structure at any one time is a compromise resulting from conflict between sub-systems, between individuals, between ideologies. In a real world conflict of some sort will always exist. A useful theory must include it.

Organizational effectiveness

Before developing the concept of organizational effectiveness Katz and Kahn divide social structures into four broad groups of which the main one for our purposes is the productive or economic type. This includes all industrial and commercial organizations. Generally this type of structure has certain characteristics which tend to differentiate it from other types such as government, schools, hospitals, trade unions, and political parties.

The more important among these characteristics that influence the effectiveness of productive or economic structures are:

(i) Structure and adaptive procedures are more attuned to things than persons.

(ii) The market for their output is a guide to action.

(iii) Generally they have their greatest problems in dealing with the people who make up the structure.

(iv) Instrumental rewards (wages, salaries, fringe benefits) do not call forth complete loyalty and commitment to organizational purposes.

(v) They are frequently more concerned with short-run rather than long-run effects.

(vi) Both the structures as a whole and their leading, managerial systems show greater tendencies towards change than do other types of structure, but even here change is more easily made in technology than in social aspects affecting people.

(vii) They are more likely to adopt the principle of maximization or growth.

Katz and Kahn are uncompromising on much of the writing on organizational success. They say that it is ill-conceived, contradictory, and open to question. Only a new concept of what is meant by effectiveness will resolve the difficulty.

To begin with, efficiency is a major part, but not the whole, of effectiveness. Organizations being open systems can only survive by maintaining negative entropy, that is by developing greater order and complexity, expansion, and growth. As open systems they draw in energy from the environment in the form of physical and mental human energy, power, materials and machines. This total energy is used in two ways – to produce the output and to energize and maintain the organization. Without the second use, called 'net energic cost', the organization would suffer from entropy and finish up as a random, purposeless distribution of elements.

Current accounting methods, which provide the main yardstick for measuring efficiency, fail to provide full answers for three reasons. There are many inputs of energy into the system which accounting completely ignores. The distinction between running costs and capital costs is inadequately dealt with and in the long run all capital costs are running costs. The only possible common denominator for costs is money which is an inaccurate and incomplete measure.

In a way Katz and Kahn seem to sidestep the issue by avoiding the concept of total, measurable cost. 'The inclusion or exclusion of any input is a problem of frame of reference'[1] and systems theory 'is not rigid about such matters'.[2] The frame of reference can be just what the theorist wants to make it. Its only top limit is the whole of human life over infinity.

Taking efficiency first, the efficiency ratio, or input units of energy compared with output, has two aspects. Any organization will have a potential efficiency related to its structural design. One may be better designed for its purpose than another and so will have a greater potential output for the same input of energy. The second aspect is the extent to which that potential is realized. Comparison between two organizations can only be valid if both aspects are considered.

Profit and efficiency are not directly related as efficiency is the input–output ratio and profit depends on market factors often beyond the organization's control.

The earlier relation of input–output ratio is not quite complete. More efficient organizations acquire a surplus of energy (as a return for their output) that is beyond their needs to produce the output and maintain the organization. This surplus can be shared between the input factors or some of them, used to expand the organization, or be held as a reserve to meet future contingencies. Over the long period the outcomes of efficiency are growth, increased survival potential, and further increased efficiency. But, 'There is, of course, that theoretical point at which size becomes a handicap'.[3]

Effectiveness for the organization is measured by its viability as a system to survive over a long period. This, of course, relates it to the next higher system in the environment of which it is a part. The boundary transactions of input and output, availability and use of information, and persuasion are key elements here.

In the wider frame of reference of the super-system the effectiveness of a single organization is evaluated by its net contribution to the aims of the super-system. The prosperity and survival of the individual organization are irrelevant at that stage, however important they may seem to the individuals directly concerned.

Organizational roles

So far Katz and Kahn have been building up their concept of social structure or organization in systems terms. Now they turn to the more direct psycho-sociological aspects of what goes on within the system. The concept of a 'role' is the link between psychology and sociology – 'the building block of social systems'[4] and 'the sum of the requirements with which the system confronts the individual'.[5] Although the concept of a role has been defined earlier (p. 146) it needs further amplification before we proceed. Organization is an open system of roles, contrived and designed by people, with a structure consisting primarily of acts and events. Stability occurs in the relationships between units and not between the units themselves which can change. These relationships are psychological and are fragile in the sense that they can easily be upset but at the same time durable in that they can survive change in the people involved. Role behaviour, that is doing what is expected by others, is neither an inborn nor an automatic characteristic of the individual in the role. It involves learning, accepting, and fulfilling the wishes of others. In many cases the sole reward for doing so is the payment in money or kind for the service rendered. In others there may be additional psychological rewards. The role behaviour of an individual is never an isolated action. It is more or less a recurrent pattern of actions inter-related with the recurrent actions of others so as to form a predictable pattern with a predictable outcome.

Roles then fulfil the function of substituting a pattern of expected behaviour for random action. Each occupant of a role has a series of expectations of the actions and reactions of others as they have of him. But role expectation goes further than a set of ideas about actions. It includes also expectations about the role occupant's attitudes and skills, preferences as to the way he should carry out expected acts, and expectations as to how he should relate to other members of the organization.

In so far as role expectations are already well known, understood, accepted, and followed by all, nothing further is required. But when new members join the organization or conditions change so that existing expectations are no longer valid, then information has to be transmitted and influence exerted to get new expectations to be accepted and followed. Katz and Kahn call this process 'role-sending' from the role-sender (initiator) to the incumbent, focal person, i.e. the person to be influenced.

The incumbent will have role expectations 'sent' to him by many, if not all, of the people with whom he is in contact. Many will, of course, come from his superior. The 'sent role' can be assessed on the bases of do or do not, of strength, of generality or detail, and of degree of freedom of choice left to the incumbent. Behind the 'sent role' there is usually an implication of rewards or sanctions for following or ignoring the expectation.

As communication between individuals is often imperfect the concept of a 'received role' is required as the incumbent's version of the 'sent role'. The 'received role' will depend how the incumbent perceives the 'sent role' and for many reasons his perception may be faulty. But it is essential to remember that it is the 'received role' which motivates and influences the incumbent's actions. In addition to the 'received role' there may be other influences affecting the action taken such as the actual situation itself, the incumbent's own attitudes, beliefs and long-term motives, and, sometimes, the personal satisfactions he gets from his work. As a result it can often happen that the action taken is quite different from the expectations of the role-sender.

While this sounds complicated enough in itself it is, in fact, only a part of the story. Many individuals in holding one job will have many roles relating to different aspects of their job, to different people, and to different times and circumstances. The pattern of roles is not a one-to-one between individuals but a complex interweaving that becomes more and more complex as organization structures become more and more sub-divided and develop more and more levels. Conflict between the roles of different people and between the 'received roles' of individuals becomes a virtual certainty.

While these concepts of expectations, role-sending, role-receiving, and resulting action are very useful tools for analytical purposes it must be remembered that they are a theoretical abstraction from an extremely complex, ongoing situation.

On the other hand, although Katz and Kahn do not specifically draw the conclusion, their analysis of types of role-conflict seems to give very useful guidance on some causes of difficulty in operating an organization. These types are given as:

(i) *Intra-sender*. Inconsistency in his role-sending.

(ii) *Inter-sender*. Different expectations and conflicting sent-roles from different role-senders to one incumbent.

(iii) *Inter-role*. Where an incumbent holds more than one role.

(iv) *Personal-role*. Differences between role-requirements and personal values, attitudes and norms of behaviour.

(v) *Role-overload*. Where the incumbent holds more roles than he can cope with.

It is not difficult to turn all these into the everyday language of common experience.

Power and authority

In order to continue existing and functioning an organization has an endless need to attract, retain, and motivate its individual members. As they will all be *individuals* and therefore more or less different the organization must try to reduce 'the variability, instability and spontaneity of individual human acts'.[6] Obviously this reduction does occur to a reasonable extent but it is never complete and at times may be negative. The more complex the organization the more difficult this problem becomes.

Katz and Kahn say that the organizational answer to the problem starts with 'passing laws' as to what should or should not be done at three levels – general to everybody in the entire organization, limited general applying to particular sub-units or groups, and individual applying to particular roles.

If perfect foresight as to all possible future conditions, a completely stable environment, and automatons rather than individuals all existed, the passing of the laws would ensure that the organization would function like a perfectly designed, frictionless machine and no further action would be needed for it to behave perfectly. But not one of these conditions do, in fact, apply. Therefore a continuous process of adaptation and adjustment of the structure and of the laws is essential for the survival of the organization.

In order to try to ensure the adaptability and adjustment the management sub-system adopts and applies the concept of authority. It observes whether the operation of roles meets the requirements of the 'laws' passed about them. If not, it applies sanctions or punishments to the incumbents. When new members join the organization it stipulates directly or by implication that the new member will accede to the legitimate requests of superiors as prescribed for the role or roles he is to occupy.

This stipulation is in general terms accepted and so it legitimates the authority and the right to influence but it does not imply either perfect or continuous acceptance or perfect performance. In addition to the negative sanctions, rewards are, of course, used to help ensure good performance.

Authority may be charismatic arising from a dominant personality. More often it is what is called rational-legal. In this last sense it is impersonal in that it is prescribed to a position rather than an individual, is limited to a given area, and builds up in an hierarchy. It must be limited in scope and area if it is to be effective. This limitation involves successive layers of authority, the hierarchy, and Katz and Kahn are obviously not entirely happy with this proliferation. They suggest that fewer levels of authority might be more effective if other ways of ensuring role performance and compliance could be found, and that the Classical hierarchy hides many deficiencies.

Communication

Communication, or the flow of information, between individuals and/or sub-units (and, for that matter, between the organization and its environment) is essential to the continued existence of any organization. The real problem is to ensure that such communication as does take place is relevant to the problem and to the real needs of the system and subsystems concerned, and is limited to what is required. A further problem is to prevent random communication.

Even if communication were limited to only that which was necessary all individuals, sub-units and organizations would still find it necessary to analyse and sort out what they receive into a limited set of categories. This process, called coding, involves more than just sorting the wheat from the chaff. Selection or sorting out what is needed and discarding the rest is, of course, a major aspect but other important ones are refining, elaborating, distorting, and transforming. The last two arise from a psychological need for security so that information which appears new and threatening is re-interpreted to fit existing patterns or altered to minimize or remove the apparent threat. Inevitably different people and groups will at times interpret the same information in different ways and will seek information that meets their own particular needs. The different backgrounds and frames of reference of different individuals and groups will usually involve some form of translation process as information passes across the boundary between one and the other.

Too much information passing to an individual or a group will result in overload. The reaction to this situation may be one of coping with it in some way or of acting defensively for self-protection. The effective answer is to reduce the flow where overload occurs. Self-protection by omission, error, filtering, approximation, and escape has dysfunctional consequences for the organization although it may bring some relief to the individual. Coping by dealing with one thing at a time, selective filtering, and using multiple channels usually provides organizationally effective temporary measures.

The flow of information along circuits or channels is the other important aspect of the process. The possible directions are up and down the hierarchy and laterally across the organization. The involvement may vary from single man-to-man to the entire organization. The actual flow may be repetitive, in which case the identical message is passed from one to another, or modified, in which case the message is adapted to suit the new receiver, coloured or filtered to match the needs of the sender, or part of the message is withheld for some reason. There is also the possibility that the flow may be stopped at some point by a decision not to pass the message on.

In general more links in a communication channel mean less effective communication. From the point of view of organizational effectiveness the essential thing is that correct information flows to where it is needed and not elsewhere.

Probably most communication in organizations does flow down the hierarchy. This can be divided into job instructions, reasons behind the job, information on procedures, feed-back on performance, and indoctrination in organizational goals. But too often it is limited to job instructions, the other aspects being either neglected or badly handled. Another frequent difficulty with down-the-line communication is that when it starts high up in the hierarchy it is meaningless or misunderstood by the time it reaches the shop floor. People at the top too often have inadequate and incomplete information, their frame of reference and their mode of expression are completely different from those at the bottom. Unless their directives or statements of information are suitably translated on the way down their effect is likely to be worse than useless.

Lateral communication between equals can be a difficult and also a fruitful area. Bureaucratic, machine organizations tend to restrict it to a minimum by their insistence on the use of vertical channels. On the other hand where it can operate it makes for effective co-ordination between sub-units, it provides psychological, emotional, and social support, and it can act to check excessive power at levels above.

Communication upward is an essential requirement for effective operation but is often difficult in view of the superior–subordinate relationship. Really it all depends on the superior. If he encourages it, acts in what Likert calls a supportive relationship, can listen to good news with praise and approval and to bad news and failure without making the subordinate feel insecure, he will receive adequate and truthful information. If he does none of these things or, rather, if subordinates do not perceive that he does them or do not feel trust and confidence in him he will get minimal information and what he does will tend to be distorted and coloured.

Apart from the information generated in the communication patterns given above, larger organizations, particularly, may need to set up formal structures and sub-units to discover and feed information into the organization. Systems for reporting the results of activities are one form. Operational research is another whose purpose is to find and generate information leading to improved operational methods and systems. Very large organizations may have sub-units specifically to survey the environment, trends in events, long-term possibilities and their relationship to the organization.

Policy formation and decision-making

So much has been written about policy and policy-making that Katz and Kahn seem to find it difficult to do much more than change the phraseology. Their main interest, of course, is in its effect on behaviour and the structure of relationships. From this point of view there are two or three relevant comments. One is that policy-making may be related to the future and will therefore cause some change in future structure and behaviour, or it may be retrospective and confirm and legitimize forms of structure and behaviour which were already existing as deviations from previous policy. Such *deviant* change may, in fact, be the very mechanism that enables the structure to survive.

Katz and Kahn follow March and Simon (see Chapter 20) in dividing policy into operational which has measurable effects, and non-operational whose results cannot be measured. They also give criteria for measurement which would be much better described as criteria for assessment as most of them cannot possibly be measured accurately. If anything, this adds to their usefulness as they are more directly related to the structural and behavioural changes that should be the result of effective policy. They are:

(i) The feed-back arising from transactions with the environment.
(ii) The amount of internal conflict and dissension.
(iii) The number and quality of new ideas generated.
(iv) The development of capable leaders.
(v) Cost accounting.
(vi) Longer run profitability and growth.

Decision-making again owes much to March and Simon and here we shall limit ourselves to the more specific psycho-sociological aspects. The need to make a decision arises from pressure felt by the decision-maker which may arise from within himself, from colleagues (subordinates, equals, and superiors) or from the environment. This pressure must rise at least to the level of psychological consciousness to have any effect. When the pressure experienced is urgent and very heavy it is likely to result in hasty, ill-considered decisions and expedients that are unlikely to be adequate.

A useful distinction is borrowed from Rapoport between problems, that can be solved within the decision-maker's and others' frames of reference, and dilemmas, that need new thinking and the reform of accepted assumptions. The solutions to problems that, by definition, are inside existing frames of reference are unlikely to create much resistance. The solutions to dilemmas are, however, restrained only by the overall organizational context and are much more likely to run into difficulties with sub-units wanting to maintain the *status quo* and the resistance that individuals tend to show to major change.

Another point that tends to be ignored in rational decision theory is that the decision-maker may be affected not only by his objective view of the situation but also by his subjective assessment of the effect of the decision on the social approval or disapproval likely to be accorded to him and its effect on his own feelings of self-approval or disapproval. This obviously leads directly into important questions of status, self-esteem, dependence on or independence of others, sets of values, in fact, almost the whole gamut of psychological theory. But this is not followed through. It would need another book. However a short list of psychological limiting factors on decision-making and the decision-maker is given:

(i) His position in social space.
(ii) His identification with outside groups (e.g. professional associations).
(iii) Projection of his personal attitudes and values.
(iv) His capacity to make valid distinctions, avoid either – or thinking, and recognize new situations and factors.
(v) His personality type (e.g. power or ideology orientated, emotional or objective, creative ability or common sense, active or contemplative).

Leadership

It is perhaps inevitable that this topic starts with a description of the very varied thinking and lack of agreement which it has generated. In trying to find common ground Katz and Kahn define it as 'the differential exertion of influence [within the formal structure, so that] more than mechanical compliance with routine directives of organization occurs'. (Author's note: It seems fair comment to suggest that this definition excludes informal leaders and informal organization. As these are so often an important characteristic of the total organizational situation their omission must limit the value of the theory.)

Almost equally inevitably the analysis of power is the starting point. Three sorts of power arise from the occupation of a position above the bottom level of the hierarchy. They are legitimate power, reward power, and punishment power. All three are inherent in the psychological contract of employment and involve at least tacit acceptance by the subordinate. In addition there is referent power based on personal liking and expert power arising from greater knowledge.

Legitimate, reward, and punishment power may or may not be used by the holder although they are inherent in his position. The way they and other means of influence are used may affect the holder's referent power, by influencing the way subordinates think about him. Expertise makes acceptance of directives and suggestions more likely. From the point of view of organizational effectiveness the ideal is legitimate, reward, and punishment powers used in such a way as to be acceptable; referent, and expert power used in parallel to reinforce and be reinforced by legitimate power. In addition as referent and expert power are not dependent on hierarchical position they should be allowed to exercise influence wherever and whenever they appear (provided they are exercised towards and not against organizational objectives).

Much earlier it was suggested that in a perfect, stable world once the organizational structure was set up with perfect foresight the job of the management system would be finished. But these conditions do not hold. The total situation is dynamic and ever-changing, static organization structures cannot cope, no organization is ever perfect, sub-systems and individuals have their own dynamics. For these reasons, say Katz and Kahn, the need for leadership arises.

From this they draw the rather arid conclusion that the functions of leadership are to introduce structural change, to fill out the gaps and incompleteness of the formal structure, and to use this expanded structure to keep the organization in motion and effective operation. Introducing major change is an occasional, top-level activity usually related to pressures from the environment. Filling out the structure is a continuous function of middle management and keeping the whole thing going effectively is the continuous function of supervisory management.

Leadership arises when the formal structure is effectively used, when people are influenced to behave in organizationally rational behaviour. Its effectiveness can be measured in terms of specific criteria such as growth, efficiency, stability of membership over a period of time. Outstanding short-term results are by no means necessarily effective long-term ones.

The different levels of leadership need different qualities in the leaders. At the top level the ability to take overall, long-term views, to recognize the need for and carry through major structural change when necessary, and some element of charisma are required. Middle managers should have a thorough understanding of the sub-units, their functioning and inter-relationships and a two-way orientation, upwards to top management and downwards to supervision. At the supervisory or administration level knowledge of technical aspects, of rules and the effects of their application, and consistency, fairness and 'the spirit rather than the letter' attitudes are the foremost needs.

The two contradictory needs of stable administration and change as a reaction to the environment and a condition of survival and growth exist in differing proportions in all organizations. The problem, it is suggested, is most acute at the top level which should switch its attention from one aspect to another according to the relationship between the organization and the environment. But in times of very rapid major change innovation will affect all levels directly. In any case research seems to show that the most effective organizations are those in which the power to influence (show leadership) is widely spread throughout all levels in the organization.

The psychological basis of organizational effectiveness
At the end Katz and Kahn seem forced to two conclusions. Organizational effectiveness is not simply a matter of better motivation of members. Better technology, a better situation, and a better role-system or structure may also be large contributory factors. The second is that the question of motivation in complex organization structures has not been effectively studied.

The analytical framework for an adequate theory must look at both individuals and groups in real-life organizational settings and must find answers to these questions:

(i) What types of behaviour are required for effective organization functioning?
(ii) What different motivational patterns are and can be used?
(iii) What are the conditions required for eliciting a given motivational pattern in an organizational setting?

There are, however, partial answers that can be given and do show some advance in understanding.

Patterns of individual behaviour that further organizational effectiveness can be summarized under three headings:

(i) Joining and staying in the system.

(ii) Dependable behaviour; meeting quantity and quality standards, reducing somewhat the range of human variability.

(iii) Innovative and spontaneous behaviour beyond role requirements; active co-operation, protective actions directed at the system or sub-system, creative suggestions for improvement, self-training for responsibility, external support for the organization.

Motivational patterns more or less understood and used fall into four categories:

(i) Legal compliance. Rule enforcement, acceptance of implied contract. Probably gives only minimal performance.

(ii) Instrumental Rewards. System rewards and individual rewards. Personal identification with leaders. Social approval from affiliation with peers. Produces varied effects which from the organizational point of view may be positive or negative.

(iii) Self-determination and self-expression. Sense of accomplishment and use of abilities. Provides direct satisfaction and identification with the job.

(iv) Internalization of organizational goals as representing own values and self-concept. Probably the ideal.

The objective conditions, psychological variables and probable outcomes of these four patterns are reiterated as a summary that does not really add to existing knowledge.

Organizational change

The emphasis on change which occurs throughout the book ensures some consideration of it as a separate topic. There is a suggestion that consideration of change has been handicapped by confusion between change in the individual and the change in organizational variables which are due to the systemic properties of organizations themselves. The individual subjected to change from outside sources, e.g. a training course, is more likely to revert and suppress the change if he still finds himself in the same structural pattern in the organization. Only if he is at the top of the hierarchy and has the authority, the power, and the skill to initiate organizational change is it likely that personal change will lead to changes in the structure of organization.

There are a number of possible approaches for bringing about change in the organization. Supplying information about it, to the people concerned, has real value, if done properly, in providing reasons for the change but it is not primarily a positive motivating factor for acceptance and implementation. Individual counselling can be used to provide new insights, change attitudes and probably to change individual behaviour while leaving the structure unchanged. Group methods may produce group norm changes provided their effects are not over-ridden by role and authority structures. Sensitivity training and group therapy may have their uses in increasing insights and removing emotional blocks. But Katz and Kahn conclude that direct manipulation of the variables in organization structure, such as changing decision-making points or bringing the technical work system into a better fit with the social system, is the most powerful and effective way of bringing about organizational change.

Conclusion

Modern industrial society with its tendency towards mainly bureaucratic structure has produced four major problems for organizations:

(i) The insistence on maximization has produced rapid growth, has vastly increased the general standard of living and, at the same time, has produced the monolithic corporation and the 'nightmare of totality'.

(ii) Role-systems have increased efficiency at the expense of impoverished personal relations and loss of self-identity.

(iii) Standards of conformity, the emphasis on empiricism and compromise are an apparent threat to the moral and ethical integration of society.

(iv) At the very time when improving standards of life and education are increasing the expectations and aspirations of the rank-and-file, sheer size and complexity are making their fulfilment more difficult.

Neither the past nor the present have been or are perfect. Our greatest need is still to determine the overall best forms of organization taking both efficiency and humanity into account.

References

(1) Katz, D. and Kahn, R. L. *Social Psychology of Organizations* (New York: Wiley 1966), p. 153.

(2) Ibid, p. 153.

(3) Ibid, p. 159.

(4) Ibid, p. 171.

(5) Ibid, p. 171.
(6) Ibid, p. 199.

Bibliography

BOOK BY D. KATZ AND R. L. KAHN
The Social Psychology of Organizations (New York: Wiley, 1966).

15

R. Likert
1967

Single-mindedness, the persistent following of one theme is not always a virtue. It may be either the quality of a saint or of a crank. Rensis Likert would certainly claim to be neither, but single-minded he certainly is. Why, then, should we include *The Human Organization. Its Management and Value* in this volume when his *New Patterns of Management*[1] has already been dealt with in *Developments in Management Thought*?[2]

In his Preface to *New Patterns of Management* Likert claims to present 'a newer theory of organization based on the management principles and practices of the managers who are achieving the best results in American business and government'.[3] In the next paragraph he says 'The few partial tests of the theory . . .'.[4] Good scientific practice requires that the principles enunciated in a new theory should be tested and re-tested against new situations and by using them for prediction. Only if, and for as long as, a theory stands up to this rigorous scrutiny can it be said to remain viable. From our point of view *The Human Organization. Its Management and Value* provides confirmation of the theory of New Patterns and, more importantly, shows where the ideas have been further developed.

New foundations for the art of management
The very first word of the title of the first chapter is 'New'. This is not obsession on Likert's part it is the bare statement of the fact that he and his co-workers at the Institute for Social Research at Michigan have a 'new science-based management' on which the practical manager can build the art of good, effective management. 'Of all the tasks of management, management of the human component is the central and most important task, because all else depends on how well it is done.'[5] Likert claims that most current management is based on key assumptions drawn from managers of the past. A form of folk-lore that has been updated in places but only now has been explained, confirmed, or refuted by the

new scientific base, by quantitative research that can be, and has been, repeated, re-tested and verified.

A look at management systems
In order to test the hypotheses put forward in *New Patterns of Management* a large-scale survey of several hundred managers was carried out. The earlier evocative titles for management systems or styles were dropped and replaced by numbers 1, 2, 3, and 4 to avoid 'suggesting' appropriate answers. Otherwise the pattern had been used before. It required the managers to rate the management of the most productive department and of the least productive one on a twenty-point scale under seven main headings. The details are irrelevant here, the findings are important. They confirmed overwhelmingly that the least productive departments tended under all headings to use managerial practices that came within systems 1 and 2, exploitive and benevolent authoritative management and that the most productive departments tended to use practices within systems 3 and 4, consultative and participative group management. Further insights were that the managers questioned generally used practices nearer to systems 1 and 2 than those used by the best department known to them, that some managers thought that consultative and participative methods could only be used after high production had been obtained by authoritative methods, and that top managements consistently reverted to system 1, authoritative exploitive, to increase efficiency and reduce costs.

Productivity and labour relations under different management systems
Much fuller questionnaires were used to obtain more detailed answers that again confirmed the previous results, while another one showed that most managers would prefer, given the opportunity, to operate under system 4.

While questionnaires are useful and, when properly designed and used, reliable ways of getting information, the proof of a theory is its use in practice. Laboratory experiments do not reproduce the conditions of a factory and real-life factories are not easy to come by. The Institute was fortunate to become involved over a period of two years in monitoring and helping in a deliberate change of management system and practices in a newly acquired subsidiary company. Likert gives a full account of the case. The outcome was that the management of the parent company that had used system 4 succeeded in two years in changing the existing management of the subsidiary from systems 1 and 2 to 3 by processes of training, guidance and support. The effects of this showed as increasing productivity and earnings, improving management–labour relations and co-operation, increased motivation, improved morale, reduced costs and labour turnover, a changed image in the community, and substantial losses converted into profits.

Other examples quoted are an extremely successful plant which, on investigation, was found to be using almost entirely style 4, participatory management, a group of companies that had adopted the Scanlon Plan and which showed management practices approaching system 4, and large-scale field experiments involving deliberate shifting of management practices towards system 4 which improved a very bad labour relations history in a quite remarkable way.

One swallow does not make a summer and these are only a few examples. Many others appear in works by other members of the Institute. Likert is happy to rest his case. The hypotheses in *New Patterns of Management* work in practice. The development is that they have been shown to work.

The interdependent, interacting character of effective organizations
This section expands and sets out more clearly the basic concepts involved in managing under System 4. In summary they are:

(i) The use by managers of the principle of supportive relationships.
(ii) The use of group decision-making and group methods of supervision.
(iii) The use of high-performance goals throughout the organization.

Supportive relationships are a central feature. They are relationships and behaviour which enhance the self-esteem and build up the ego of the individual instead of destroying them. But a supportive relationship will only work if the subordinate 'in the light of his background, values and expectations' (sees it as one which) 'contributes to his sense of personal worth and importance, one which increases and maintains his sense of significance and human dignity'.[6] Where these are used non-economic motives will reinforce, harmonize with, and be compatible with economic forces. The combination will increase co-operative behaviour directed to organizational goals.

It is one thing to use a phrase like supportive relationships which could so easily become a glib bit of jargon. It is another to spell it out. Likert does just that. Behaviour is supportive in so far as it includes the following: mutual trust and confidence, expectations of good performance, help in maintaining a good income, understanding and doing something about work problems, real interest in personal and family problems, help when needed in doing the job, training in the job and for promotion, information on job matters, information on the company as a whole, seeking and valuing others' opinions, giving credit where credit is due, and being friendly and approachable.

System 4 involves the use of the overlapping group with the link-pin as a member of his own and the next superior group and, where necessary, of peer-groups. At the level of all groups it is claimed that group decision-making improves the quality and the carrying out of all decisions. This increases rather than diminishes the responsibility of the group leader. He remains fully responsible for the results but has the additional responsibility of ensuring that his group is trained to become capable of reaching good decisions. At the same time the group also becomes responsible for carrying out its own decisions, they are no longer something imposed from above.

The third condition of high-performance goals seems to be more typically American than British. Likert claims, and can back the claim with evidence, that generally employees want stable employment, job security, opportunities for promotion, and satisfactory compensation. But, he goes on to claim that generally they want to be proud of their company, its performance and accomplishments. Supportive behaviour by management must meet these needs of the workers and to do so the company must be successful. (Author's comment. It is an interesting thought that the differences here may be in many cases more fundamental than skin-deep. The histories and cultures of the two peoples and particularly the history, growth and attitudes of trade unions in the two countries have been, and still are in most cases, so completely different. This opens too wide a field to be discussed here as we are only trying to get the gist of Likert's contribution. But it is a point to be borne in mind when transferring American ideas into a British background.)

High aspirations and expectations are not sufficient in themselves. To be fully effective they must be held at all levels and, most important, must be set by some participative mechanism which involves the people who have to reach them in setting them.

These three basic principles of system 4 have been shown by many studies to be essential to high levels of success but it is recognized that the specific methods and procedures used to carry them out will vary according to the nature of the work and the traditions of the company concerned.

A long-range research project carried out by a team from the Institute for Social Research in a large insurance company showed clearly the effects of different systems of management when the systems were deliberately manipulated. The results are summarized in Figure 2.

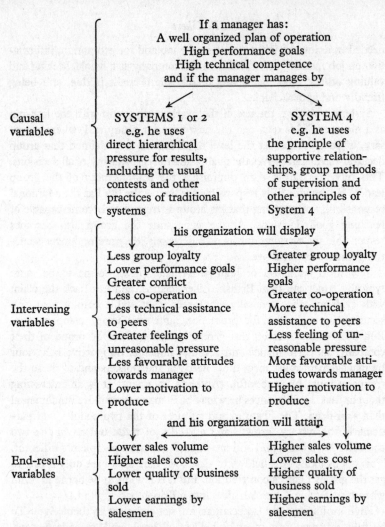

Causal variables
{

If a manager has:
A well organized plan of operation
High performance goals
High technical competence
and if the manager manages by

SYSTEMS 1 or 2
e.g. he uses
direct hierarchical
pressure for results,
including the usual
contests and other
practices of traditional
systems

SYSTEM 4
e.g. he uses
the principle of
supportive relation-
ships, group methods
of supervision and
other principles of
System 4

his organization will display

Intervening variables
{

Less group loyalty
Lower performance goals
Greater conflict
Less co-operation
Less technical assistance
to peers
Greater feelings of
unreasonable pressure
Less favourable attitudes
towards manager
Lower motivation to
produce

Greater group loyalty
Higher performance
goals
Greater co-operation
More technical
assistance to peers
Less feeling of un-
reasonable pressure
More favourable atti-
tudes towards manager
Higher motivation to
produce

and his organization will attain

End-result variables
{

Lower sales volume
Higher sales costs
Lower quality of business
sold
Lower earnings by
salesmen

Higher sales volume
Lower sales cost
Higher quality of
business sold
Higher earnings by
salesmen

Figure 2. Sequence of developments in a large well organized company.

Reproduced from Warshaw M. R. (Ed.) *Changing Perspectives in Marketing Management* (Ann Arbor: University of Michigan. Bureau of Business Research, 1962).

Time: a key variable in evaluating managerial systems
A major cause of the tentativeness of the conclusions of *New Patterns of Management* was that often the direct correlation between causal variables and end-result variables which was expected did not materialize. Of the several explanations put forward at the time, research since then has convinced Likert that the important variable is time. The interval between causal variables and the expected end-result variables has

proved to be much longer than expected. As illustration of this a change to or a tougher enforcement of systems 1 and 2 will probably show an increase in output and reduction of costs over the short period, that is, up to about a year. The long-term effects of reduced morale, higher absentee rates, higher costs, lower quality, and lower production will not start showing in all probability until about eighteen months to two years. Even then they may be improved again by a further increase of pressure in systems 1 and 2. On the other hand a movement towards system 4 takes time to become accepted and to work its way through to end-result variables but when improvement does show it goes on increasing and building on itself. So, at the end of, say, twelve months after a move either towards a tighter system 1 or to a system 4, the end-result variables will look very much alike. But after two years there will be no doubt whatever about the long-term direction of the changes, system 4 favourable, system 1 unfavourable.

But even this, although it has been shown to be the case, is still something of an oversimplification. Managerial behaviour is by no means always and in every way a shift in one direction and of the same order of magnitude in all aspects. This makes even more complex and less predictable the changes in the intervening variables which are the immediate causes of change in end-result variables. The usual measurements of results are often unreliable as indicators of cause and effect. Often the initial changes in causal variables occurred so long before the final changes in end-result become apparent that the cause–effect relationship is lost and some other more recent, but irrelevant factor, gets the credit or the blame.

A system of management that exists and remains unchanged will not, of itself, cause changes in end-result variables *if* the whole system of operations is in a stable state reflecting accurately the system or style of management. But, at any one time, the operations system may be in the process of change moving towards a match with the management system. The operative factor is the movement of the management system from one position to another, either nearer to or a tighter imposition of systems 1 and 2 or nearer to system 4.

The data from many studies of change towards systems 1 and 2 have been amalgamated into general measurements of the changes in causal variables, intervening variables, and end-result variables. The results are more or less consistently in the same directions: short-term improvements in end-result variables, slow but certain deterioration in intervening variables resulting in long-term deterioration in end-result variables. Variations about the norm have been observed to be due to the particular history of the firm, the degree and duration of increased management pressure, the general labour climate of the community, and the fact that a badly organized and loosely controlled firm will always respond favourably to improved organization and tighter management.

Similar data have been compiled from firms where the shift in management observed has been towards system 4. The results again are as would be predicted from the theory. Favourable increases in causal variables as managements have acquired more skill in new methods, slow but continuous improvements along all intervening variables and, a little later, continuous improvements along all end-result variables.

It is admitted that these are generalized patterns and that individual cases could and did vary about the norm. One possibly significant fact that seems almost to slip into the account without emphasis is that the system 4 firms are described as having labour forces from about a hundred to several hundreds. It would seem that larger firms of a thousand or more employees have not been studied or are not included.

Likert suggests that top management fails to recognize the value of system 4 because its results are slower to show in traditional accounting and cost records and because what he calls human asset building does not show at all in traditional figures (except as costs incurred). He also maintains that socio-metric measurement of causal, intervening and end-result variables must be kept up for much longer periods than were first thought necessary to show results. Ideally they become a permanent feature of control but with less frequent measurement than accounting procedures.

In concluding this section he says that when all factors are taken into account and proper analyses made 'consistent, positive relationships can be expected among the causal, intervening and end-result variables in every organization'.[8]

Better fiscal management

Likert insists that there is an essential need for altering and increasing accounting records to show *total costs* and *total asset values*. It would then be possible to show the difference between genuine reduced costs of increased production and these same items obtained at the cost of running down the value of the firm's most important asset – its managers and workers. Similarly many items such as training, regarded at present as pure cost and, at best, a necessary evil, would be seen to be investment for the future in building up the value of the human asset. The case for it is, he says, irrefutable.

How to do it is not, however, quite so clear. It is claimed that procedures to ascertain the current values of the human organization and customer goodwill are now available using psycho-metric and socio-metric measures of the intervening variables. The traditional end-result variables of cost, profit, and turnover are of very doubtful value and often misleading.

The need for a systems approach

There is a need right at the start to qualify Likert's use of the term 'Systems Approach'. He is using it in the context of a system or style of management, his system 1 to system 4 or authoritative exploitive to participative systems.

Throughout all the years and the many thousand of questionnaires the responses on the styles or systems of management used in hundreds of firms have been consistent. If some main items of management behaviour fell into system 1 then the rest would be in system 1 or at most just spreading in a few cases into system 2. Very careful steps were taken later to avoid conditional response but in spite of this the patterns remained cohesive. This consistency and cohesiveness tends to run throughout the organization and the patterns of behaviour. For instance communication methods and patterns consistent with system 1 would not be found in a firm with a system 3 or 4 general pattern.

This has great significance when the question of change arises. There are only two viable possibilities. Either the proposed change must be consistent with the existing system and resulting patterns or the whole organization must be shifted to a new system which is consistent with the change. Any other alternative is doomed to fail.

Likert lays down specific guidelines for introducing major change. First the most influential causal variables related to the change must be located and altered. At the same time the operating procedures which will need changing to confirm the change need to be reviewed and systematic plans must be made and put into effect to modify these procedures. Only in this way can the consistency necessary for success and survival be obtained.

Measurement

Likert makes the now common assertion that every organization is in a never-ending state of change but he takes this somewhat further. The usual variations due to changes in the environment, technology, and products are mentioned but additionally he gives changes arising from internally initiated adaptation and from movement from one system of management to another.

The capacity of an organization to function well under such conditions depends upon the quality of its decision-making processes. But even the best decision machinery can only function as well as the information on which decisions are based. If such information does not contain reliable measurements of the state and trends of causal, intervening and end-result variables it is, Likert maintains, dangerous and incomplete. Effective decision-making depends on knowing the state of the system, information which traditional end-result measures cannot possibly supply. The social sciences using the techniques of mathematics and statistics as measuring tools for their own disciplines are claimed to have developed the methodologies required for measuring the variables necessary for showing the state of the human organization, in particular the intervening variables which are predictors of trends. More refined and accurate end-result variables must be monitored continuously, intervening variables at regular, but less frequent, intervals allowing for the time lags involved. Changes in causal variables must also be monitored through the system.

Measurements such as these used with system 4 management not only put the real emphasis on long-term results rather than possibly spurious short-term ones but they also do two other things. They monitor the progress of change so that mistakes in decisions can be put right before lasting harm is done and they provide advance warnings of the need for decision so that last-minute panic measures become generally unnecessary. But it is emphasized that such measurements can only produce favourable results if allied to system 4 management. With systems 1 and 2 the information obtained would be distorted and incorrect and its use for autocratic control and repression could only make a bad situation worse.

Likert claims, and quite obviously believes, that this book justifies the initial theories of *New Patterns of Management* because it is based on research and experiment which is backed by empirical data and measurement. At the end of the chapter he makes the proviso that this sort of measurement is a complex task for specialists and that interpretation of the data obtained is even more so. The explanation of how to do it requires another book 'as yet unwritten'.

Human asset accounting
In the middle 1960s accountants and top management if they were forward-looking were just beginning to realize that the human resources, the men and women, the managers and workers, were assets in the organization which should be taken into account in assessing its value. £10,000 spent on acquiring a machine with a life of ten years automatically appeared in the books and the balance sheet as an asset with a value adjusted each year. £10,000 spent on acquiring, training, acclimatizing, and producing a manager on whom the effectiveness of the machine and all that went with it appeared only as expenses!

The same problem appears in another approach by Likert. As was said earlier, systems 1 and 2 management could produce effective end-results over relatively short periods at the expense of a demoralized work-force, absenteeism, and high labour turnover. In the long run system 4 management would get better results with improvements in morale, absenteeism and labour turnover. Systems 1 and 2 reduced the asset value of the work-force, system 4 increased it. Traditional accounting shows neither result directly. That good records of these facts should be available is one of those obvious facts that is only obvious when it has been pointed out.

The comparative human values of two firms of about the same size and using similar technology, machinery and processes would represent the difference in their future earning power which was attributable to their human assets. Likert suggests eleven different aspects on which comparison could be made, from performance goals to co-ordination, from decision-making to training.

To say that such valuation and comparisons are obviously necessary is one thing. To make accurate measurements of them is quite another. It will take years to develop sophisticated measuring techniques but in the meantime a start could be made by linking variations in causal and intervening variables with improved financial and cost data.

Achieving effective co-ordination
Likert certainly has the courage of his convictions. At this point he puts forward the massive claim that system 4 is a science-based theory of organization which provides formal solutions for organizational difficulties that, he claims, cannot be solved under traditional organization theory. Frequently these problems are handled by informal methods which run contrary to the formal organization theory of the firm.

The problem of achieving effective co-ordination is set out under seven headings:

(i) Whether to organize the large company by function, product, geography, or some combination of these.

(ii) Economics of scale tend to push firms towards a functional form of organization.

(iii) But highly functionalized firms run into problems in achieving effective co-ordination.

(iv) New knowledge and technologies are complicating the problem.

(v) The limits of human capacity to cope with new knowledge and technology are adding to the problem.

(vi) Decentralization becomes more inadequate as a solution as technology becomes more complex.

(vii) Generally attempts of co-ordination have been limited by adherence to systems 1 and 2 principles.

Having defined the problem Likert sets out the conditions that must be fulfilled for a satisfactory solution. They are, in effect, a restatement of the claims made for system 4. There must be high levels of co-operative behaviour between superiors and subordinates and especially between peers. Favourable attitudes, confidence and trust are essential between all members. Differences and conflicts are inevitable and the organization structure and the interaction skills of members must be adequate to produce creative solutions. There must exist a capacity to exert influence and to create motivation and co-ordination without the traditional lines of authority. Finally the decision processes and superior–subordinate relationships must be such that, where necessary, people can work effectively within the one man–two bosses situation. Categorically these conditions cannot be met under any one of systems 1, 2, or 3 and where high-producing managers are producing these conditions under any management set-up other than system 4 they can only be doing so by deviating from their firm's management style.

The essence of system 4 management lies in two concepts. One is overlapping groups joined by the link-pin man who is a member of both groups. The other is effective influence-interaction processes throughout all groups at all levels. The overlapping group works vertically by having the leaders of related subordinate groups as the members of the next higher group with their common superior as leader and so on up the hierarchy. Lateral co-ordination is achieved by lateral representative groups of link-pins led by the next higher superior of the product group. Co-ordination between functional specialisms and production and other aspects is dealt with by having functional specialist link-pins.

Fundamental to the system is the use of effective group decision-making methods in all groups. Only in this way can an effective influence-interaction system be set up which provides for the free flow of information throughout the system, for the maximum influence upward and downward to be generated, and for the right motivational forces for co-ordination to be created.

The co-ordination link-pin system creates an additional formal structure over and across the usual functional line and staff structure. Where the load is not too heavy it is recommended that the additional co-ordinating roles be added to the roles of appropriate functional managers. If this is impossible new co-ordinating roles must be created.

Decision-making also takes on a new form. In every group decisions must be reached by consensus so that an individual, a workgroup, or a specialist group cannot impose solutions on others. At all levels these decisions must be in the interests of the firm as a whole and not of any one particular section or group. Problems that relate specifically only to one unit must be settled within that unit. Problems that affect other units in a larger group and arise in terms of one unit or sub-group must be restated in terms of the environment of the head of the whole group. All members of the larger group, which will be made up of the link-pins of all the sub-groups with the head of the next level, will contribute to the decision process the situational requirements which they face and between them they must find the solution considered best for the whole group and its sub-units.

Idealistic though this may sound Likert does not have to leave it at mere theorizing. Having set out the requirements he goes on to give chapter and verse of firms met by members of the Institute who are working to system 4 or are approaching near versions of it.

The next step

Three specific major experiments are used as examples of what can be done by carefully planned, deliberate training of managers in moving management systems over to system 4. There are three provisos. One is that it is useless for an individual manager or a group to try to shift to system 4 while the rest of the organization stays on systems 1 or 2. So it is essential that the 'conversion' must come right at the top of the management tree and spread from there throughout the entire organization. The second is that quick results cannot be expected. A shift to system 4 management will take at least a couple of years which seems to be the time for changes to be produced in the intervening variables and for these changes to show significant, permanent improvement in the end-result variables. Likert himself gives the time required as 'a few years'. The third proviso must be that a great deal of professional help will be needed to carry through and monitor the change. Much of this help will have to come from outside the firm.

Likert ends on a cautious note as he did at the end of *New Patterns of Management*. But it is a very different sort of caution. Then he was being cautious about the whole concept of system 4 – it was so revolutionary. Now his caution is not about the system but how to apply it. 'The Institute for Social Research is working intensively with a limited number of companies in widely different industries helping them to shift to system 4.'[9] He adds that the Institute is still learning more about the system, how to apply it to specific conditions, and how to train managers to adopt it.

References

(1) Likert, R. *New Patterns of Management* (New York: McGraw-Hill, 1961).

(2) Pollard, H. R. *Developments in Management Thought* (London: Heinemann, 1974), Chapter 17.

(3) Likert, R. op. cit., p. vii.

(4) Likert, R. op. cit., p. vii.

(5) Likert, R. *The Human Organization. Its Management and Value* (New York: McGraw-Hill, 1967), p. 1.

(6) Likert, R. *New Patterns of Management*, p. 103.

(7) Likert, R. *The Human Organization. Its Management and Value*, p. 76.

(8) Ibid, p. 99.

(9) Ibid, p. 191.

Bibliography

BOOK BY R. LIKERT

The Human Organization. Its Management and Value (New York: McGraw-Hill, 1967).

16

F. Herzberg
1968

Most of the psycho-sociological ideas current before 1960 seem to have taken one of two courses during the decade of the 1960s. Either way they have generally been subjected to much empirical research which has led on the one hand to confirmation and extension and on the other to serious modification or even outright rejection. Of course this is no more than a demonstration of the way in which knowledge is increased.

Herzberg's book *Work and the Nature of Man* is a good example of the first course. The ideas in *The Motivation to Work*[1] of which he was part author, were published in 1959. Herzberg claims in *Work and the Nature of Man* that further research has confirmed and extended the original theory.

The book is extremely positive in its approach and is built round four fundamental ideas:

(i) It develops the idea of the dual nature of man as a logical base for the concepts of hygiene and motivator factors.

(ii) It confirms empirically the theory of *The Motivation to Work* and extends it from the narrow confines of professional employees to all ranks.

(iii) It develops a specific plan of action for improvement based on the theory backed up largely by practical work.

(iv) It is critical of much of the psycho-sociological school in a way that may explain the scepticism of many managers towards 'the school's' ideas.

There is, however, one proviso that Herzburg himself puts forward and then largely seems to ignore. It is the admission that the psychological growth of any individual is conditioned by *all* that happens to him both before as well as during his time at work. This must have two effects. In so far as the experience is stultifying the worker's personality it must, to some extent, limit the amount managers can do to improve the situation. Secondly the manager's own experience will at least partially condition his own approach. Stressing these conditions does not invalidate the essential nature of Herzberg's proposals but it does prevent their being viewed as the herald of a perfect world.

Herzberg suggests that what was currently going on in industry was '. . . a silent revolution in which man is protesting not merely the treatment society accords to him but the very conception of his nature as it has been fostered by the prevailing institutions. He (man) seems to demand a more realistic appraisal of his nature than the myths about him that have so conveniently and over so long a period been provided'.[2] In addition the amount of real knowledge about the nature of man has fallen far behind the knowledge and application of technology. The results have been the industrial monolithic corporation and well-meant efforts by many sincere managers to improve the happiness of society and individuals which have actually prevented the very thing they were trying to do.

Adam and Abraham
These two Old Testament characters are used as a starting point for an elaboration of the discussion that every individual has two sets of quite different basic needs. The first set comprises 'animal' needs related to the environment in which he lives, the second are 'human' needs related to tasks in which the individual is uniquely involved.

The discussion also leads to the claim that whenever society has lacked concrete knowledge it has resorted to accepted myths to fill in the gaps, to provide some form of understanding of the individual's place and purpose in society. Of these myths those dealing with human nature have been the most far-reaching and useful ones.

In any social culture support has only been given to those needs of the individual which match the needs of the controlling forces in that culture. In the industrial era of the last two centuries the major controlling force has been the organization directed to industrial or commercial ends. Industrialization has been based on two main concepts – the replacement of the direct man–tool–work relationship by the machine–machine minder relationship in which the worker becomes an interchangeable, specialized instrument, and the alienation of the worker from his conception of the value of work.

The needs of the organization based on these two concepts have been used to create myths about human nature which, while fundamentally wrong, have enabled the industrial society to survive. The fact is that the human being is the most adaptable form of life. This has made it possible for the individual to exist at the same time as industrialization and its related myths but it does not validate the myths. It only proves the power of survival under adverse conditions.

Industrial myths

Before we look at Herzberg's view of the prevailing and recent myths it would be as well to remember that as long as myths are accepted they are regarded not as myths but as truth, and that different sections of society may well hold fiercely to contradictory myths.

Herzberg seems to be primarily concerned with the myths of one dominant class in society, namely the managerial group in industry. They consist of the following:

(i) Business is religion and religion is business.

(ii) The captains of industry are the leaders of men and nations. Without them the workers would live in squalor and want.

(iii) Virtue is economic success and success is economic virtue.

(iv) The indolent and lazy lack ambition and are predestined for perdition.

(v) 'Economic man' and rationality are the cornerstones of society.

(vi) Paternalism, capitalistic welfare, and social welfare are the products of the revolt of the worker and middle-class philanthropy.

(vii) Human relations theories of physical well-being, comfort, happiness, and pay applied by managers will produce correct motivation to work in the worker.

Two other myths are worthy of mention. Scientific Management is a self-fulfilling prophecy. Efficiency requires the breakdown of work into the smallest possible units. These make minimal demands on human abilities and require immature and childish behaviour from the worker. This causes workers to behave in immature and childish ways, therefore these requirements match people's needs. The other is that a manager by definition is a rational person while a worker is not.

The basic needs of man

Herzberg admits that the psychological nature of man has been the most difficult area of all in which to substitute scientific knowledge for myth. The roots of psychology go back to philosophy and physiology. The rational, scientific approach of the nineteenth century in particular produced an explosion of scientific knowledge and discredited the philosophical approach to the question 'what is man?'. So, while psychology has given well-documented answers to problems about the behaviour of man, questions of what is his real nature have been largely ignored.

In human beings the early period of life during which the individual only slowly loses complete dependence on others for the satisfaction of needs is relatively protracted. This dependence on others for the meeting of primary physiological and psychological drives leads to feelings of inferiority and later the primary drives lead to learned patterns of behaviour that are transferred to other unrelated areas. The sources of the feeling of inferiority or being 'less than' become virtually unlimited. The primary drives and their derivatives are cyclical, their satisfaction only lasts a short time so they are constantly recurring. Present failure to meet them and, because the brain can link the past, the present, and the future, the anticipation of future inability will both cause present discomfort and foreboding.

While animals are limited by biological growth human beings are able to break these limits by mental growth and psychological ability. To a greater or lesser extent they are themselves determiners and masters of their own destiny. The over-riding intention is survival. A major means to this end is the setting up of cultural evolution as the main determinant of human behaviour.

Throughout this personal and evolutionary development mankind has needed myths to explain the mysteries of the unknown. A little too optimistically Herzberg suggests that all the mysteries have now been explained by rational analysis except the central one of man himself, his self-awareness, his ultimate aloneness, his potential for self-actualization, and self-realization. With the abandonment of the philosophical approach these areas are still largely unexplored.

In brief the human animal has two distinct sets of needs. One derives from his animal nature and is based on avoiding the loss of satisfaction of primary drives and learned drives derived from them. The other set comes from an urge to satisfy the need to realize his own potential by psychological growth. Their origins and forms of satisfaction are quite different. They are not simply different points on a single scale of needs.

Psychological growth

The relatively recent and by no means complete shift of attention in psychology from disturbed, abnormal behaviour to a study of normal behaviour patterns has brought the question of psychological growth into greater prominence. The most crucial question is the extent of the capacity of the individual to grow psychologically. Two aspects are the potential of the individual and his ability to develop it. Both are variable from one individual to another but only in the mentally ill can they be assumed to be completely absent.

Psychological growth has a number of aspects that can be ranged in some approximate order of development. The earliest is a growth in knowledge, learning from experience both of success and failure. Mere knowledge can be just more disconnected scraps of information so the second stage is an increased ability to develop relationships between bits of knowledge, to fit new information into the right place in existing patterns, to modify or abandon patterns when this is seen to be necessary. So far the individual has been on the receiving, but not inactive, end. The next stage is creativity, the conversion of knowledge into new patterns of behaviour and into new ideas. This may range from quite simple adaptations to meet minor situations in everyday life to the greatest works of art or the most earth-shattering discoveries.

The three higher levels show much more complex forms of behaviour. The one certain thing about the world around the individual is its great uncertainty. Life is full of ambiguities. The psychologically mature person accepts and can live with uncertainty, can remain effective in the face of ambiguity. The less mature individual oversimplifies, fails to consider more than the fewest variables in a situation, and is only too glad to hand over the responsibility for decision and action to some more mature 'father-figure'. Herzberg calls the fifth stage 'individuation'. This involves becoming a separate individual, distinct from the mass. In this there is a paradox to be resolved. Each stage of psychological growth involves more differentiation between individuals but mankind can only survive by combining into groups and societies which necessarily involves some surrender of individuality. The solution for the mature individual is to have his own feelings, beliefs, ideas, judgement, and patterns of behaviour while at the same time co-operating with others to enhance the group and help to achieve its purposes and using this co-operation to further his own growth. The final stage of psychological growth is expressed very briefly. It is the complete surrender and discarding by the individual of all illusions about himself.

This is, of course, a counsel of perfection and like all perfect states is unlikely to be realized in practice. It is equally unlikely that many people have gone as far along the road to psychological growth as their potential could take them. It is a main plank in Herzberg's thesis that society as it is organized today seems designed to prevent the majority from growing at all.

The motivation–hygiene theory
Probably as a result of eight years of explaining the motivation–hygiene theory Herzberg sets it out in much more detail here than in *The Motivation to Work*.[1] It is worthwhile taking a look at the new version.

The factors at work which can lead to dissatisfaction and satisfaction have not been altered. The dissatisfiers are company policy and administration, supervision, inter-personal relations, working conditions, salary, status, job security, and the effects of all of them on personal life. These are the hygiene factors. The satisfiers or motivators are achievement, recognition, the work itself, responsibility, advancement, and the possibility of personal growth.

Hygiene factors are related to the human needs of man as described earlier. They lead to a need to avoid unpleasantness. Primarily they are related to the conditions surrounding the job. When these conditions are good they avoid dissatisfaction arising but they do not create positive satisfactions, positive attitudes to work or personal growth. When they are less than good dissatisfaction will be felt.

Motivators are related to the need for psychological growth. They are derived from the nature of the job itself. They provide positive satisfactions and job attitudes because they provide the opportunity for personal growth.

The two sets of factors reflect different, but parallel need systems that operate independently in opposite directions. They are not opposite ends of one single set of needs. The opposite of job dissatisfaction is no job dissatisfaction and of job satisfaction no job satisfaction. Taking the idea a little further Herzberg suggests that there are two different aspects to mental health. The one goes from extreme mental health to no positive mental health and the other from no mental ill-health to extreme mental ill-health. On the one hand adjustment to the environment or a satisfactory environment avoiding unpleasantness leads to a state of no mental ill-health. Mental health, on the other hand, comes only from adjustment to oneself and consequent psychological growth.

Taking a pessimistic, but probably realistic, view Herzberg suggests that in modern society very many people are hygiene seekers motivated only to satisfy needs which avoid unpleasantness and whose satisfaction can only be temporary and requires constant renewal. Such people suffer from chronic unhappiness, continual dissatisfaction, and a failure to grow or even to want to grow. This, he suggests, is a learned process resulting from the value systems endemic in modern society.

From this analysis people can be placed in one of seven categories:

(i) Positive mental health. Motivator needs paramount and adequately met. Challenges related to ability. Tolerance for delayed success. Realistic attitudes towards achievement, ability, and situation. Avoidance of poor hygiene factors.

(ii) Positive mental health linked with poor hygiene factors. Satisfied with work itself despite reason for complaint about surroundings. Vocal about complaints. Probably comprises large numbers of workers who do a good job of work in spite of constant grumbles.

(iii) Sympton-free adjusted. Relatively small personal growth needs due to lack of opportunity to grow. These diminished needs met on a routine basis. Hygiene needs adequately satisfied.

(iv) Outright losers. Growth seekers denied opportunity to attain growth and having unsatisfied hygiene needs. Miserable but too balanced mentally to obtain relief by neurotic behaviour.

(v) Maladjusted. Seekers of positive satisfaction from hygiene factors who have had a significant number of positive achievements but have failed to appreciate them or to make any psychological growth as a result.

(vi) Mentally ill. Lifetime hygiene seekers who see themselves as failing to get any satisfaction from it. Use purely defensive mechanisms.

(vii) Monastic. Unfulfilled hygiene seeker who has given up altogether and withdrawn psychologically into an unreal world.

The analysis is taken a stage further into a detailed comparison of the characteristics of hygiene seekers and motivation seekers. The main differences seem to be these. Hygiene seekers are primarily concerned with their environment, are generally dissatisfied, over-react to changes either way, are generally apathetic to work. Motivation seekers are primarily concerned with the nature of their work and the opportunities it provides for them, obtain great satisfaction from achievement, profit from their experience, react less to hygiene conditions, and have balanced, sincere belief systems.

Verification

For our purposes here the detail is unimportant. What does matter is that the doubts that followed the publication of *The Motivation to Work* because it was based solely on research into accountants' and engineers' attitudes have been largely dispelled by subsequent research.

There have been two lines of approach. One followed Herzberg's original method of open-ended interviews on events which caused particularly good or bad feelings and extended the research to all levels of workers. The other approach assumed that Herzberg's method preconditioned the result and was therefore self-fulfilling so other methods were used. Herzberg claims that all the researches without exception endorse his theory to some extent and none contradict it.

What should we do?

Herzberg is now prepared to go much further in suggesting what should be done than he and his co-authors were in *The Motivation to Work* in 1959.

First there are some general guidelines on the background to the situation. Management should look at the worker and his job twice. The first question is 'what does the worker seek, what makes him happy?'. The second question is 'what does he want to avoid, what makes him unhappy?'. It is central to Herzberg's approach that the answers to these two questions will be on quite different planes. Management actions that deal only with hygiene factors will only result in preventing dissatisfaction and this only for a relatively short time as these factors are recurrent. The generally current ideas in the predominant forms of large-scale industry and commerce lead to the reduction of creativity in the individual in the name of rational organization. This may lead to organizational goals which have as one element, at least, the fear of creativity or the insistence on conformity.

The final guideline has about it a certain air of ambiguity. In effect Herzberg says that the industrial organizations as the dominant form of institution in which the majority of people are involved *must* treat them in terms of their *whole* nature if it is to use them effectively. The critical word is, of course, 'effectively'; the question 'effective to what purpose?'. It is, by now, widely accepted that industry in general, and any one firm in particular, has at any time more than one goal and that these goals may be contradictory and mutually incompatible. If Herzberg's theory is correct and could be applied in practice on a wide scale then its application would produce a much greater productivity per man, much lower unit costs, higher wages, and salaries, more output, greater profits or lower prices and some improvement in profits, *and massive dislocation and at least temporary unemployment.* This, of course, is taking the argument to its extreme while, in reality, the application and the results would be a long-term process. But the logic is there and, given the truth of the theory and its successful application, management must decide, one hopes in consultation with workers, to what ends effectiveness is required. And while the final responsibility rests, and must rest, on management's shoulders, the results must inevitably spill over into moral, ethical, and political fields.

To return to Herzberg's prescription. Deciding on and implementing specific measures can only be the task of practising managers. It seems rather odd that, when increased self-actualization, responsibility, commitment, and so on are so essential to Herzberg's ideas, he seems completely to ignore, at this prescriptive stage, any question of worker participation on decision-making.

Drucker in *The Practice of Management* quoted with some approval the opinion of some wit that Personnel Departments did all things which were not connected either with the work or the management of workers.

Herzberg wants to expand them and their functions into much wider spheres. Actually he calls them Industrial Relations Departments but he means Personnel Departments and not just the sub-division which deals with negotiations with trade unions.

The first stage is to follow the idea of the difference between hygiene factors and motivation factors to its logical conclusion. They deal with completely different aspects of the situation, with completely different goals and so they must be different divisions. The hygiene division should carry out most of the present work of the Personnel Department with the emphasis on dealing with aspects of the work situation which act as dissatisfiers. The aim would be to prevent conditions arising which could cause dissatisfaction. At the same time this division would do most of the essential, but routine, clerical work involved in keeping records and so on. This division would not be simply a negative affair. It must be given the responsibility of continually improving levels all round in its area of operation because the satisfaction of hygiene needs is, by definition, short-lived and higher achieved standards lead to yet higher aspirations.

The second division of the Personnel Department, the motivator-needs division, will for many organizations be almost completely new, certainly in its aims and objectives. It is to be deliberately charged with the objective of providing opportunities for psychological growth for all employees at all levels of a kind that is appropriate to their present, potential, and future state of growth. This is the key to positive motivation, to improved performance. Its first task is to be the re-education of workers *and* of management.

That is the broad scheme so we turn to more detailed aspects. A first priority must be to deal with the problem of the de-motivating process which so often occurs during the first year at work. At the shop-floor level the youngster may come in from school already indoctrinated with the disillusioned myths of a working-class background or he may come in full of the starry-eyed enthusiasm of youth. His first year at work may confirm and strengthen his disillusionment or it may destroy his enthusiasm. The graduate trainee after twelve months of 'sitting with many Nellies to gain experience' is often among the most disillusioned and bitter men on the staff. Prevention is better than cure and the task of the motivator-needs division will be to prevent this appalling waste.

Another major task will be to alter, or even create, the base for loyalty to the company. Where it does already exist it is often for negative reasons. It is a good company to work for because the dissatisfiers are kept to a minimum. It is hygiene-based. It must be altered by providing conditions where the loyalty of the individual comes from the opportunity for self-fulfilment that the job provides.

The re-orientation of workers will be a big task in terms of changing the content and methods of communication. It must be matched by a corresponding change in the attitudes and actions of managers and supervisors to ensure that communication is not distorted on its way down and, equally important, that there is no credibility gap between what the company is trying to say and what managers and supervisors are doing throughout every day.

So much for the essential background 'atmosphere' which will be the first (and most difficult?) aspect of the motivator division of the reconstructed Personnel or Industrial Relations Department. With this under way it must also turn its attention to more detailed work. A major task will be a complete review of all jobs to re-structure them so that, as far as possible, they will provide the appropriate level of psychological rewards from performing the actual tasks. These are, of course, the opportunities for real psychological growth. Herzberg agrees that perfection is asking the impossible but the motivator division must be continually reviewing, especially at trouble spots when they develop, to obtain improvement and a better fit of job to worker. The question of fit is vital. Whatever may be said to the contrary people are not all equal so they will not all require the same level of self-actualization or the same degree of psychological growth.

This approach to job structure and constant review necessarily involves a flexible form of organization able and ready to adapt easily. Two questions arise from this. Different schools argue that depending on the environment and/or technology a stable *or* a flexible organization structure will be the most suitable. Herzberg would probably argue that by the organization itself creating a state of continual change a flexible structure is essential irrespective of technology or environment although both of these could provide additional reasons for flexibility. The second question arises at a very different level. Many psychologists would argue that the individual has a basic need for stability and security and for the reduction of ambiguity in his situation. Herzberg contends that structure and stability are necessary if an individual is to accommodate himself to bureaucracy, but it is not a basic need and certainly does not apply to anyone motivated by psychological growth needs. Both arguments seem to suffer from over-generalization. At another point in his book Herzberg admits that each person is unique so the tolerance for instability and uncertainty could also be unique. While it may be possible to raise the general level of tolerance this is not the same thing as making all people highly tolerant.

Remedial work also must come within the scope of the motivator division. This seems to involve a realistic assumption that the organization run on Herzberg's ideas can be neither Heaven nor Nirvana. Cases of technological obsolescence, of poor performance and of management failure are expected to occur and when they do it will be the motivator division's job to locate, analyse and correct them.

Finally the motivator division will be required to carry out periodic reviews of the many things that are usually taken for granted until some major catastrophe calls them into question. Company policies, practices, assumptions, rules, and regulations will all be put under the motivator microscope to assess their continuing value.

The totality of Herzberg's approach is new and has probably still to be applied. But, as he points out, there is 'much scattered evidence' that the implementation in practice of some of the ideas of the motivator division has given quite marked increases in productivity at the higher creative levels of work and, perhaps somewhat wryly, marked increases of errors at the operator or shop-floor level. He remains unrepentant, however. If genuine responsibility for the consequences of their actions were shifted lower down in cases where the workers already have some semblance of a human job then the challenge of motivator problems at lower levels and the release of time and energy at higher levels for more creative work in providing a more positive climate would start the ball rolling at least in the right direction. The completely rationalized worker as the pure adjunct to the machine with a completely dehumanized job must be removed by complete automation. We can neither afford nor should we ask that human beings submit to being used in non-human ways.

Somewhat as an afterthought there is a little string of recommended imperatives:

(i) Sabbatical leave periodically for managers to renew psychological strength.

(ii) Review jobs for growth potential as well as work performance.

(iii) Reduce any over-emphasis on human relations procedures at the expense of motivator ones.

(iv) Reject psychological testing as at present practised.

(v) Abolish once and for all the ideas that no one must ever fail or create unpleasantness by a challenge.

(vi) Abolish the rules, regulations, and practices used by middle and higher levels of management as protective screens against visible failure.

(vii) Once and for all get rid of the inability to see that man lives at two levels and is motivated by two sets of quite different needs that involve two separate approaches.

(viii) Equip managers with the ability to tackle the challenge involved in managing responsible adults.

'There is no theoretical barrier to the implementation of the dual nature of man. The studies reviewed in this book show that this concept can be demonstrated in real-life situations and, if it can be demonstrated, it should be possible to implement it.'[3]

Today, more than ever before, society has a stake in mental health.

References

(1) Herzberg, F., Mausner, B. and Snyderman, B. B. *The Motivation to Work* (New York: Wiley, 1959) and

Pollard, H. R. *Developments in Management Thought* (London: Heinemann, 1974), Chapter 18.

(2) Herzberg, F. *Work and the Nature of Man* (London: Staples Press, 1968), p. viii.

(3) Ibid, p. 189.

Bibliography

BOOK BY F. HERZBERG
Work and the Nature of Man (London: Staples Press, 1968).

17

E. H. Schein
1970

A first reading of Schein's book *Organizational Psychology* gives the early impression that we have been here before. Ideas, concepts, and names which we have already met and others which would have been included if there had been more space seem to crop up with great regularity.

If this were all there would be little point in including the book here. But it is not all. There is a deliberate and obvious attempt to draw together many threads that have been developed by others, and by Schein himself, and to weave out of them a pattern which begins to outline the picture as a whole. It represents not the culmination but the start of a process which must surely be inevitable if a useful theory of management is to be developed. The author himself says in his Preface that he has only covered and illustrated selected topics so the book is not claimed to be a final picture but it certainly seems the best one to occupy this place in our book.

The field of organizational psychology

The development of organizational psychology has been the result of a number of traditional psychologists who over nearly fifty years have transferred their attention to particular industrial problems. Gradually the field has widened and spread into more and more areas of organization and behaviour at work. Schein traces the development through assessment and selection problems, measuring aptitudes, job design, reward and punishment systems, motivation, factors in individual and group behaviour, to the concept of organization as a total system, as a psychological entity to which the individual reacts.

The organizational psychologist, as distinct from the industrial psychologist, is concerned with the organization as a complex social system which influences *all* behaviour and not just particular aspects of it. The concepts of totality, complexity, and interdependence are the tools of the organizational psychologist. New concepts in the more general social psychology, new research methods, multiple causality instead of simple cause/effect assumption, changes in technology, and field research in live organizations have all contributed to and brought about this movement towards totality, the beginning, at least, of the integration of many different viewpoints into a more realistic general view.

The organization

Schein's opening definition is 'an organization is the rational co-ordination of the activities of a number of people for the achievement of some common explicit purpose or goal, through division of labour and function, and through an heirarchy of authority and responsibility'.[1] This is only a starter and, as Schein says, it will be modified later.

At this point the subject matter is obviously *formal* organization. Its characteristics are:

(i) Co-ordination is of activities not people.

(ii) Only limited aspects and activities of the individual are relevant to the organization.

(iii) Organization is concerned with roles, but the individual filling the role may influence performance.

(iv) The organization as a pattern of roles and co-ordination can survive any or all of the individual members.

(v) In principle the organization only changes when 'the blueprint' of roles is changed or the roles re-defined by authority.

In addition to the formal organization there may be two parallel organizations existing at the same time. The first he calls 'social organization' consisting of spontaneous groups arising to meet their own goal or goals but without formal, rational co-ordination processes. The second is the 'informal organization' or the additional pattern of role functions and relationships between members of the formal organization which is not specified by the 'blueprint' of formal roles and relationships.

Psychological problems in formal organizations

In broad outline these fall into five main areas. The recruitment, selection, training, and allocation procedures may pose considerable problems in psychological areas. Organizational policies and practices may mean that individual needs and expectations will not be met. Both fitting the worker to the job or the job to the worker can create problems.

Although the concept of a psychological contract between the employee and the organization has replaced the earlier idea of rewards and sanctions it has not solved all problems in the areas of motivation and performance. The contract itself is often more implicit than explicit and may, therefore, leave differences in expectations on both sides unresolved. Fundamentally the contract is embedded in the concept of authority and acceptance which is, as yet, by no means an area of sweet truth and light.

Formal organization necessarily involves departmentalization and sub-division of tasks. These produce means–ends chains, sectional aims, variations in interpretation, gaps, conflicts, and cross-purposes. Here Schein goes a step further by maintaining that these problems are rooted in psychological problems of the informal organization, loyalty, hostility, and the aspects of the total personality that are not required and are ignored by formal organization. It is, therefore, impossible to solve them simply by a one-sided improvement in the formal structure.

Finally, there are inevitable problems in the survival, growth, and adaptation of the organization in a changing environment. Maintaining an effective work-force and a successful management team present problems in themselves. Innovation, which is vital to survival and adaptation, involves psychological problems whichever way it is tackled. If line management and the workers are to innovate, problems of attitudes and motivation may arise which are very deep-seated. If specialist depart-ments are to innovate, then rivalry, conflict and integration will provide problems in plenty.

As the general rate of change in the years since the 1940s has increased so quickly and created so much unpredictability the most essential characteristics of managers and workers have become flexibility and adaptability. It is one thing to say this. To achieve it presents perhaps the biggest psychological problems of all.

Selection, testing, and recruitment

Right at these very first stages there is an immediate and important problem with deep psychological implications. With what end in mind should the linking of jobs and individuals be carried out? Traditionally it has been by selection from a number of apparently suitable people. Behind this method lie a number of assumptions. The characteristics and requirements of the job are presumed to be known, as are the qualities, aptitudes, personality, etc. of the person required to fill it. It is, of course, a further assumption that these can be discovered and adequately described. It is assumed also that it is possible to assess people along the various criteria required. Although all these assumptions have moved nearer to at least potential realization they have not yet destroyed the fundamental assumptions that organizational needs are supreme and that the individual selected will adapt to the requirements of the job.

The other possible aim in matching jobs and individuals is to assess all members of society on the basis of *their* characteristics, abilities, and needs, channel them into jobs that are the most suitable for them and which will provide them with the best opportunities for psychological growth and satisfaction.

It is not unnatural that Schein considers that the use of applied psychology and appropriate testing is likely to give better results in selection than the 'ten minute interview'. But he does not let the excessive enthusiasm of the developers of tests run away with him. He gives a detailed description of how to set and to validate tests before they can be properly used and the conditions under which they are more likely to succeed. Even then, he maintains, the problem is not entirely solved because greater interdependence between jobs and greater complexity make it difficult to be sure that today's job can be adequately defined for today let alone for the future. This is particularly true of managerial jobs. Consequently even with ideal testing and selection the correlation between short-term and long-term performance may well be low and long-term effectiveness should be the organization's aims. Another difficulty is that, while testing for present qualities and aptitudes is problematic enough, testing for potential for development is even more doubtful.

From another angle, test procedures for selection may create the impression in the individual that the organization is in a fundamental way an impersonal system, emphasizing organizational needs and designed primarily to exert influence and put pressure on the individual. It may create the seeds of alienation, the very thing it wants to avoid by correct placement of individuals in the structure.

Schein prefers tests to no tests but is realistic enough to insist that their limitations, the possible consequences for the organization, and the assumptions on which they are based must be recognized and taken into account.

Job design and human engineering

Job design, starting as it did with Taylor and Gilbreth, has probably created as many problems as it has solved but at a different level. Physical and production volume problems have been met at the cost of a whole syndrome of psychological problems. The three fundamental errors in job design based on work study were the extreme sub-division of jobs into meaningless routine; the assumption that workpeople were adaptable and interchangeable; and that the individual worker was the appropriate unit of analysis. It failed to recognize the influence of organizational practices and the informal organization on the performance of the job.

Through ergonomics which is the study of the man-machine relationship, job enlargement or increasing the variety and scope of the job we have now moved on to human engineering. This envisages the complete design of the job and its environment to match the physical, psychological, and social needs and abilities of the person in the job.

Both Argyris and McGregor are quoted to support the view that the worker, especially in large organizations, feels and accepts as reality the view that he is merely a cog in a large machine that ignores most of his abilities, his limitations, and his needs. As a result he replies by doing the minimum required and uses his ingenuity to 'beat the system'. If, under conditions of increasing change, the organization becomes more dependent on the individual for performance, loyalty, and creativity the psychological problems involved in changing apathy and indifference into extra co-operation will be enormous.

Training and development

Even with good selection and recruitment procedures some training beyond work skills is required. If the employee, whether worker or manager, is to be fully effective he will need to absorb the orientation and the basic beliefs of the organization, and to learn the appropriate attitudes to his job and to fellow members of the organization. Over suitable periods of time he should be given opportunities for further education and self-development.

For success the motivation and attitudes of the trainees must be positive and favourable. If the hiring process has created feelings of impersonality then apathy and defensive attitudes will be the probable response to training. But if hiring has created expectations of a challenging future then poor training can only produce frustration and alienation.

Specific goals for training such as obtaining a manual skill generally lead to better results. The assumption in the 1950s and 1960s in America that the knowledge and skills required for effective supervision and management could be *taught* like manual skills has been proved to be false according to Schein. Attitudes, motives and perception are now realized to be vital aspects of training at these levels and the problems involved are of a completely different order from those of manual skill training. At the same time the vital importance of effective supervisory and management training is being more fully realized as are the facts that the company philosophy and the ideas and practices of senior management must also be geared to the training programmes.

To meet this almost endless series of problems Schein proposes a systems view of selection and training as parts of the overlapping, complex, interdependent system that is the whole organization. Within this context there are three major problems. One is the uncertainty of the future which really requires training in attitudes, capacity, adaptability, and general knowledge, rather than specific skills, with long-term viability as the objective. Another is that training in one or some areas may lead to pressures for change in other areas which are not prepared for it. Thirdly the questions of recruitment, selection and job design are all inter-related to and interdependent on training. No one can be effectively considered in isolation.

Organizational man and the process of management

By 1970 most writers had accepted what practising managers had been saying all along – 'There is "no one right way" to manage'. Schein accepts the 'no one right way' thesis and suggests that the reasons for difference lie in the history of the organization, its mission or purpose, and the goodness or otherwise of the fit between the managers' assumptions about people and the actual characteristics of the organization's members.

(Author's note. Very oddly for a psychologist Schein does *not* make the very necessary distinction between perception and reality. The two may be the same but very often they are not and people tend to react to a situation as they perceive and understand it. The second point is that Schein speaks of the employee and the organization which seems to reify the organization and give it an existence of its own. In fact in this section he seems actually to be talking of the relationship between employees and management. While there are difficulties in this, it is more realistic to accept a dual aspect for managers than to create an abstract, non-existent reification of the 'organization'.)

To return to Schein, the interaction between the employee and the organization is regarded as the practical reciprocal process of working out the psychological contract. Both 'sides' (employees and managers) have certain expectations of each other and both sides generally have more or less power to achieve satisfaction of their requirements.

Etzioni's basic variables of power, which may be coercive, utilitarian, normative, or mixed and involvement, which may be alienative, calculative, moral, or intrinsic, are quoted as a base from which to work. The type of authority/power used will elicit one appropriate type of involvement that will produce workable and 'just' psychological contracts. These combinations are coercive – alienative, utilitarian – calculative, normative – moral, intrinsic. These are the pure combinations but in practice most organizations will have some sort of mixture with one combination predominating. More recently with changes in management's viewpoint (or enlightenment) there have been trends towards a normative – moral and utilitarian – calculative combination which uses less authority or power-over (Follett) and tries to create moral commitment and involvement.

Management's assumptions about people are a vital factor in the working out of the psychological contract. These assumptions may be conscious or sub-conscious, true in the sense that they mirror reality or false in that they do not but, whatever the case may be, they are the basis on which managers act. The effectiveness of these actions depends (among other things) on the congruence between the assumptions and reality.

There have been considerable changes in assumptions about the nature of the worker but it must be said that changes have taken place much more thoroughly and quickly in psychological theory than in the manager's office.

Economic theory provided the first set of assumptions in the 'rational-economic man'. These assumptions are, as yet, by no means dead and it must be admitted that they have been usable assumptions in that they have worked to build up an industrial structure. Whether other assumptions would have worked better is another question altogether.

With such assumptions as the basis for management action the strategy generally would follow this pattern:

(i) A system of authority and controls to protect the organization and the individual from irrationality.

(ii) A structure of positions having official authority.

(iii) An emphasis on task performance.

(iv) Job design, incentives, and control used to maintain morale.

(v) The task of ensuring organizational effectiveness entirely one for management.

Schein comments that this is far too much of a black versus white picture to be truly representative of reality. At the same time he follows Argyris in regarding it as a very self-fulfilling prophecy and therefore not likely to be easily challenged by management. So far as workers are concerned many, in mass production particularly, do not expect any more from their work than a routine job, non-involvement and a wage packet at the end of the week. But from practically all viewpoints this set of assumptions is becoming increasingly unrealistic.

The second set of assumptions is based on Mayo and the Hawthorne investigations and is that of 'social man'. Its hypotheses are:

(i) Social needs form the basic motivation of the worker.

(ii) Work-study and rationalization have taken the meaning out of work.

(iii) Individuals respond more to their peer-group than to management.

(iv) Supervisors must meet the social and acceptance needs of their workers to get effective response.

This set led to the Human Relations approach to management. The strategy for management was to pay more attention to people as individuals and as groups than to work, to encourage feelings of acceptance and belonging among the workers, and for supervisors and middle management to act as intermediaries between workers and top management. The psychological contract was extended to imply that management would meet some social as well as economic needs in return for loyalty, commitment to and identification with the organization by the individual.

In practice this overshot the mark almost as much as economic man but in the opposite direction. As the theory and the practice developed it was found that social needs that could not be or were not being met led to informal groupings, but also that the informal organization was not necessarily against management aims. At times it could correlate with them.

The next step, self-actualization theory, really centres on Maslow's theory of an hierarchy of human needs in which, as the lower orders of needs become reasonably satisfied, higher orders of needs come into operation. It made the assumption that something higher than social needs as assumed by the Human Relations school was needed.

Drawing on Maslow, Argyris, and McGregor, Schein summarizes the assumptions of the self-actualization theory as:

(i) Motives and needs are arranged in an hierarchy and as lower ones are met the higher ones come into play. These are self-realization and self-actualization.

(ii) Man will seek to be and is capable of being a mature personality at work provided he is given the opportunity. Much of the way in which work is organized as routine, small, meaningless units, prevents this and causes the individual to behave in immature ways.

(iii) Man is primarily self-motivated and self-controlled. Incentives and controls that are imposed on him from above threaten and reduce his personality.

(iv) There is no inherent conflict between self-actualization and more effective organizational performance. Under proper management assumptions and practices, the employee will voluntarily integrate his personal goals with those of the organization.

The implications of these assumptions for management strategy are very considerable. Not only must management provide a situation in which the basic economic and social needs of workers are met but it must go further and design work and jobs so that meaning is restored to work, and feelings of self-esteem and self-respect can develop. Authority shifts from the personal fiat of the supervisor or manager to the needs of the work situation itself. Motivation arises from the intrinsic satisfactions in doing the job and from high quality performance. Power and influence are shared between management and workers.

These assumptions are as controversial as the earlier ones. There are two main grounds for criticism. The first is that they are the result of the projection of the feelings and attitudes of the academic or research worker on to the industrial worker. The second criticism comes from the hard-headed realists. The evidence for the wish for self-actualization on the shop floor is by no means clear and, in any case, a utilitarian, calculative psychological contract may be, in fact seems to be, right for many people so why go to all that extra trouble and complication if it produces an adequate organizational result. Certainly there is a more convincing case to be made out at managerial levels. Schein quotes Argyris's view that this practical, hard-headed view is a compromise that wastes human resources.

The fourth, and most recent, set of assumptions are those of Complex Man. Needless to say complex man implies correspondingly complex theory and in doing so probably comes nearer to reality than previous ideas, all of which were partial views.

The assumptions which are used to justify complex man are:

(i) High variability. The hierarchy of needs is not universal. It varies between individuals and over time for the same individual. Also motives need not be single, they may combine to form very complex patterns of behaviour.

(ii) The individual can learn new forms of motivation as the result of experience so the ultimate pattern is the result of the interaction between individual and organization.

(iii) The same individual can be motivated in different ways in different organizations or sub-units.

(iv) The individual can become involved in production through different motives and his own satisfaction and the success of the organization do not depend entirely on the nature of his motivation. The task, his own abilities, and other people with whom he comes into contact all have some influence on the outcome.

(v) The individual is adaptable enough to respond to many different managerial strategies.

Certainly this looks more like the real, everyday world which is the experience of most people. Schein claims that earlier research leads up to it and quotes half-a-dozen writers and researchers who specifically support this point of view. Unfortunately Schein does not develop here a managerial strategy to cope with complex man.

Groups and inter-group relationships

The criteria for the existence of a group, whether formal or informal, are interaction between the members, psychological awareness of each other by members, and recognition by members that they are a group with a boundary of some sort around them.

Formal groups are officially created within the organization to carry out specified tasks and reach goals related to the organizational goal. Usually they are more or less permanent structures but the development of project organization has produced temporary, *ad hoc* structures.

At this point Schein gives as the other type of group the informal group. Somewhere his distinction at the beginning of his book into formal, social, and informal organizations (*see* p. 190) seems to have been lost.

Informal groups now can almost always be said to exist although the nature of the work, physical barriers and distance, and time may hinder their development. They are the result of people coming together with the purpose of meeting needs which are not met by the formal organization structure.

Groups fulfil different functions according to their type. The function of the formal group is to carry out its share of the task specified to reach organizational goals. It involves sub-division of labour and allocation of individual tasks.

Informal groups generally fulfil psychological and social functions. Among the more usual ones are providing for affiliation and support needs, developing and confirming identity and self-esteem, providing the means of testing reality against personal perception, and increasing the security and power of members.

Schein claims that research is now showing that many formal groups also perform informal functions and so, while this adds greatly to complexity, it may also provide the key to the reduction of conflict.

The question of conflict or integration between formal and personal needs must be very near to the centre of organizational psychology so it is not surprising to find it analysed in some detail. The factors affecting it are divided into three groups. First there is the environment at work. The nature of the work, the way it is organized, the physical location of people in relation to each other, and time schedules for work are prime factors. Organizational tasks involve logical groupings but how far these foster informal groups which can become defensive and anti-management depends largely on the managerial climate and practices. Assumptions such as rational-economic man will usually cause conflict between group and organizational needs. Social-man or human relations practices tend to deal with matters outside the actual task itself and are therefore irrelevant to integration. Self-actualizing man assumptions, through their concern with the reintroduction of meaning into work, are more likely to produce integrated groups provided they do not fall into the trap of only considering the individual. Practices based on complex man should be the most effective in bringing about integration. They involve looking at each situation in terms of task, history, people available, their attitudes to and ability to form groups, and leadership capacity and skills before deciding what will be the most suitable form of action in each case.

Within the group there is a whole collection of factors that can influence integration. The consensus on and direction of the group's basic aims obviously have a major influence, e.g. whether they are towards, neutral to or against integration. The effectiveness of communication within the group (and between the group and other parts of the organization) is vital. Individual status, backgrounds and behaviour especially of key individuals in the group all influence the situation. The possession of and the ability to use leadership skills that are appropriate to the group and to the situation at the moment are essential factors also.

Schein, as might be expected, delves a little deeper into the question of groups and produces a collection of dynamic factors influencing the effect of groups on the integration of organizational and personal needs. These will have occurred within the life of the group and affected its development or retardation. The induction, conditioning, and orientation of individuals as they have joined the group, the development of its structure, its previous successes and failures in achieving its own and the organization's goals will all have had some influence on its present effectiveness. Looking at this another way the history and traditions of a group cannot be altered overnight by a new leader with different ideas. The major norms and attitudes will persist for some time and he must, if he is not to destroy the group, adapt to them and introduce change slowly when he has helped the group to become ready for it. Sudden, unwelcome change forced on to a group can only produce an inevitable backlash.

The leadership function comes in for its share of attention. On a somewhat limited base the effectiveness of a group can be predicted by taking into account the group task, the position of the leader in the group and the orientation of the members towards the leader. Task and emotional or social leadership are both required in an effective group and may well be split between two individuals, e.g. formal and informal leader, or may even rotate among members according to the needs of the particular situation.

Some research into individual performance and group performance is quoted but is shown not to be conclusive. Examples are that groups are not necessarily slow and inefficient in action, more conservative in judgement, or more creative than individuals. Group decisions are more likely to produce commitment among members than imposed decisions. Group effectiveness is greatly affected by the leader having sufficient knowledge and understanding of the important factors in membership, environment, and group dynamics and being able to use them.

Intergroup problems in organizations

These are regarded as being second in importance only to problems of group effectiveness. The very fact of individual groups developing commitment to their own objectives and a sense of their own cohesion and self-realization tends to lead directly to inter-group rivalry and conflict.

Schein suggests that the results of inter-group rivalry are universal at all levels of organization and of society itself. Within the group rivalry with another group or groups will produce the following effects:

(i) Members of the group close ranks, increase their loyalty, and forget internal differences.

(ii) The group climate shifts towards task accomplishment.

(iii) Leadership tends to become more autocratic.

(iv) The group becomes more highly structured and organized.

(v) The group demands more loyalty and conformity from its members.

Between the groups the results are equally predictable:

(i) Each group sees the other as 'the enemy'.

(ii) Each develops a negative stereotype of the other, probably with little semblance to reality.

(iii) Hostility increases. Communication and interaction between the groups diminish.

(iv) When forced into interaction each group tends to listen only to its own point of view and to ignore the other group's case.

When inter-group conflict can only be resolved by a win–lose situation the effects on both the winning and the losing group tend to be undesirable.

The winning group retains and may even increase its cohesion. But the tension has been released and the group may become casual, complacent, less concerned with accomplishing its task. Its stereotype of 'the enemy' will remain unchanged and it is unlikely to carry out any re-examination or evaluation of its own operations. After all, it won, didn't it?

In a way the loser can get more out of losing. The immediate reaction is to rationalize and deny the reality of losing. Finding a scapegoat becomes a pre-occupation. The group itself may splinter over allocating blame or through internal unresolved conflicts coming to the surface.

Working harder becomes a palliative. In the end the losing group will probably learn a lot about itself, its weaknesses, its perceptions and the errors in its stereotypes. With luck it will re-organize to 'win next time'.

Inter-group competition is by no means entirely negative in its consequences. Often it can produce useful effects for the organization as a whole. But negative consequences can be reduced by the groups finding a common 'enemy' or, better, a super-ordinate goal to which they can both subscribe. Also if means can be found to bring sub-groups of competing groups into interaction with each other this can help.

But when all is said and done conflict is bound to be produced by the very fact of formal organization and sub-division. At best attempts can be made to minimize it by putting the emphasis on total organizational effectiveness and somehow assessing and rewarding groups and departments on their contribution to the overall result. The practice of a high degree of interaction and direct communication between groups can be actively encouraged. Members can be rotated between groups to increase understanding of each other's points of view. Finally wherever possible win–lose situations must be avoided.

The organization as a complex system

At the beginning of his book Schein gave a fairly traditional definition of organization with the promise that it would be updated later. Throughout the book the case for a new definition has, he claims, been built up. As a reminder the points made are summarized as follows:

(i) The complex interaction of selection, induction, training, job assignment, and management assumptions and practices.

(ii) The interaction between formal and informal (social?) groups.

(iii) The informal mechanisms that counteract the disintegrative forces of formal mechanisms.

(iv) The realities as opposed to the stereotypes and assumptions about how members function.

(v) The real complexities of interaction as compared with the simplifications of Classical theory.

(vi) The increasing instability and change in the environment bringing greater pressure for change and adaptation in the organization.

Other views and researches are brought in to strengthen the case. The organization–environment boundary is no longer regarded as being easily and clearly definable. There is in the boundary area a two-way process of primary and secondary functions in which the organization serves and is served by the environment. The organization itself contains members who function both within the organization and within the environment and who may have divided loyalties and at times or for special purposes members of the environment may become temporary members of the organization.

The technology of the industry is now generally recognized as having a close relationship with organization structure. The Tavistock Socio-technical model developed by Trist and Rice (1963) implies that any organization is made up of a technical system inherent in the technology of the industry *and* a social system dependent on the needs, feelings, attitudes, history, etc. of the people who are members.

The Homans (1950) model of the social system of an organization showed that any organization exists in a three-part environment, physical, cultural, and technological. This total environment specifies and imposes activities and interactions on members of the organization which comprise the *external* system. Between these activities, interchanges, and the feelings which result there is a constant interaction going on. But, because the interaction is taking place within and between members of the organization, new sentiments, new norms of behaviour, new shared frames of reference will develop inside the organization. These are not directly specified by the environment and constitute the *internal* system. Although the causal link between them is indirect they are, in fact, mutually dependent and sooner or later a change in one will result in a change in the other. The important thing for the organization is the explicit recognition by members of this mutual dependency.

More recently Likert's Overlapping Groups and Link-pin model also supports the need for change in ideas. In this model the starting point is the individual group.

A modification to Likert's thesis is suggested by Kahn with the Overlapping Role-set model. Likert's idea of groups is held to miss the vital point that the formal groups may not coincide with the psychological groups, so that the real link-pin may not be known. The unit of organization should be the role-set. The occupants of a role must, in order to fulfil it, have contacts with and be associated with people occupying other roles. This pattern of association and contacts for any given role is called the role-set and the whole organization consists of the total number and patterns of role-sets. This leads on to concepts of role expectations, role ambiguity, role conflict, influence, and perception and their relationship to organizational, personality, and inter-personal factors.

Schein pushes on still further to bring in what he calls the Neo-Structuralists. Lawrence and Lorsch, Burns and Stalker, Woodward and Galbraith all put the emphasis in some way on technology or environment structuring the organization.

Having marshalled his evidence Schein suggests that both theory and research are pushing almost inevitably towards systems concepts. Their use makes it easier to describe what actually happens in organizations and a general systems theory can be used for prediction. But for the moment his redefinition of organization is a promise that he does not fulfil. Instead he gives half-a-dozen propositions leading towards a redefinition:

(i) An organization is an open system, interacting with the environment, dealing with inputs, processing, and outputs.

(ii) An organization has multiple purposes and functions and multiple interactions with the environment.

(iii) An organization consists of sub-systems in interaction with each other. Subsystem behaviour, groups, roles, and sets are becoming more important than individual behaviour.

(iv) Changes in one sub-system will affect others.

(v) An organization exists in an environment which is made up of other systems and super-systems and is dynamic.

(vi) The multiple links between the organization and the environment makes precise definition of its boundary extremely difficult.

Organizational effectiveness

Having successfully demolished or extended beyond recognition the Classical view of organization Schein obviously cannot accept the Classical criteria of effectiveness, profit maximization, efficiency, productivity, and morale. Seemingly rational (Classical) organizations behave ineffectively, others behave effectively in spite of multiple and possibly conflicting goals.

At the level of systems theory effectiveness in a system is shown by the capacity to survive, maintain itself, adapt and grow, regardless of particular functions. From another angle Bennis (1962) is quoted as showing that effectiveness is measured over periods of time by the organization's ability to solve problems. Continuing with Bennis a healthy organization is one that is able to react flexibly to its environment, has a sense of identity and insight into its real nature which is shared and understood by its members, and is able to test its ideas against reality.

Integration along various lines provides various criteria of effectiveness. Argyris proposes integration of sub-groups so that they are not working at cross-purposes, McGregor suggests the integration of personal and organizational goals, and Blake and Mouton the integration of concern for individuals and concern for production.

A systems-level criterion cannot be single, it must be made up of multiple related criteria.

Still at systems-level a major measure of effectiveness is the ability of the organization to succeed in the adaptive-coping cycle. Starting with a sensing of change, internal or external, the organization must collect the necessary information, inaugurate change in line with the information, stabilize the internal changes and minimize undesired consequential results, and obtain feed-back on success or failure.

Successful coping implies certain preconditions in the state of the organization and its members. The first is the ability to find, take in, and communicate information reliably and without distortion. Internal flexibility and creativity are essential, as are the willingness on the part of members to accept change and to integrate their goals with those of the organization. Finally the internal climate of the organization must be one of support and freedom from feelings of threat.

Schein summarizes his own ideas and draws together those of others in four guidelines for success. They are:

(i) Recruitment, selection, and induction procedures which make members feel wanted and secure. Job structures which provide meaningful tasks. An atmosphere which leads to positive commitment to organizational goals. A management which is trained to stimulate personal growth.

(ii) A psychological contract of employment and assumptions about people which match reality and not false stereotypes.

(iii) Conditions in which groups can form, interact effectively and have efficient and appropriate leadership.

(iv) Leadership as a function of organization not a personal characteristic. Shared leadership moving around according to the situation. Leadership at all levels managing relationships, setting goals, and establishing the values and norms around which the organization develops a sense of identity and belonging, and doing this by participatory methods rather than imposition from above.

References

(1) Schein, E. H. *Organizational Psychology* (Englewood Cliffs. N.J.: Prentice Hall, 2nd ed 1970), p. 9.

(2) Likert, R. *New Patterns of Management* (New York: McGraw-Hill, 1961) or
Pollard, H. R. *Developments in Management Thought* (London: Heinemann, 1974), Chapter 17.

Bibliography

BOOK BY E. H. SCHEIN
Organizational Psychology (New Jersey: Prentice Hall, 1970).

PART III

Decision and Control

18

An Overview

The basic topics of Parts I and II of this book largely chose themselves. Part III has been much more difficult. There were so many other topics, so many approaches that the question of what to include and what to leave out seemed almost insurmountable. In the end the fact that decision-making and control are and always will be central aspects of management and that the two are in many ways interlinked led to the conclusion that they, at least, could not be left out. Even with this limitation the ground that can be covered is lamentably small.

The question of decision-making has attracted a great deal of attention both in terms of developing a generalized theory underlying the process and in terms of a more esoteric mathematical-statistical analysis. The latter is outside the scope of this book but three Americans in particular, Simon, March, and Cyert, have between them developed a fairly comprehensive general theory. They form the subject of the next three chapters.

Simon's book *Administrative Behaviour* starts the ball rolling with his view that choice and decision-making are the very core of the management process. From this it is only a very short step to seeing organization as an interlinked pattern of decision-making points. Another short step and we have managerial action and influence as the means of putting decisions into effect. A very useful distinction is drawn between decisions resting on value judgements and those that have a factual base. The former cannot be *proved* to be right or wrong and generally comprise policy decisions. Factual decisions have right and wrong answers provided enough facts are available.

A year later March and Simon developed and extended the theory of decision very considerably in their rather curiously titled book *Organizations*. It purports to deal with behaviour in organizations starting from the concept of the total human being. They do not invalidate Simon's own version. They complement it with a number of new ideas. The decisions of the individuals making up the organization, in particular whether or not to join, to remain in, to produce are shown as essential to organizational survival. Perhaps more importantly the economic assumptions of full knowledge and completely rational decisions are put under the microscope and shown for what they are. In place of full knowledge there are important concepts of evoked and unevoked 'sets' from memory, experience, and the environment. Complete rationality is replaced by limited or bounded rationality and optimizing of results by satisficing. These are not steps, they are huge strides into the reconciliation of theory and practice.

In 1963 March with the third of the trio, Cyert, delved even more deeply into the actual processes of decision in *A Behavioural Theory of the Firm*. Coalitions between members of the organization, bargaining, side-payments and the order of search for solutions becoming building blocks of the theory as to how decisions are reached. The inevitable uncertainty with which every organization has to contend produces a very complex organizational learning process leading to the adaptive rationality essential to the prime objective of large organizations – survival.

Sayles, in 1964, gave an account of and drew conclusions from a very large research project into the behaviour of middle and lower managers. He started with the premise that the real job of a manager was either misunderstood or not understood at all. The proof of his analysis was that when the results were put to the managers concerned they did recognize the pattern as the real nature of their work and such preconceived ideas as they had as myths and folk-lore. According to this analysis, managers do not basically manage people. They manage complex patterns of relationships between the job and the environment, between organization structure and behaviour. Primarily their job is a constant process of adjustment and readjustment of these relationships. Both conflict and compatibility are facts of life with which the manager must learn to live. Decision-making is 'playing the organization' for minor adjustments here and minor gains there. In case this sounds too cynical it must be remembered that Sayles was concerned with 'life as it was' for middle and lower managers in large corporations and one thing it certainly was not was 'the ivory tower'.

The second half of Thompson's book (1967) moves on from an analysis of structure, dealt with here in Part I, to bring together structure, behaviour, decision-making, and control.

Finally *Control in Organization* written right at the end of our allotted time span, 1970, brings together a wide range of empirical work on control, the factors involved and the forms it can take. From these Tannenbaum drew his own conclusions on the overall 'state of play'. His main contribution seems undoubtedly to be the conclusion that the amount of control in an organization is not a fixed quantity such that more control by one party or group must mean less for another. Mary Follett implied this fifty years ago, but it needed saying again and it is doubtful whether the lesson has yet been learned.

19

H. A. Simon
1957

It may seem strange when we are supposed to be covering the decade 1960–70 to backtrack to a second edition in 1957. There can be little doubt, however, that, in the context of *Developments in Management Thought* and of this book, Simon's *Administrative Behaviour* belongs much more to the 1960s than the 1950s.

Fundamental principles

Simon puts forward the new thesis that management theory should be based primarily around the question of choice and decision-making as the core of management. While the art of getting things done, of implementing decisions is an aspect of management that cannot be neglected, it logically follows after and is subordinate to the decisions on what is to be done, how, when, where, and by whom. The question of choice or decision-making is not confined to the top ranks of the heirarchy, but goes right down through all ranks of management although, of course, the nature and scope of choice varies between different levels.

While the actual work of the firm or institution (e.g. making and selling shoes or assessing and paying out social security benefits) is carried out by the lowest levels, the administrative staff (management and supervision) operate in the organization to the extent that they influence the decisions of the workers. (Author's comment. Simon uses 'administration' and 'administrative' as synonymous with 'management' and 'managerial'. In view of the connotation of red tape and bureaucracy attached to 'administration' on this side of the Atlantic 'management' and 'managerial' will be used throughout this chapter.)

In a management structure all levels except the very top are subject to influence arising from choices or decisions made at a higher level. Each level transmits, elaborates and modifies these influences in passing them down.

All behaviour is said to involve choice, but such choice is not necessarily rational. It may be conscious, unconscious, deliberate or accidental choice among alternatives. This seems to omit habitual, reflex behaviour but this, presumably, is based on an earlier pattern of choices which, by a learning process, produce ultimately reflex action.

Within an organization it is assumed that activity is purposeful and is directed towards the goals of the organization.

. Decisions in an organization can be divided into two broad groups. Those on the final goals of the organization are 'value judgements' and are more general. The other group consists of decisions on implementation of the goals and are called 'factual judgements'. These are more specific in character. The fact that organizations have goals to achieve implies an hierarchy of decisions ranging from the most general down to the most detailed instructions. The distinction between 'value judgements' (goals) and 'factual judgements' (implementation) is somewhat blurred by the statement that at each stage down the hierarchy the manager must set 'goals' for the level below him. Simon says distinctly that this hierarchy of goals does not imply that they will be perfectly integrated and organized in actual behaviour. This integration is the job of management (elsewhere called co-ordination) although even without conscious effort by management some degree of integration will occur by itself.

All decisions are to some extent a compromise on three grounds. In real life no one course of action among the alternative possibilities will perfectly achieve the objective. Secondly the available alternatives as determined by the environment may not include the best possible, so something less has to be accepted. Finally the decision may depend on value judgements on the relative importance of conflicting objectives and on the efficiency of different means of achieving the objective.

Decision-making in the management process
At this stage the influence of Classical thought seems to be still operating. Management is said to be always of group activity rather than individual activity. Management processes are processes of decision and they take away most discretion and decision from the operative level. These management decisions specify the function or job of the individual, specify the extent of authority and to what positions it is allocated, and set the limits of discretion for all levels except the top one. The pattern of organization, which determines the decision-making points, is a combination of horizontal division based on division of work and vertical division which provides for the hierarchy of decisions, for co-ordination of lower levels, for specialization, and for accountability for results.

As the essence of organizational functioning is group behaviour, correct decisions and the adoption of these decisions by all concerned are vital to effective operation. Such co-ordination is achieved by authority and other forms of influence and by centralizing decision-making.

The exercise of influence within the organization is much more involved than simply the issue of orders. Effective communication between individuals and between individuals and groups is essential to the process. Much regular and continuous influence can be obtained by establishing patterns of attitudes, habits, and states of mind that lead to habitually correct behaviour. The use of authority to impose decisions is another method but recently it has been tempered by suggestion and persuasion as more effective methods. Any means of influencing people implies that the desired behaviour lies within a 'zone of acceptance' or, as Barnard called it, a 'zone of indifference'. Authority, persuasion, and suggestion will all fail if the required behaviour is unacceptable, although what is or is not acceptable can vary greatly for a large variety of reasons. Simon suggests that authority can, at times, be exerted upwards and side-ways in the organization although influence would perhaps be a better word than authority.

Other important aspects of influence in ensuring conformity to decisions are:

    (i) Identification by the individual with the group or sub-group. Sub-group loyalties may shift conformity to sub-group rather than whole-group objectives.

    (ii) Advice and information, especially if backed by specialist knowledge, are important influencing factors.

    (iii) Training, frames of reference, indoctrination, and approved forms of action all help to improve conformity.

Some problems of managerial theory

The first problem consists of the so-called 'principles' of Classical theory, such as hierarchy, specialization, span of control. Simon shows that for each of the classical 'principles' there is an opposite and equally valid principle. This does not deny the classical view but restates it in terms of appropriateness to particular circumstances. In order to get a set of valid concepts all the relevant diagnostic criteria must be identified and used. The approach suggested is that a scientifically relevant description of an organization will, as far as possible, define for each person the decisions he is required to make *and* the influences that bear on him when he is making such a decision. This is, perhaps, a more precise way of saying that the theory of decision-making is the theory of management.

Using the necessary decisions as a base the theory should demonstrate how the organization structure should be built up to do its work efficiently. With the emphasis on efficient performance the main factors determining the degree of efficiency attained are the limits on the individual's capacity to do his job and on his ability to make correct decisions. There is a kind of determinism about this as Simon says, 'Two persons, given the same skills, the same objectives and values, the same knowledge and information, can rationally decide only on the same course of action.'[1] But, of course, the key word here is 'rationally'. Rationality is seldom, if ever, complete. It is limited by the individual's subconscious skills, habits, and reflexes, by his own values and concepts of purpose, and by the relevance of his knowledge to the job. If he is aware of the limitations on his rationality he is likely to be more rational as he can guard against known weaknesses.

The aim of the organization is rationality but, in fact, it has to be limited or bounded rationality due to the fact that the organization consists of people not omniscient automatons. The limits indicate the criteria by which to judge the organization structure. Such criteria must then be 'weighted' for relative importance. It is suggested that, although it would be difficult to do, a valid theory of organization and management can only be built up from empirical research into alternative structures and patterns to provide the concepts of limits and weights followed by the measurement of results against quantifiable objectives.

With this as the ultimate aim Simon bows to the inevitable and says that his book '. . . will attempt only the first step in the reconstruction of administrative theory – the construction of an adequate vocabulary and analytic scheme'.[2]

Fact and value in decision-making

Fact and value are given as the basis for the distinction between managerial and policy decisions. Factual propositions are statements about the observable world and the way in which it operates and, as such, can be proved true or false. Decisions are more than factual propositions firstly because they must relate to the future whether it be ten seconds or ten years and secondly they have an imperative quality in that they are bases for action. In addition they have a sort of ethical quality as they accept one and reject other alternatives.

Provided a proposition can be compared directly with experience it can be shown to be true or false. If it cannot, it can only be described in ethical or value terms such as 'good', 'bad', 'ought', etc. From this Simon deduces that decisions cannot be described as right or wrong, correct or incorrect, but they may be good or bad. Then some confusion seems to be added to complicate the situation. Decisions usually are part factual and part ethical and also may be said to be correct if the results meet the required aims and objectives.

At the top end of the decision pyramid the aims and objectives decided on cannot in themselves be described as correct or incorrect. Lower level objective and/or means decisions can be evaluated in terms of their contribution to the higher aim and as this contribution is factual these decisions can be labelled correct or incorrect. Top level decisions can only have an ethical basis which, to be useful, must have definite values for subsequent comparison with performance. It must also be in such form that it is possible to judge the probability of particular courses of action attaining the required result.

The division between ethical and factual decisions is not, however, watertight. There is nearly always room for judgement both because of future uncertainty and because many factual decisions have some ethical component.

Rationality in managerial behaviour

This section presents Simon's view of a theory of decision-making. The modifications required in practice are set out in the next section.

A rational decision involves the choice of one alternative from a number. (Author's comment. It might be worthwhile making a point here which Simon obviously takes for granted but which the author has often met in discussion. It is often argued that situations arise where there are no alternatives. If this is genuinely true then there is no question of choice and no decision to be made. Apart from this limiting case there is the case where there are only two courses of action – one positive course of new action and the alternative of wait and see, or do nothing. Doing nothing is a perfectly admissible alternative and, in fact, Drucker ranks the ability of a manager to know when *not* to interfere very highly.)

Returning to Simon's argument, alternatives vary in the consequences that will follow according to the one selected. A 'good', i.e. rational, decision is in theory one that is realistically adapted to the ends or consequences required. Rationality, then, is concerned with the construction of means–ends chains, the links being the action or behaviour undertaken and the consequences that naturally follow. It follows that an hierarchy of means–ends chains in theory integrates all the behaviour involved and directs it to the ends required. Ideally the structure of organization should parallel the basic pattern of means–ends chains required, so that any particular sub-unit of organization will match a particular set of broad means to attain particular ends.

But theory must take some account of the fact that complete rationality is just not practical. So some qualifications are necessary to validate the theory. The first is that rationality in an organization is what is left with an incomplete and possibly inconsistent hierarchy of means–ends chains.

This concept of incomplete or bounded rationality is the essence, and the value, of Simon's approach.

Any particular alternative chosen may well have side effects which produce ends or results which are not required or even expected. Rational decision-making involves the widest possible consideration of all possible ends likely to result from all possible alternative means.

While judgement on ends has been described as value orientated while means are factual judgements, in practice different alternative means frequently have value considerations attached to them.

In most decision-making the question of time is involved. Only one state of the situation is possible at any one time, but over a period of time many states are, at least theoretically, possible. However the choice of one end and therefore state of the system at one time means that other alternatives at that time have been sacrificed and, further, it may limit the possible number of alternatives at a later date. Simon suggests that such limitation will increase rationality.

On the question of comparison of alternatives it is likely that different means often produce largely the same end but will differ from each other only in certain respects. Rationality implies that only the differences need be considered.

It is recognized that decision-making in an organization is not purely concerned with one individual. The decisions and actions of other people which may be competitive or co-operative have to be taken into account. Co-ordination, says Simon, can be described as the means of ensuring that everyone has sufficient accurate knowledge, and good planning and organization as ensuring that each decision-maker can anticipate the decisions and actions of others.

The theory concludes with some final comments on rationality. 'Roughly speaking, rationality is concerned with the selection of preferred behaviour alternatives in terms of some system of values whereby the consequences of behaviour can be evaluated.'[3]

It is not so determined as this definition might imply. It may be conscious, sub-conscious, deliberate or non-deliberate. If wrong information is the base then a decision may be wrong although still rational. A decision may be rational for one purpose and irrational for another.

In competitive situations and co-operative ones where knowledge is inadequate the rationality may be unstable.

The psychology of management decisions

Simon maintains that a single individual in isolation could not cope with the large number of alternatives and possible consequences and therefore it is impossible for his behaviour to show a high degree of rationality.

Presumably it must be assumed here that he is thinking of an organizational rather than a 'Robinson Crusoe' situation. With this restraint the question is how is it overcome.

(i) It is assumed that there will be a large number of 'givens' in any situation – premises that are accepted without question and limit the range of adaptive behaviour available.

(ii) Because knowledge is never complete the organization is assumed to be a closed system with a limited range of variables and consequences. The degree of correspondence between the assumed closed system and reality is a limiting factor on rationality.

(iii) There is a limit to the ability to recognize alternative behaviour patterns.

(iv) The learning process arising from the experience of the individual and the communicated experience of others modifies altertives and behaviour by eliminating undesirable patterns.

(v) Leading on from (iv) personal and organizational memories (e.g. files and records) and habitual patterns of behaviour and routine reactions lead to conditioned responses so reducing the area of choice.

(vi) The stimulus that creates hesitation while a choice is made often directs attention into the appropriate area and so puts its own limitation on choice alternatives.

(vii) Organizations develop mechanisms to integrate behaviour into a broad, acceptable pattern.

Expanding on the last point one of the main mechanisms for integration is planning. Substantive planning at higher levels in the organization involves the broad decisions on values and aims. Procedural planning at the lower levels creates mechanisms that are intended to ensure that information, attention, and action are directed so as to conform to the aims provided by substantive planning.

While a decision made now on a choice between present alternatives influences future behaviour it is itself to some extent limited by the past. Past decisions may have ruled out alternatives that might otherwise have existed. Also they may provide guidelines for present decisions by having selected particular values as criteria, particular items of knowledge as relevant, and particular forms of behaviour as the only ones admissible.

Because of their much wider influence ends/results decisions need to be based on a much wider range of factors than means decisions or procedural planning.

The integration of the behaviour of individuals within the organization is vital to the effective outcome of decisions. Social organization as a pattern of group behaviour will influence the individual who belongs to it because it does, or should, provide a pattern of stable expectations of how other members will behave. At the same time it provides stimuli and directs attention in the required direction. The behaviour patterns which result are fundamental to the achievement of rationality. More specifically the formal organization exerts influence on the individual by division of labour, standard practices, authority and influence systems, communication channels, and training. The formal organization must use special measures such as these to achieve integration or co-ordination on a wide scale. Self-co-ordination, it is claimed, can only occur in small, face-to-face groups where all members are in a position to observe each other.

A final word on the individual and the sub-group is required. So far the question of integration of means and ends has seemed to revolve round the individual and the ends of the whole organization. However, in any but the smallest organization the individual will first and foremost be a member of a sub-group and only more remotely a member of the whole organization. For the individual the question of choice will be affected by the decisions of others in his sub-group. Only if these can be taken as given will the question of choice be purely a personal one for the individual. The group or sub-unit within the organization will have its own problems and alternatives for choice. If the group is to be stable it must develop a plan of behaviour for all members of the group which is communicated as relevant to each member and which will be acceptable to each and every member.

The equilibrium of the organization

In explanation it should be pointed out that by 'equilibrium' Simon appears to mean the ability of the organization to continue to exist, to adapt, to grow and to prosper rather than equilibrium in the sense of a stable situation to which it returns after any interruption or deviation.

Continued existence depends on the willingness of members of the organization to remain as members and to contribute to the organizational objectives. That they do so depends on one or both of two conditions – that by meeting the organization's objectives they are directly or indirectly achieving their own personal goals and/or that they are offered inducements to participate which are felt by them to make it worthwhile.

Three groups can be shown to make decisions which determine the destiny of the organization. Customers decide whether or not to buy, workers whether or not to belong and work, and controllers, the management group, whether to belong and work and what the values, ends, and objectives of the organization shall be. But both the other groups can veto the objectives by refusing to buy or to belong and work.

All these decisions, if favourable, involve contributions of money, work, effort, and so on to the organization. The sum of these contributions must be at least sufficient to provide the inducements necessary to call forth the contributions. If they are not, the organization dies. If they are more, they provide the resources for growth and prosperity.

Within business organizations management can normally be expected to consider profits and survival as the primary ends and the adaptation of output to match customer demands as the main means. At the same time it will endeavour to ensure the most efficient use of resources. So that the question of efficiency in operation becomes the main overall criterion by which to judge management decisions.

The role of authority

Having established the position of decision-making as the keystone of the management process Simon turns to the implementation of decisions. First to be considered is the role of authority.

Implementation is a complex two-sided process. On the one hand management makes decisions that are drawn from value premises and factual premises. By its actions and the basic organization pattern management provides stimuli to the individual and at the same time determines some but only some of the premises on which the individual decides. On the other hand the individual has a psychological 'set' or pattern of experience, preconceived ideas, attitudes, and aims. These determine his response to the stimuli received.

The superior-subordinate relationship required by the concept of formal authority depends on the appropriate forms of behaviour on both sides, the expectation of obedience, and the willingness to suspend judgement and to obey. This means that the command becomes a criterion of choice. While it limits the choice to an obey or disobey alternative it still may leave a wide range of choice as to how well or otherwise to carry out the command.

While authority is given as the main difference between the work situation and the rest of the individual's personal life, other means of influence such as persuasion and suggestion are recognized.

At one time authority vested in birth, position, or property would not have been questioned. Today with the erosion of its traditional bases others have been found.

(i) Custom, or socially expected conduct. There may be wide variations here between groups and between societies.

(ii) Social sanctions. Sanctions imposed by the group or society on deviant behaviour.

(iii) Acceptance of a psychological basis for a leader–follower situation.

(iv) Acceptance of a joint purpose and the assumption that the person exercising authority will by his orders further this purpose.

(v) Formal sanctions available within the organization.

(vi) The preference of many, perhaps most, people to avoid the responsibilities that must go with the possession of authority.

Authority is seldom, if ever, absolute. It is limited on the one hand by the subordinate's area of acceptance. At some point the individual (or the group) will say 'so far and no further' and leave the organization, strike, go slow or whatever. The superior, too, is likely to impose limits on his own exercise of authority in order not to lose the respect, confidence, and goodwill of his subordinates.

On the question of psychology and authority Simon takes a very specific point of view. He maintains that propositions about rational behaviour do not involve propositions about the psychology of the person behaving. Leaving on one side the concept of bounded or limited rationality and assuming complete rationality he maintains that given a particular set of values and a particular situation there is only one course of action which an individual can follow. Psychology, then, is not a part of the theory of authority or of management. It is needed, however, to explain why actual behaviour departs from the rational norm and it does this by explaining the determination of value systems – presumably irrational ones. So psychology is a part of the environment in which management operates. It is, presumably, a question of boundaries. Where are the boundaries of the management system, of the organization system, of the relevant theory system? There are still wide differences of opinion on these questions.

For some reason which is not altogether clear Simon deals with the question of informal organization under the general heading of authority. Formal organization is a set of more or less permanent relationships intended to govern behaviour within the organization. In practice the ideal formal pattern is never realized either because the ideal is seldom, if ever, formulated, or because what is formulated is to some extent ignored. Also, of course, as conditions change the formal organization should change. Either it does not or there is a time lag before it does.

To fill the gaps, to make up for deficiencies people set up other inter-personal relationships which are not in the formal pattern and which constitute the informal organization. Simon takes a jaundiced view of informal organization unless it specifically furthers organizational objectives. He goes so far as to say formal organization '. . . performs no function unless it actually sets limits to the informal relations that are permitted to develop in it'.[4] It must not allow internal politics to become harmful, or duplication of function to occur, but it should encourage informal organization which is constructive.

Communication

Communication here is clearly and directly linked to the decision-making process. It is '. . . any process whereby decisional premises are transmitted from one member of an organization to another'.[5]

The techniques (and channels?) of communication used will largely determine where decision functions should be located. Ideally this involves upward, downward and sideways channels. For decision-making to function adequately communication in all three channels must be a two-way process – information to the decision point, and decisions from there to where they are to be carried out. This claim for two-way communication is supported by the argument that not all the information required will be located at the point where the decision is to be made. Conversely it may be necessary, because of the volume of information needed or the specialized knowledge required, to break down a major decision into parts that can be delegated as sub-decisions to be taken and communicated back to the higher decision point for co-ordination and onward transmission. Simon appears to assume that generally the point of information will tend to be high in the hierarchy and this leads to centralization of decision-making with the advantages of responsibility, expertise, and greater co-ordination. On the other hand decentralization of decision-making nearer to the point of action has the advantages of local knowledge, speed, and lower manpower costs.

After seeming somewhat unhappy about informal organization Simon is almost completely in favour of informal communication channels. They and formal channels are 'equally important' but they perform a different complementary function. Informal channels are based on the social as distinct from the formal pattern of relationships and carry advice, information, unofficial 'orders', and the norms and values of the informal organization.

The criterion of efficiency

While most of this section discusses local authority administration where ends and results cannot be objectively measured, it is at this point that Simon seems to react most strongly against the Human Relations/Psycho-sociological schools. Business organizations are largely guided by the profit motive so efficiency is measured by the net money return (profit) to the organization. The simplicity [*sic*] of profit as a criterion is that both inputs and outputs can be measured in the common denominator of money.

The reaction, however, is not absolutely complete. He does admit that non-monetary considerations may enter into management in so far as it is not solely concerned with the profit motive. He also seems to be not quite happy with money terms as an absolute measure. Perhaps costs and results should be measured in terms of foregone alternatives – the economist's 'opportunity costs'.

Loyalties and organizational identification

In the early stages individual behaviour in the organization is based on values and objectives corresponding to organizational ones and imposed by authority. Gradually these values become internalized and accepted as the individual's own provided, of course, that he stays in the organization. As this happens he develops a loyalty to the organization which automatically ensures that his personal decisions will be consistent with organizational objectives. (Author's comment. Argyris would certainly disagree violently with this last statement and it must be a matter for speculation whether Simon is stating a 'fact' in his ideal completely rational organization or whether he does intend it to represent the real world of bounded rationality.)

As the argument proceeds it does become clear that Simon has certain reservations. The organization provides the individual with a frame of reference but even so there will be difficulties in making subsidiary objectives conform to higher ones. In particular this problem arises when the individual identifies with the sub-group of which he is a part and the sub-group's own objectives do not conform to those of the organization as a whole.

From the organization's point of view, given its system of values, there can only be one best response to a situation and this does not depend on the personal motives of the individual making the decision. But the individual has, in fact, a degree of freedom as to whether he uses the values and frame of reference of the organization, of the sub-unit he belongs to, of some other group or his own. His decision then is, in practice, a variable and not a completely definable, rational outcome. Rational, that is, from the point of view of the organization.

This question of identification by the individual is obviously of crucial importance in operations. In so far as organization is rational it will be so designed that the activities of a function which is likely to produce local identification are made as far as possible independent of the rest of the organization. It will also arrange activities in groups so as to ensure a minimum of side effects. On a more positive level purely local identification can be lessened by ensuring adequate communication between all units in the organization so that the broader issues become well known and local issues can be set against the broader background.

The anatomy of organization

Simon is quite definite that his book does not advise on how organizations should be designed or operated. He provides the 'anatomy' of organization which is the complex network of the decision-making process and the physiology which consists of the processes by which the organization provides the premises and influences that affect members' decisions.

Decision-making is a complex process involving components that can be traced back through the formal and informal processes to many individuals. While one person may carry the final responsibility for a decision the determination of it is seldom totally a one-man job.

The influence exerted by the organization can vary from absolute authority to the most marginal. Often it only provides goals and guidelines and so leaves considerable room for discretion. Control is achieved by determining the major value premises at the top of the hierarchy and by each succeeding lower level specifying the objectives of the next lower level and ensuring co-ordination of their efforts and results. This hierarchy of decisions will be backed up by standing orders, standard practices, training and review procedures.

The modes of influence used are authority, advice, information, efficiency criteria, and the creation of identification with the organization. As other forms of influence become effective authority can be used less.

Planning procedures can be used to bring together a great deal of information and to involve wide participation but Simon insists that the resulting decisions must remain with the hierarchy.

The review of the results of decisions serves four purposes. It establishes the quality of the decisions. It shows where modification is needed in subsequent decisions. It demonstrates the need to correct incorrect decisions. It shows where sanctions need to be imposed (and rewards granted?). In general the arguments favour centralization of the decision process rather than decentralization.

Final lessons

The so-called 'principles' of management current at the time the book was written are mutually contradictory. They are dependent on the conditions under which they are applied.

Real understanding is obtained by analysing the managerial process in terms of decisions. If complete rationality were possible then the whole theory of decision-making and management would be 'Always select that alternative, among those available, which will lead to the most complete achievement of goals'.[6] The need for a theory of management arises from the fact that human rationality is incomplete. Behaviour depends on environment, values, skills, habits, and purpose. It includes irrational and non-rational elements. Management theory is concerned with the area of rationality as bounded by the adaptability to non-rational elements.

References

(1) Simon, H. A. *Administrative Behaviour* (New York: Macmillan, 2nd Edn, 1957), p. 39.
  (2) Ibid, p. 44.
  (3) Ibid, p. 75.
  (4) Ibid, p. 149.
  (5) Ibid, p. 154.
  (6) Ibid, p. 240.

Bibliography

BOOK BY H. A. SIMON
  Administrative Behaviour (New York: Macmillan, 1957).

20

J. G. March and H. A. Simon
1958

March and Simon's purpose in *Organizations* was to begin to build a theory of organization that would first ask and then try to answer the many questions which begin with the word 'why'. It is this basically new approach for its time which marks the watershed between 'The Work Approach' and 'The Experience Approach' of *Developments in Management Thought* and the lines of approach in this book.

Their claim was to impose order on existing knowledge without imposing their own particular point of view. Later references to *Organizations* by other authors confirm that it did more than they claimed. In fact, they set a new direction.

They bring us to the idea that organization is one of the most universal aspects of modern society. It is virtually impossible to get away from its impact on human beings whether at work, at school, in church, at the social club or dealing with one of the many national or local government offices. Social behaviour, a shorthand term for the many aspects of living and working together, is influenced more or less by every part of the environment in which he lives but, for twentieth-century man, his contact with organization has the greatest and most direct influence on his daily life. It is in belonging to an organization that a person finds his role to be most defined, elaborated and stable. 'Role' means the pattern of duties and responsibilities allotted to a person in a given situation, together with the relationships with other people which he is expected to maintain.

The heart of the theory is expressed in the idea that 'Propositions about organizations are statements about human behaviour'[1] and that this involves showing which characteristics of human beings are relevant to the theory. In general, Classical theories of economics and management have assumed that the human being in an organization was a passive instrument reacting to an external stimulus. In reality members of organizations at all levels are by no means passive. They are complete human beings possessing their own individual sets of attitudes, values, and goals, needing in some way to be influenced to co-operate in the purposes of the organization, and inevitably bringing more or less conflict and dissension into its working. The propositions put forward by March and Simon throughout the book relate to both these points of view about people but most of them relate to the second and more realistic version. Additionally there are propositions which relate to members as problem-solvers and decision-makers. *Passive* man belongs to Classical management, *emotional* man to psycho-sociology, *decision* man to economics. March and Simon intend to bring them together as *real-life* man under the umbrella of a theory of organization.

Pre-conditions for the theory

Certain basic ideas underlie the whole analysis and construction of the theory. Somewhat briefly stated they are:

(i) Over very short periods of time the behaviour of any organism is the result of its internal state at the beginning of the period and the environment which surrounds it during that period of time. This does not imply complete determinism and lack of free will as either the organism or the environment may contain elements of uncertainty or probability.

(ii) At any one time the internal state of an organism is the combined result of its history. Again, this does not mean that every single event or circumstance will have equal effect; some may be extremely important while others have only very marginal effects. Also some later event or circumstance may modify or even wipe out earlier ones. In the human being the past is stored in memory, but at any one time and under a given stimulus only a part or some parts of that memory will be at a conscious, operating level. This concept, the part of the total memory of an individual which is recalled at any one time, is extremely important in the theory and is called the *evoked set*. The remainder of the total memory which is not operating to influence particular behaviour is called the *unevoked set*. What is evoked or not by any given stimulus or event depends upon its nature and the interpretation put on it by the individual. In this connection a 'set' is a psychological term for a particular pattern of interrelated ideas.

(iii) The total content of a memory increases relatively slowly by learning over a period of time. But as events, stimuli and even a person's view of them can change very rapidly the operating parts of memory, the evoked set, can also change very rapidly by bringing in other parts of total memory or discarding back into the unevoked set parts no longer thought to be useful.

(iv) Changes in people's behaviour can thus be brought about in two ways, by a learning process that increases the total memory or by changing the evoked (i.e. operative) set by changing the stimulus or presenting it in a different way.

(v) In a similar way the total environment surrounding an organism can be divided into a relatively small part that at any one time is exerting an influence and a relatively large part that under the circumstances prevailing is having no effect.

(vi) These two ideas of only parts of the total memory and only parts of the total environment being operative at any one time are the essential characteristics of organisms which distinguish them from what are called the 'natural systems' of physics or chemistry.

(vii) Time is an essential concept for understanding the theory. Over short periods of time the evoked set from total memory and the operating part of the total environment will both be relatively small. As the time period considered gets longer and longer so more and more aspects of total memory can come into the evoked set and more and more of the environment becomes operative.

(viii) Because man has a brain and is not simply a collection of reflex actions his memory has two important aspects. One consists of a pattern of values and goals that he has built up for himself from experience and which form his criteria for judgement. The other consists of recollections of actions taken in the past and their results which build up into generalized beliefs of causes and effects. Without entering into discussions of free-will it is possible to see that different combinations of criteria and beliefs lead to alternative choices for action.

Classical theory

With their own basic groundwork laid down March and Simon devote a whole chapter to a careful analysis of Classical theories. For our purposes a brief summary of their conclusions is all that is needed. In essence they say that Classical theory takes the human being in organization for granted as a passive, docile individual reacting in predictable ways. This, as everybody knows, is by no means always borne out by the facts of life. In a little more detail Classical theory makes wrong assumptions on why people behave as they do: ignores conflict of interests; ignores the constraints imposed on the individual by the complexity of his nature; largely ignores a person's ability to know and see facts, to develop ideas; and finally, as a result of all these, virtually ignores the fact that management's programmes and plans have to be elaborated and modified as they go into action.

In other words, man being what he is imposes constraints on the organization by joining and being part of it. These constraints must be recognized in any valid theory of organization and it is to these that we now turn.

Planning, influence and motivation

This section brings us to the very heart of the difference between Classical views of organization and the new trends. Henri Fayol is, perhaps, the best of the Classical writers to use to illustrate the change. His four functions of management were to foresee and plan, to organize, to command and to control. Implicit in this there seems to be a sort of foregone conclusion, a law of nature, a statement of cause and effect. In this way everything would go 'according to plan', provided the foreseeing and the planning were appropriate to the situation that developed. But even in Fayol's day people did not *always* do exactly as they were told or work as effectively as management wished.

March and Simon's view is that Classical theory is not entirely or always wrong, and in this they would include much of the early psycho-sociological theory of before and after the 1939–45 war, but, because it does not explain many of the current difficulties that managers have in carrying out plans through other people, it is incomplete.

The starting point of the new theory is that the influence process over a person's actions is one of a stimulus of some kind leading to a response. This process can, in many cases, be extremely simple and direct. In other cases due to the complex nature of man himself, of his perception and beliefs about his environment, of his personal goals and motives the process is anything but simple and direct and may often produce undesired or dysfunctional results from the point of view of the organization's objectives.

Two different kinds of decisions are required from the individual. These are decisions to produce and decisions to participate, i.e. join, stay, or leave the organization. These are influenced by quite different factors.

Taking first the decision to produce, March and Simon again develop a long and very detailed argument to build up their case. The conclusions which form the new theory seem to be:

(i) If an organization is treated in a way that assumes that people react like machines then unexpected consequences will result.

(ii) The motivation of the individual is a constraint on his actions.

(iii) Motivation is the result of a combination of:

    (*a*) The stimulus or stimuli present.

    (*b*) The perception of (*a*) by the individual.

    (*c*) The evoked set of ideas.

(*d*) The perceived consequences of the alternatives available.

(*e*) The individual's personal goals, attitudes and values.

(*f*) His identification with the organization and its objectives.

(*g*) His identification with his workgroup, its ideas and its objectives.

(iv) The stimulus may produce the expected evoked set of ideas, a larger one, a smaller one or none at all. Its purpose may be mistaken by the individual.

(v) Bureaucratic forms of organization are less effective in promoting organizational ends.

(vi) In making decisions the individual may not always be concerned with present satisfaction. The anticipated future satisfactions resulting from present alternative courses of action may be more important.

(vii) The lower the present satisfaction the greater the search for alternative courses of action.

(viii) The individual's reaction to a situation will change if:

(*a*) His values relating to the situation change.

(*b*) His estimate of the consequences of alternative actions changes.

(*c*) His evoked set of ideas relating to the situation changes.

(ix) The nature of supervision, the work itself, the rewards and the workgroup all have more or less influence on the individual's evoked set of ideas.

(x) Individual goals can be altered over time by experience, training, and indoctrination, provided the individual is willing to accept change and sees it as being to his advantage.

(xi) Identification with the group depends on shared goals, the amount of interaction, the prestige of the group, and the satisfaction of the individual's needs by the group.

(xii) Identification with the organization depends on the extent to which it satisfies the individual's needs.

(xiii) The influence of the organization and of sub-groups may reinforce or detract from each other depending on the extent to which they share goals, attitudes and norms.

Turning now to the other decision for the individual, whether or not to participate at all, March and Simon make the point that the very survival of the organization is dependent on enough people of the right kind deciding to participate. Fortunately the theory here is more easily stated. In return for the individual's agreement to participate the organization offers rewards – pay, status, and other forms of satisfaction. The individual will participate if and for so long as, in his opinion, the rewards offered are greater than or as great as the 'cost' to him of participating and no other better alternatives elsewhere are open to him and known to him. 'Cost' here will be measured in terms of effort, time, stress, other undesired effects that he is willing to offer or accept in return for the benefits to be obtained for participating.

It is, perhaps, not quite so obvious that contributions resulting from members' participation are the total source of the rewards the organization can offer and must be enough to meet them if the organization is to survive.

For the member the difference between the total rewards he receives and the total 'cost' to him of participating can vary between extreme satisfaction and extreme dissatisfaction with a zero point of indifference somewhere in the middle. At or below the point of indifference he will be willing to and will leave if he can see, as he thinks, a better alternative.

The decision to participate by members is widened rather beyond the normal idea of the organization by including among members not only employees but also suppliers, customers, investors. While all do make contributions in some form or other to the organization the most obvious participants are 'the employees including the management',[2] but the others must be included in a complete theory of organization.

It might be as well at this point to digress for a moment from March and Simon's views to explore the very basic question of what *is* the organization as distinct from its members. In part the trouble stems from the very general and therefore imprecise words we are compelled to use in this field of knowledge and 'organization' is one of the worst offenders. In ordinary conversation it may be used very loosely to mean the company, the firm, the people responsible for running the business, but a cricket club, a hospital, a church are also organizations. In a more precise context organization can be defined as a pattern of duties and responsibilities for and between people working together to achieve some common purpose – the organization's purpose! March and Simon have just been dealing with people's contribution to the organization and the question of whether they join or leave it to take just two examples. So, can we reify the organization, in more everyday language give it a separate existence of its own? The answer must be no if only because the organization would cease to exist if all the people left it. But it is more than just the sum of the 10 or 10,000 people who participate in it.

Perhaps one main value of March and Simon's book is that it extends, by implication if not specifically, the meaning of the word. It is very like a long and complex algebraic equation with many unknowns. It is the sum of those aspects of the individuals participating which is contributed towards the common purpose, their ideas, skills, aptitudes, work and attitudes, of the past and present decisions made by individuals and groups of individuals within the organization, of the patterns of relationships and interactions between individuals and groups and the effects of its history and of past and present environments. To paraphrase King Charles's retort 'The organization's attributes are its own, its deeds are those of its members'.

If an organization is anything like the summation in the previous paragraph it is easy to assume that conflict is inevitable and it is to this that March and Simon next turn their attention. Within the organization, conflict can occur within the individual member, between members, between groups and between any of these and the overall objectives of the organization.

At the individual level the member may experience conflict in making his own decisions when he is in a situation that he sees as unsatisfactory but the alternative courses of action do not contain one that is clearly better than the others or when none of them are regarded as being good enough. These are states of incomparability and unacceptability. It may also happen that conflict for the individual will arise when he is unable to identify the possible results of different alternatives. This is uncertainty.

Very rarely does one alternative possess all the advantages and no disadvantages as its probable outcome. In between the two extremes an alternative may have very little of one or the other – it is 'bland'.

It is assumed that under different circumstances the individual will take different sorts of action and that he has previously learnt how to generate responses that are likely to be acceptable. If all the outcomes are uncertain or unacceptable he will try to find new alternatives. When time is short he will search more vigorously for alternatives and is more likely to choose on the basis of the first alternative found that just meets his most important criteria. This last idea of the order of search and accepting the first satisfactory solution rather than continuing the search until the best possible solution is found is to occupy a key place in March and Simon's theory.

While the way in which an individual resolves his own conflicts will contribute to the functioning of the organization in some way, conflicts between individuals and groups are usually regarded as more important. For considering these problems two general assumptions are made although it is obvious that they are not universally true. The first is that there is at least a general agreement on the desirability of finding a solution that is acceptable to all. The second is that all individuals can assess accurately the probable results of all possible known alternatives. But, of course, conflict between individuals may arise because they want different things or because they cannot make up their minds as to what they do want. It is argued that greater past experience and less complex decision situations make inter-personal conflict within the organization less likely. Also when individuals see their environment as becoming more favourable or when there is a considerable difference between the levels of their achievement and their aspirations conflict between them is more likely.

Paradoxically conflict between groups must start with agreement. The individuals within a group must at least agree on what the fight is about, on what they want and that they should fight as a group. Obviously it is possible for any larger group to split into smaller groups that then fight each other. The alternative to inter-group conflict is joint decision-making by the groups. Conflict is more likely when the groups have different goals or different perceptions of reality. Joint decision-making to resolve the difference is more likely when members of both groups feel that it is necessary, when they are in situations of interdependence or mutual dependence on some outside condition, that is, outside the groups' control, and when the groups concerned are relatively high up in the organization hierarchy.

In more general terms conflict, or the likelihood of it, within an organization depends on how far members accept the organization's aims as being rational, the type and size of the organization, the extent to which members have similar backgrounds, attitudes, training, ideals, etc., the system of rewards to members within the organization and the total amount and type of resources available. It may well be that, in fact, because many conflicts arise because people 'see' things differently, anything that affects their perception also affects the likelihood of conflict. March and Simon mention the amount of information available and who it is available to, the interaction between goals and knowledge and formal and informal channels of information. They hypothesize that the greater the number of independent sources of information the greater the risk of people seeing the same thing differently. (Curiously they omit the point that differences in individuals' background, experiences, memories must affect their interpretation of what is going on around them.)

If we assume that conflict when it arises will be resolved, what ways are available of doing so? Four basic methods are given. Problem-solving is the rational way involving the search for new information, new alternatives and the acceptance by both sides of a new solution that meets both sides' needs. Persuasion of one side by the other causes the first to accept a solution proposed by the second but it is peaceful persuasion and implies that as a result of appeals to reason or to higher level goals the first group's goals can be changed. Bargaining assumes that each side is prepared to give way on some aspects of its original goals in return for similar action by the other side and that at some level of 'trade-off' an agreement of sorts can be reached. Playing politics involves one side gaining allies and support from outside to strengthen its case.

Problem solving and persuasion are suggested as more likely to be used for inter-individual conflict, bargaining, and playing politics for inter-group conflict. The use of power is not directly mentioned as a resolver of conflict although, together with the strains and pressures, and the implicit acceptance of differences of group objectives, it is given as having a disruptive effect on the organization.

Conflict between organizations themselves is only too obviously a fact of life which must have a direct effect on the characteristics, structure, and behaviour of any organization involved in it. It is mentioned as largely unexplored territory with a brief reference to the theory of games.

Rationality

Most economic theory has two fundamental assumptions as a bedrock on which the whole edifice is built. First, the behaviour of man in business or at work is entirely rational. Second, the aim of all activity is to optimize to achieve the best possible result. Anything other than these is a deviation. There may (and must) be reasons for it, but it is still a deviation and can be ignored in building up the theory. Classical management adopted these two assumptions as its own.

March and Simon will have none of it. A 'good' theory explains what *is* and not some imagined ideal state of affairs that has to be modified again and again to match the everyday experience of every single person. Organizations do not behave as if they were completely rational and they do not always or, perhaps, even often go on searching until they find the one best, optimum solution to problems.

The attack on rationality comes first and substitutes limited rationality for perfect rationality. Complete rationality would be possible if there were in any given situation a given set of alternatives all of which were known and which have predictable outcomes, and if in addition the decision-maker had a given set of ranked preferences for all posssible outcomes and had a rational method for comparing the values of outcomes with his preferences. If the outcomes are only probable then he must match outcomes and preferences to get the greatest probable utility. If the outcomes are uncertain rationality is at best a doubtful starter. But the argument for complete rationality is only valid with all facts known, all outcomes certain and perfect judgement for the decision-maker, and, in any case, rationality is itself a slippery term.

So, what is needed to bring the theory into line? The starting point is man himself. At any time when he is faced with a choice he can only use as a base his own 'limited, approximate, simplified model'[3] of the real situation. He defines the situation for himself and the elements that go into that definition are the result of psycho-sociological forces together with the background and activities of both the one who has to choose and of those around him in so far as *he* sees them as being relevant to the situation. This extends by a great deal the coverage of the theoretical base. It does not exclude complete rationality but it does at the same time include all possible states to complete irrationality.

To extend the theory further into reality the need for a decision arises because of some stimulus to which reaction is needed. At one extreme the reaction may be almost automatic; a decision, if such it can be called, to put into action a learned, routine response that may vary from very simple to very complex. The point is it is routine and once the decision is made the rest follows automatically. At the other extreme there may be no easily recognizable response to the stimulus and long and complicated search and decision processes may be brought into action that may result in very complex programmes for action. Stimuli that occur frequently tend by a process of learning to produce routine, acceptable responses. (One point that must be implied here, although it is not specifically stated, is that one possible decision or choice is to do nothing, to ignore the stimulus for one reason or another.)

Having disposed of complete rationality what about optimization, the other sacred cow of Classicism? This fares neither better nor worse. It is possible but unlikely. First, to get the optimum involves scanning and evaluating *all* possible alternatives and *all* their possible consequences. But one thing that is limited for everyone is time. The second factor is the ability to search, recognize, and evaluate. Finally outcomes may be indefinable or, at best, probabilistic. So in the light of the stimulus and the known conditions, which may be incomplete, the decision-maker sets what are, in his estimation, the minimum criteria on which he would accept a solution. The search for alternatives goes on until a solution is found that meets these minimum criteria and this is then adopted. It may not be the best but it is at least minimally satisfactory. Optimization generally becomes 'satisficing'. What is considered to be satisficing depends on the criteria set and on the order in which possible solutions are found. The order in which areas of possibility are searched becomes a vital factor in the result.

The theory now does not exclude optimization. Provided the criteria set are those of the optimum result and search continues until a solution meeting these criteria is found, optimization occurs. But it is not unfair to describe it as unlikely under everyday conditions.

Performance programming

Many actions which have to be performed to meet the organization's objectives and to keep it in being can be reduced to more or less repetitive, routine responses. To take a separate, new decision each time one of these cropped up would soon grind the whole thing to a halt. The answer lies in a collection of decisions that lay down detailed programmes or guidelines as to what is to be done under given circumstances until the decisions are countermanded and new ones set up in their place.

A 'performance programme' specifies an action or a series of actions, which may be extremely complicated, that are to be carried out in detail as laid down. Guidelines, which March and Simon call a 'performance strategy' give guidance on the ends to be achieved but allow discretion as to how they should be reached.

These very general statements are developed into a number of hypotheses of which perhaps the more important can be summarized as:

(i) Greater routine leads to more programming and more predictable behaviour.

(ii) The greater the co-ordination needed between individuals and/or groups the more likely are programmes to be used.

(iii) Once they are established programmes are more likely to be modified to meet new situations than new ones are likely to be developed.

Sub-goal formation

The division of work and the resulting formation of sub-units of the organization are an essential feature of all but the very smallest of organizations. Similarly the overall goals of the organization have to be sub-divided by means–ends chains into sub-unit goals. At the highest level of the organization there are certain ends or goals to be achieved. Broad ways of achieving them are decided, e.g. for a given goal of profitability 'means' in terms of production, costs and sales targets will be set. For the marketing division the sales target becomes the goal and means are devised to meet it by sales budgets, advertising allocation, merchandizing programmes, etc. These again become goals for the appropriate sub-departments who develop means or plans to achieve them and so on down to the man who is given an instruction to design the layout for a particular advertisement, or achieve £X of sales of a particular line.

This splitting into sub-units and sub-goals is due to the sheer physical impossibility of one man doing all that is necessary and also to the fact that the individual's ability to take in and comprehend a situation is limited. In fact the real situation is even more limited than that. The individual substitutes for the reality about him a simplified and more or less adequate model of the situation as *he sees* it. The result is that the individual tends to identify with the sub-goals of his sub-unit rather than the overall goals of the organization.

Further complications arise because sub-units often develop sub-goals of their own that may conflict with those assigned to them by the means–ends chain as their contribution to overall goals. Also the defined goals in a situation will affect the means used only if some real or illusory connection is seen between them by the people concerned. And what people will do depends not on reality but on the conclusions they draw from the reality around them as modified by the processes of screening, colouring, filtering, bias in passing on information from one person to another.

We are a long way from the early theories of motivation and light-years away from Fayol's 'Command'. But the point is made, behaviour in an organizational situation is not just a simple response to a stimulus, although it *may* be that. It is a response as modified by what people think they know of and the way they interpret that view of reality, by the influence of other people and groups and by the individual's own goals and personal motivation. This brings into clearer focus the question of interdependence within the organization and highlights the need for continuous co-ordination to achieve it.

Communication

The need for communication within an organization is obvious, the conditions for and results of its degree of effectiveness are less evident. It is needed to supply information for non-programmed activity, to determine strategies of action, to determine, initiate and establish programmes, to evoke them when the need arises, to adjust and co-ordinate them, to provide information on progress.

For it to be effective it must be adequate in volume and in direction, it must be free from 'noise' – suppression, filtering, colouring, bias – and it must match the conditions where it is intended to be received and understood. Where communication is effective it is possible for the sub-units of the organization to be more independent of each other. Information that comes in from the environment, whether the 'outside' environment of the organization or the intra-organizational environment of the sub-unit, must come through some individual in a boundary position, that is, in contact with his own unit and with the 'outside world'. The occupant of the boundary position must decide how much to pass on, i.e. filter, and how much uncertainty he must absorb, i.e. convert evidence into inferences that, in turn, as they are passed on become 'fact'. The routes or channels by which information is passed on may be formally laid down by programming, but these or other unofficial ones will tend to persist and grow if they are effective and lapse into disuse if they are not.

Organization structure and boundaries of rationality

Before turning to innovating or changing the form of an organization March and Simon draw together and summarize the threads so far. Summarizing still further they are:

    (i) The characteristics of human problem solving and of (bounded) rational choice are the basic features of organizational structure and function.

    (ii) (Bounded) rational behaviour involves simplifying reality.

        (*a*) Optimizing is replaced by satisficing.

        (*b*) Search involves sequential discovery of alternatives and consequences.

        (*c*) Programmes of action are laid down for repetitive events.

        (*d*) Each programme is designed for a restricted situation.

        (*e*) Each programme can be treated as semi-independent of the others.

    (iii) (Bounded) rational behaviour deals with one or at most a few components of a situation at a time.

    (iv) Organization structure consists of aspects of behaviour which are reasonably stable and change only slowly.

    (v) (Bounded) rational behaviour in an organization will be adapted to stable aspects of the environment or will be going through a learning process of adaptation.

    (vi) Stability in behaviour is a relative term. Programmes for action are the least stable as they may have to be adapted to sudden changes in circumstances; rules for switching from one programme to another are more stable; procedures for developing and installing new programmes are the most stable aspect.

[Author's note. In the text March and Simon do not use the word 'bounded' which has been inserted in brackets. That they intend it is basic to their theory of bounded rationality and, in fact, at this point they go on 'Organization will have structure . . . in so far as there are boundaries of rationality'.[4]]

Planning and innovation in organizations

There are costs involved in innovating new programmes, in modifying existing ones and in continuing with existing ones. In this order they are also in inverse order of magnitude. The greater the cost of change the more likely are existing programmes to be continued, so the stimulus required to produce change must be greater than the stimulus to stay put. Innovation involves producing new solutions to new problems or new and better solutions to old problems. Doing nothing or carrying on as before is not regarded as a simple alternative to innovation. It involves no increase in activity so there is no limit to the amount of doing nothing an organization can absorb – at least until it collapses. As innovation involves additional activity there is, at any one time, a limit to the amount the organization can take.

In so far as it involves new programmes and criteria, planning is innovating activity. In the model given it has four main characteristics:

(i) Its main purpose would be satisficing.

(ii) It will be initiated when one or more criteria are not being met.

(iii) Changing a programme involves choice of new procedures and choice of how to initiate them.

(iv) Usually different programmes are related to different criteria and the link between them is their joint demands on scarce resources.

Innovation can be regarded as the result of achievement falling below aspiration levels or what is desired, but aspiration levels generally change only slowly, rising if the situation remains steady. One standard for aspiration levels is previous achievement but other standards can exist. Marked differences between aspiration levels and achievement produce stress if they are not resolved but if there were no difference nothing could ever improve so it is thought that there could be an optimum level of stress which produces the best amount of innovation. Too much stress by its psychological effects could result in regressive behaviour and no innovation.

This 'natural' process of innovation may be too slow for organizational purposes so additional stimuli can be brought into operation by establishing criteria for rates of innovation, by deliberate allocation of resources to non-programmed activity and by setting deadlines.

March and Simon think that most innovation in an organization is done by borrowing from the environment, either imitating what others are already doing or taking on people from outside who will have new ideas. This limits the rate of innovation to the amount of exposure to the environment. The second source is a search through the collective 'memory' of the organization to find clues to possible solutions. Solutions whatever their source, will be reached by taking one aspect at a time and evaluating it in terms of means–ends chains. At the higher end of the hierarchy it will take the form of non-operational goals, lower down it becomes operational goals, means, and contributions.

References

(1) March, J. G. and Simon, H. A. *Organizations* (New York: Wiley, 1958), p. 6.
(2) Ibid, p. 89.
(3) Ibid, p. 139.
(4) Ibid, p. 170.

Bibliography

BOOK BY J. G. MARCH AND H. A. SIMON
Organizations (New York: Wiley, 1958).

21

R. M. Cyert and J. G. March
1963

With the title *A Behavioural Theory of the Firm* it might be expected that Cyert and March's book would correctly belong in Part II of this book. 'Behavioural' would seem, however, to be something of a misnomer. The subject is actually a theory on how business organizations reach decisions so although individual and group behaviour is one aspect considered, this seems to be subsidiary to the decision theory aspect.

A model of business decision-making has existed in economic theory for a long time. Its basis is the entrepreneur as the maker of all major decisions in the firm and maximization of profit as the criterion of decision. As an exercise in logic based on these assumptions it is a satisfactory model but even with the addition of the ideas of imperfect competition and economic friction it falls very far short of explaining what really goes on in practical business decision-making. Cyert and March, by empirical research and by hypothesis, make an attempt to produce a more realistic theory.

For them the economic model fails on many counts. Maximization of profit is not always the only or even the prime goal. Knowledge is never complete and often is no more than probabilities or even guesses. The basic characteristics of the firm such as complexity, control, standard practices, multi-level management, interaction, and survival are all ignored. Marginal analysis, which is central to the economic model, is often replaced in practice by rule of thumb, guidelines, and standard operating procedures.

Organization theory, if anything, fares even worse. Cyert and March consider that it has been built up from three sources with three main lines of development:

(i) Sociological – based on concepts of bureaucracy.
(ii) Psycho-sociological – experimental base with efficiency as its criterion.
(iii) Administrative – based on the problems of the executive.

239

This theory largely ignores the questions of targets, deals mainly with processes with only the third approach dealing with decision-making, does not (according to Cyert and March) deal with aggregates and so only provides a partial theory of the firm.

But if these are not adequate theories of the firm what would be? The list of requirements is long and explicit:

(i) It takes the firm as the basic unit.

(ii) It takes as its main purpose the prediction of the firm's behaviour on decisions in major areas such as prices and output.

(iii) Its basic commitment is to research the processes of organizational decision-making.

(iv) It must provide a theoretical language for describing explicit models.

(v) It must decide in terms of this language what questions need answering and in how much detail.

(vi) It must include objectives, overall and sub-goal formation, the influence of interaction, competition, and planning within the organization.

(vii) It must discover what characterizes objectives and under what conditions one or other will be preferred.

(viii) It must examine how far the environment determines decisions, how far the firm has discretion, and how this discretion results in strategies and rules.

(ix) It must investigate what conditions the firm takes as given and what conditions it can manipulate.

(x) It must investigate the processes of information gathering, communication, and interpretation, and of decision-making and implementation.

(Author's note. Items (iv) and (v) are dealt with in mathematical terms and illustrated in considerable detail. It is not thought possible to handle them within the purposes of this book and they have been omitted.)

Organizational goals

Cyert and March come down straight away on the idea that the organization as such has its own goals. 'People (i.e. individuals) have goals – collectivities of people do not.'[1] But something analogous to personal goals is needed at organizational level. An organization is described as a coalition of individuals for a general purpose. The coalition will be divided into sub-coalitions relating to the particular purpose of the moment. Sub-coalitions arise either as major groups related to a relatively short period of time or as major groups related to a particular purpose or decision. The boundaries of either the whole coalition or of sub-coalitions cannot be regarded as fixed. The prime factor determining their membership will be the purpose in question. From the point of view of Cyert and March's discussion short-term models are used so that the more complex processes that determine coalition membership over a longer period can be ignored.

Between members of a coalition or sub-coalition or between sub-coalitions conflict and difference of opinion are at some time inevitable so a satisfactory theory of organizational goals must include this aspect. The two possible solutions of entrepreneurial decision with the consensus of other members obtained by rewards and sanctions, and of only common consensus goals being used are both rejected as unsatisfactory. The way out is a somewhat jaundiced view of what organizational goals really are although in large complex organizations it is probably more realistic than other views leading to neater theories.

Actual organization goals cannot usually be described in terms of a joint preference order related to the preferences of all members of the coalition. Usually they tend to be highly ambiguous. This ambiguity, while getting formal agreement from coalition members, in fact hides disagreement and uncertainty among members at the level of general goals and also at the lower level where sub-unit goals have to be determined from the ideas people have about the general goals. Further, most goals are expressed in terms of aspiration levels, they are, in fact, hopes rather than clearly set out targets. Aspiration levels themselves will change with time and experience and will change differently for different sub-coalitions. All this rules out the idea of consistent goals achieved by consensus and a bargaining process between sub-coalitions or between members is postulated as the means of arriving at organization goals.

The bargaining process

Bargaining also takes place to determine the actual membership of the group within the coalition which will arrive at a decision and the general terms under which it will operate. Within the group two processes must operate. One to set up controls to stabilize and elaborate objectives, the other to modify objectives in the light of experience.

This bargaining process requires some elaboration. Bargains require two parties either of which may be an individual or a group. The bargain consists of one party getting the agreement of the other to support a line of action in return for some side-payment. This means that the party wanting the agreement must have some benefit to offer to the other as the side-payment. These can take many different forms from increased pay or other perks right through to a simple offer to support the other party on some other matter in which it has an interest. Those members and sub-groups who by virtue of their position have the greatest range and quantity of benefits to offer will tend to be in a controlling position.

While this process of bargaining will define or clarify many objectives it is unlikely to ensure that the objectives will be mutually consistent. Skill in negotiating, the sequence in which demands on others for agreement are made, the aggressiveness or otherwise of sub-groups, and the scarcity or otherwise of resources tend to be the determining factors in any one decision rather than its consistency with other decisions. Further, in view of the need for apparent consensus and the involved way of getting it, often objectives will be decidedly vague and will be expressed either as hopes (aspiration levels) or as 'non-operational' that is at a level which does not specify targets or the action to be taken.

But the process does not end there. While organizational objectives are usually reasonably stable over considerable periods of time their related side-payment agreements are neither complete nor do they identify all future possibilities. Breaking down the overall objectives into operational terms involves sub-goals and further bargaining and secondary side-payments to develop mutual control systems to elaborate and enforce them. This secondary bargaining may be limited by standing orders, standard practices, and customs which have come to be accepted.

So far the processes described are presumed to produce relative stability in goals over reasonable periods of time but in spite of this stabilization process change is likely to take place over longer periods in the demands made on coalitions. Attainable goals may lead to higher aspiration levels and so to increased demands. Also Cyert and March suggest that at any one time only some limited number or sub-set of the total possible demands are operating. In the light of experience the contents of the sub-set that is operating may change, in which case the demands will change. Also the widely used practice of dealing with one thing at a time will bring different sub-sets into play and, incidentally, make possible the illogical situation of conflicting and/or mutually contradictory objectives existing side by side.

The relation between the total side-payments people and groups are able to offer and the demands that have to be met to obtain consensus is not by any means constant. Demands are likely to be relatively slow in adjusting up or down. In times of prosperity the benefits available are likely to increase considerably giving a surplus over demands. While everyone may benefit to some extent from this surplus those who are in positions of relative power and most likely to know of the surplus's existence are likely to ensure that they get the lion's share of it. This surplus is called 'organizational slack' and by 'storing it away' during good times organizations are able to draw on it during bad ones and so reduce to some extent the result of major changes in the environment.

The framework and process
It is admitted that this outline provides only a partial theory and that much more research into the actual behaviour of coalitions is required to substantiate it. But it is thought to provide a sound basis of framework and mechanisms or processes on which to build. The framework consists of the following:

(i) A set of actual and potential coalition members.
(ii) A combination of members which is viable and able to meet the requirements of the environment.
(iii) A set of demands for each member, part of which is operative and part inactive at any one time.
(iv) A set of problems for each member again with some being active and others not at any one time.

Within this framework there must be five mechanisms or processes to achieve the following results:

(i) To change demands over time so as to achieve mutual control by members and also to match changing aspirations.
(ii) To focus the attention of members on the appropriate sub-set of active demands while ignoring sub-sets that are not active or not considered.
(iii) To focus the attention of members on relevant problems.
(iv) To relate demands on people with human capacities.
(v) To choose among potentially viable coalitions.

By simply using this framework and the five mechanisms Cyert and March are able to construct a simplified model of decision-making by a firm in three areas – price, output, and sales strategy. This involves oversimplified assumptions in the shape of only these three areas having operative goals but it does allow for the goals changing in value and in the amount of attention given to them.

Real life decision-making
Two practical research studies into actual business decision-making are then described. The conclusions drawn from them support in a general way the propositions already put forwad.

Case 1. Conclusions
(i) Search behaviour for new solutions resulted from an event out-side the firm which posed a new problem. The search itself

followed severely limited lines and concentrated on local scanning in the neighbourhood of the problem.

(ii) The information produced on costs and probable returns was not comparable and led to vague, changeable estimates. These made it possible to shift the immediate focus of attention around to different aspects and to use the occasion to create organizational slack.

(iii) The resources that were available were regarded as fixed so only feasibility tests were applied to possible solutions. There was no attempt to discover whether a change in resources could produce a better, let alone an optimal, solution.

(iv) At lower levels in the organization the connection between the real stimulus and the real problem was very weak. Middle and lower level managers misinterpreted the motives of higher managers, assumed the higher managers had preferences for particular solutions and acted to conform with them.

(v) Real information on costs was not obtained until very late in the proceedings when the pressure for a solution had really built up.

(vi) Again very late in the proceedings a change in the environment showed a possible change in the resources available and this changed the order of priorities and the potential decision.

Case 2. Conclusions

(i) The original problem had been known for two years but because there was no consensus on its true nature or on possible solutions it had not been dealt with.

(ii) A new urgent problem arose that could be indirectly linked with the original one and this brought both into focus.

(iii) The search activity that occurred was limited to narrow specific events and was not related to general planning. The problems were dealt with in isolation.

In addition to the relevance which these conclusions have for Cyert and March's theory their 'true to life' nature will be obvious to anyone with a reasonable length of experience in an organization.

The firm as an adaptive institution

If a firm is to survive it must possess at least a certain amount of rationality. The question is how much. Because it exists in an uncertain and often unpredictable environment, has problems of maintaining a viable coalition of members, and suffers from limitations on the amount and correctness of the information it has, no firm can be completely and entirely rational. Cyert and March produce the concept of the adaptively rational system which has the following characteristics:

(i) At any one time it has several possible states but it will prefer some of these states to others. The number and variety of states will change over a period of time.

(ii) External, uncontrollable disturbances occur in the environment and affect the system.

(iii) Within the system there are a number of variables affecting decision. There exist some basic 'rules' for manipulating these variables.

(iv) Each combination of external shock and decision variable alters the state of the system. Given the existing state, the nature of the shock, and the decision variables invoked the next state would be predictable.

(v) A decision rule that has previously been successful is more likely to be used again than one that has failed.

This process of adaptation involves something analogous to the process of learning, but because it takes place in a complex system with coalitions of diverse sub-groups and decision-making at different points and levels in the system it will be much more complicated than individual adaptation. The actual nature of the adaptation will also depend on which existing goals are involved in it.

So long as the environment remains unstable and uncertain short-run adaptability is considered to be of first importance and long-run adaptability to omniscient rationality is 'of modest' relevance.

Reducing uncertainty

In order to maintain adaptive rationality it is necessary for the organization to do whatever it can to reduce the total area of uncertainty. The first is to build up an organization 'memory' of what has succeeded in the past so that it can be readily put to use to meet future events. This 'memory' takes the form of standard operating procedures or rules, that are based on experience and specify the conduct of individuals and groups. Additionally there will be standard procedures for the collecting, transmitting, and interpretation of information. At a higher level there should be rules and procedures for interpreting the operation of the lower level procedures so that, by a process equivalent to learning, standard operating procedures that are no longer suitable to a fundamentally changed environment can be discarded and new, appropriate ones put in their place. Over reasonable periods of time lower level operating procedures can be taken as fixed and given both for practical operations and for model-building.

A second method of limiting the effects of uncertainty is to lay down standard choice procedures. Again these are assumed to have been built up from experience and to change only slowly and in the long run. The first is to avoid uncertainty wherever possible. This is done by looking for and using procedures that minimize the need to predict uncertainty. In effect it is living from hand to mouth by taking short-term decisions where the feed-back of results will be quick and certain and errors can be corrected before any serious damage is done. The second method is to make a rule that existing rules must be followed and only abandoned under extreme duress. The third, which on the face of it appears to be something of a contradiction of the second, is to use only simple operating rules and to rely on judgement to provide the necessary flexibility to cope with complexity.

Two aspects of standard operating procedures deserve a slightly more detailed attention. Procedures for collecting, transmitting and interpreting information obviously become more important and critical as the complexity of the organization grows. In particular the routes that information should follow from the point where it arises or is collected from the outside environment have vital effects on the value it has when it reaches its destination. Routes may be too long so that the information is too late to be useful when it arrives. The people initiating the information and those along the route may all affect its value by conscious or unconscious screening, bias, alteration of emphasis, blocking or holding up its movement along the route. Where, as often happens, departments act more or less independently of each other the tendency is for formal routes to be down the hierarchical chain. Where inter-departmental co-ordination is essential the channels required between departments are more likely to be set up informally as the need is seen and to be recognized officially at a later date. Although much has been made by other authors of the occurrence and dangers of distortion and bias in passing on information Cyert and March think that after a certain amount of experience the recipients of constantly distorted information will come to recognize and allow for the distortion so that its effect may have been over-exaggerated.

The other aspect is planning as a form of standard procedure. Attention is concentrated on short-term plans because Cyert and March are convinced the long-term planning as envisaged by Classical theory '. . . plays a relatively minor role in decision-making in the firm'.[2] In particular the procedure of planning through budgetary control comes in for special mention. It is claimed that the preparation of the budget is used as a device to determine feasible programmes, and to define a set of commitments and expectations for members. By using the budget as a control device as time passes higher management are helped to turn it into a self-fulfilling prophecy.

A plan is both a prediction and a goal. Depending on the amount of detail involved it is also a schedule, specifying the intermediate steps and timing required to reach the goal. It may specify a fixed goal or a variable one dependent on one or more outside factors but, either way, it must lay down acceptable levels of achievement. Thorough planning also specifies the relationship between different aspects of the firm. Finally, and this is particularly true of budgeting, it is a precedent as, by defining the action required over one period of time, it acts as a base and precedent for the next round of planning. Planning may reduce uncertainty in two ways. The advertising budget, for instance, can help to make the real world conform to the firm's requirements by influencing sales. The other, and perhaps more dangerous, way is that it tends to substitute the plan or budget for the real world as a guide to action.

A summary of basic concepts

The discussion so far seems to have ranged far and wide and at this point needs drawing together into a more concise pattern.

The basic framework of the theory consists of two organizational devices:

(i) A set of exhaustive variables.
(ii) A set of concepts covering relationships.

The exhaustive, complete set of variables is made up of the following:
(i) Variables affecting organizational goals.
  (a) The dimensions of the goals. The views of what is important. The composition of the coalitions. The form of division of labour in decision-making. The accepted definition of problems.
  (b) Changes due to people leaving or entering the coalition.
  (c) The operative goals for a particular decision will be the goals of the sub-unit making the decision.
  (d) Goals are evoked by problems.
(ii) Variables influencing aspiration levels.
  (a) The organization's past goals.
  (b) Its past performance.
  (c) The past performance of comparable organizations.
    [Author's comment. This section should surely read 'Member's perceptions of' (a), (b), and (c).]
(iii) Variables affecting organizational expectations.

(a) The information available and the inferences drawn from it.

(b) The recognition of patterns in events.

(c) The nature, extent, and direction of search activity for information, possible solutions, advice, etc.

(d) The goals achieved (and *not* achieved).

(e) The amount of organizational slack known to exist.

(iv) Variables affecting organizational choice.

(a) The nature of the problem under consideration.

(b) Standard operating rules.

(c) The order in which alternatives are found and considered.

Cyert and March go on to say 'we think it possible to subsume any variable within the theory of business decision-making under one or more of these categories'.[3] While this claim may be somewhat exaggerated in view of their frequent assertion that they are using oversimplified models, there can be little doubt that the framework given adds some very useful insights into the process of organizational decision-making.

Turning to the relationships within the framework the authors say '. . . in many respects, they (the relational concepts) represent the heart of our theory of business decision-making'.[4] There are four of them.

(i) The quasi-resolution of conflict.

(a) Arising from the multiplicity of individual goals. The surrender of individual goals is regarded as being unrealistic so the organization continues to exist despite latent conflict of goals.

(b) Organizational goals are a series of independent constraints related to the aspiration levels of members of the coalition. Normally these aspiration levels relate to continuous operational goals but at times other goals may take preference.

(c) Decision problems become split into sub-problems for sub-units. Complex problems thus become a series of single problems in terms of one goal. Whether these sub-decisions together solve the total problem depends on their compatibility.

(d) Decision rules generally ensure that most sub-decisions will, in fact, match and that they will usually under-exploit the environment and so leave surplus resources available to meet contingencies.

(e) The usual method of dealing with one thing at a time allows mutual inconsistency between goals to arise and to continue to exist. Attention will tend to switch from one trouble spot to another rather than deal with overall consistency.

(ii) Avoiding uncertainty.

    (*a*) Organizations tend to avoid it by using short-run feed-back, negotiating environmental conditions, and, where possible, imposing plans on the environment.

    (*b*) Long-range planning depending on predicting uncertain events is generally avoided in favour of short-term plans.

    (*c*) Problems are dealt with one at a time as they arise. When a problem arises that does not conform to this sequence it tends to be 'modified' so that it will.

    (*d*) Wherever possible negotiated agreements are used to eliminate or reduce uncertainty.

(iii) Problemistic search.

    (*a*) The amount of search which occurs to find solutions to problems will depend on whether acceptable or optimal solutions are required and whether the first feasible solution is adopted.

    (*b*) Search is stimulated by a problem and is directed to the solution of that problem.

    (*c*) Search is primarily simple and assumes simple models of cause and effect until forced by failure to explore more complex possibilities.

    (*d*) Search is biased by the view taken of the environment, by the interpretation of information, and by previous experience and training.

    (*e*) Regular planned search in areas that are seen to be already adequate is assumed to be relatively unimportant.

(iv) Organizational Learning.

    (*a*) Some process analogous to individual learning has to be assumed to account for organizational behaviour.

    (*b*) The changes that take place in aspiration levels as a result of experience are one form of this process.

    (*c*) The rules for attention tend to shift in the long run to concentrate on those areas that have been seen to produce satisfactory results and to move away from areas of failure.

    (*d*) Successful methods of searching tend to be repeated and unsuccessful ones dropped.

Conclusions

After fairly detailed accounts of three experiments that do go some way in lending support to their theory Cyert and March turn to such implications as they can draw from their theory.

An adequate theory of organizational decision-making should describe how firms make decisions, should describe the behaviour and decisions required to approach optimum solutions given certain goals, should apply to industries as well as individual firms, and should help in determining economic policies. This is a massive requirement and while Cyert and March claim that their theory has most relevance to the first aspect they suggest it has some implications for the other three. With regard to the individual firm their conclusions, while only 'useful first attempts at a theory of resource allocation',[5] are claimed to be generally consistent with actual behaviour.

There can be little doubt that they are much nearer to it than economic man, profit maximization, and marginal analysis.

References

(1) Cyert, R. M. and March, J. G. *A Behavioural Theory of the Firm* (Englewood Cliffs: Prentice Hall, 1963), p. 26.
(2) Ibid, p. 110.
(3) Ibid, p. 116.
(4) Ibid, p. 116.
(5) Ibid, p. 271.

Bibliography

BOOK BY R. M. CYERT AND J. G. MARCH

A Behavioural Theory of the Firm (Englewood Cliffs: Prentice Hall, 1963).

22

L. R. Sayles
1964

In terms of sheer numbers the majority of people holding the title of 'manager' or its equivalent are probably employed as middle and lower managers in large-scale complex organizations. While their individual actions, thoughts and attitudes will not have the repercussions of those of their President or Managing Director, because of their number their behaviour as managers is of vital importance to the success or failure of their corporation or company.

Sayles's book *Managerial Behaviour* is concerned solely with analysing the results of a long period of research into the day-by-day behaviour of seventy-five middle and lower managers, backed up by discussions with the managers in open and training sessions. The managers were employed in a very large American corporation.

It is not, he says, a scientific experiment to support a particular hypothesis. It is a scheme of analysis of what actually happened. The managers concerned generally agreed that the scheme was consistent with their experience and were able to explain what was going on around them. Primarily the scheme describes the complex relationships between the managerial job and the organizational environment, between structure and behaviour.

Prospects for a science administration
Presumably from the findings of this research and, one must suppose, the writings of other people about management Sayles comes to the conclusion that the job of a manager is either not understood or it is misunderstood. He maintains that its essence is the ability to operate effectively within and between organizations. Dealing with people is a skill that is separate from the professional aspects of management. Human aspects are the frictions, the grit in the machinery which have to be taken into account in putting the theory into practice, but they are not part of the theory itself.

Management itself has progressed through a series of stages that are linked with the growth of technology, size of organizations, and the generally accepted ways of thinking of the time. In turn it has moved from owner/manager to Scientific Management, to human relations, and on (or back) to task control and operational research.

Sayles accepts none of them as a basis for a 'science of administration'. While it does matter greatly whether management is good, bad or indifferent it is by no means certain whether any one or any combination of the views above will enable us to judge what is good, bad or indifferent management. (Author's note. Throughout his book Sayles appears to use management and administration, and manager, administrator and executive as synonymous terms. To avoid possible confusion only management and manager will be used in this chapter.)

A new theory is needed with characteristics which are not typical of the earlier ones. The new theory must:

(i) Be consistent with and derived from the nature of the organization process.
(ii) Be able to describe managerial behaviour at any point in terms of functions of the position held.
(iii) Be in objective language suitable for training, counselling, and appraisal.
(iv) Have concepts which separate situational constraints (organizational pattern) from personality constraints.
(v) Relate managerial action to technology and be able to predict the effect of environmental culture on management practice.

The modern organization
It is essential to realize throughout that the whole of Sayles's version is based on the large, complex, American corporation. This differs completely in its size, nature, complexity, and atmosphere from earlier forms of organization and is regarded as typical of the environment in which modern management exists.

Modern technology, size, and complexity have produced a new element in management. This is the integration of a complex system that requires close co-ordination and the maximum of continuity, regularity and periodicity in its operations. The right contribution, whether of men, materials, finance, or decisions, at the right time and in the right place becomes the major criterion of organization. Continuous process operations have eroded the discreteness of departments and specialisms. Management is becoming increasingly a matter of managing managers as size and complexity increase the number of levels in the hierarchy. The manager manages not people but a complex system of patterns of interaction.

While this is, in fact, what managers do, Sayles maintains that most of them are, at best, only vaguely aware of the real nature of their actions and are unable to describe them in meaningful terms. They seem not to realize that their actions do not produce just a single stimulus–response reaction but have whole chains of reactions throughout all the groups around them. From this Sayles deduces that the essence of the manager's job is a continuous process of adjustment and readjustment, of participating in and influencing a series of relationships while at the same time creating and maintaining his own group to attain his objectives. 'Decision-making is not a discrete event, rather it is a *continuous* and *intricate process* of brokerage.'[1]

The individual manager consults, negotiates with, and arranges trade-offs with all sorts of people in reaching agreements on adjustments while at the same time the growth of specialists tends to curb his freedom of action.

The manager in the middle or lower ranks of the large modern organization is not just a variation on but a completely different species from, say, Fayol's planner, commander, co-ordinator and controller.

Empirical studies

As mentioned earlier Sayles bases his theory on empirical research so before developing it he lists the results of the studies on which it is based.

  (i) Formal authority and responsibility seldom resemble reality.
 (ii) Organization charts are generally pure fiction.
(iii) Job descriptions usually ignore the vital dynamic aspects of the manager's job.
 (iv) The typical manager is active in initiating contacts with others for most of his working day.
  (v) In the higher levels of the hierarchy the contacts will tend to be fewer but will last longer.
 (vi) Contacts are with equals, staff and service personnel as well as with superiors and subordinates.
(vii) Practising managers are not primarily human relations counsellors or careful planning decision-makers.
(viii) Thinking is essentially a part of interactional behaviour.
 (ix) Most of the manager's daily contacts have little to do with motivating subordinates.
  (x) Not all contacts are simply brief exchanges of facts and data.
 (xi) Some of the manager's negotiations with others take a long time and/or are spread over long periods of time.
(xii) The nature of the contact varies. Sometimes the manager does almost all the talking, at others he shares it, sometimes he mostly listens.

(xiii) The spark that sets off a contact may come from the manager himself, his superior, subordinates, equals, specialists, a piece of information, or outsiders.

(xiv) The manager must have, or must learn, a wide range of behaviour patterns and the ability to deal with a wide range of contacts.

(xv) The vertical, superior–subordinate, relationship is no longer the one primary relationship. Lateral and diagonal relationships have become relatively much more important than they were.

(xvi) The following are *myths and folklore of no further use*:

(a) Management is a unity based on dealing with people.

(b) One man must only have one boss.

(c) The manager does not do 'work'. He only gets it done.

(d) The manager devotes a large part of his time to supervising subordinates.

(e) Good managers manage by looking at results.

(f) Responsibility must be co-equal to authority.

(g) Staff people and specialists have no authority.

A statistician would almost certainly argue that Sayles's sample of managers is too small for reliable conclusions but anyone who has been a middle manager in a large firm will, if he is honest with himself, intuitively recognize most of these findings as 'life as it is'.

Programming the manager's job
Some care is needed at this stage as it appears that Sayles starts with a static view of the process of operations in which the manager's job is primarily to maintain the *status quo* or, in systems terms, to keep his share of the system in equilibrium. Later he introduces the concept of dynamic change.

The Classical hierarchy pattern with its process of managers transmitting orders downwards makes it impossible to understand and describe the manager's real function of maintaining the regularity and sequence of the work processes for which he is responsible. This can only be done by starting from the division of labour at the very bottom where the nature of the division and specialization determine the form of organization required and the content of the manager's job. As this process is continued upwards each lower layer determines the organization and the tasks of the next higher level in the hierarchy until the very top is reached. 'The objective of organizational structure is to minimize the incidence of deviations from the established interaction patterns of the work process.'[2]

From this conclusion it follows that the manager has three complex and inter-related roles to fill in order to minimize the effects of deviations on his own section's work-flow. These are:

(i) As participant in other related work-flows in order to provide the link between specialized sub-parts to hold the whole thing together.

(ii) As leader within his own group.

(iii) As monitor of performance.

It is, perhaps, the external link situation that has up to now received too little attention. Sayles identifies a very long list of relationships and aspects which can be involved here. Each involves a unique interaction pattern and foreseeable human problems. Even in summary form the list is formidable. It includes relationships concerned with the following activities: work-flow, trading, service, advisory auditing, stabilization, and innovation. These are dealt with at length later.

The manager's function as a leader is usually made up of activities by which he tries to secure a group response rather than an individual one. Individual pair (man-to-man) relationships are of less importance in large complex organizations except where the manager is one of the pair and the other is the spokesman of a group so the relationship is indirectly manager to group. In theory if the tasks within the manager's unit are correctly planned so as to integrate the individual tasks into a whole-unit task the relationship within his unit should be self-maintaining.

Internal friction and change external to the group can both interfere with the theoretical harmony of the group and in either case the manager must act as the leader to sort things out.

His leadership function has two other aspects. One consists of responding to appeals for help or support from his subordinates and the other of representing their views to or intervening on their behalf with the rest of the organization.

The manager's third function is that of monitor. Here the context is wider than the usual narrow meaning of checking performance against plan. It is a question of appraising how the internal and external relationships of the group are faring and of identifying stresses and strains when or before they actually happen. It also includes developing and implementing tactics and strategies to deal with short- and long-term disturbances and checking the effectiveness of his own performance.

The heading to this section was 'Programming the Manager's Job'. In fact, and Sayles uses this term in concluding his chapter, it is more a 'descriptive analysis' of the job in terms of the interface or boundaries at which it makes contact with the boundaries of other jobs but ignoring the emotional and intellectual characteristics of the manager and the occupants of the other jobs to which he relates. Analysis in these terms is claimed to convert management into a series of skills or 'plays' which can be learnt and whose performance can be evaluated.

In more detail it provides explicit management tools and skills. It provides motivation. It can be taught. It enables a manager to identify the structure of the parts of the system with which he and his group are interdependent. It is a means of describing and understanding the relationships he must use in behavioural terms and of predicting the feelings, attitudes, and reactions he will meet. It enables the manager to monitor relationships and to convert changes in policy into changes in behaviour. Finally it inhibits any narrow, internally directed view of the manager's job.

These are very wide claims and much of the support for them does not come to light until the consideration, that now follows, of the different kinds of relationship involved in the manager's job.

Trading, work-flow and service relationships
Primarily all these are lateral or horizontal relationships with equals or specialists as distinct from vertical superior–subordinate relationships. Their growth and importance have increased with the growth in size, complexity, and specialization in organizational structure.

Trading relationships relate to agreements which settle the terms on which managers agree to 'do business', i.e. deal, with each other. The assumption is that the manager is a 'buyer' when he wants something from another manager and a 'seller' when he is in a position to provide what another wants. Some managers may be both 'buyers' and 'sellers' of each others 'products'. As organizations are not static the pattern of buyer–seller relationships will not be constant. New relationships may need to be set up or existing ones modified or dropped. The 'terms of trade' are what, when, how, and for how much each manager will 'sell' what is required or the other will 'buy'. Initial negotiations are likely to be long and protracted as each side tries all the usual bargaining ploys. Eventually some agreement should be reached which settles the form the relationship will take and the way it will be operated by both sides. This will hold until one side or the other tries to modify it either because it is not satisfactory in practice or conditions have changed. In much writing about management the question of relationships is taken for granted, perhaps as being specified in a job description. This analysis of the way relationships are brought into operation or modified is a very useful addition to the concepts about them and explains many of the differences between 'theory' and 'practice'.

Work-flow relationships are limited to the stages where the product of the work of one group proceeds sequentially to another group and forms the work of that group. The chain of groups may be long or short but for the manager at each stage the performance of earlier stages in terms of time, quantity, and quality is vital as it will affect his own group's performance. These relationships are often difficult to work satisfactorily because when anything goes wrong or is likely to go wrong the natural tendencies are to withhold or distort information or to 'pass the buck'. Operations of this kind are subject to varying degrees of uncertainty of outcome and the greater the uncertainty the more important the relationship is and the more frequent contacts should be.

The now common practice of centralizing specialized aspects of work such as maintenance, internal transport, hiring personnel, industrial relations, and so on involves managers in service relationships. Sayles takes the view that these specialist departments are so readily accepted and so much in demand that virtually all the problems belong to the manager of the servicing department. The first of these is that he must respond to a large number of competing calls. To some extent he can arbitrate by giving priority to 'friends' or to powerful departments who, he feels, can do him most damage. In any case, under such conditions he is bound to be at the centre of conflicts between departments, and to be subject to excessive demands from departments who ask for more than they need in the hope of getting their real requirements. He is also liable to come up against departments who, either at first or in desperation, go up to higher levels in the hope of increasing the pressure on the service manager.

Service department functions are essential to the effective production patterns of their 'customers'. Perhaps the most obvious example is the maintenance department. The breakdown of a single machine can at times stop the whole production of a department so prompt service can be vital.

Sayles puts forward the view that the successful service manager can and does do something to help maintain stability in his own department by initiating action himself, e.g. planned maintenance. It would seem, however, that the best service manager will spend much time on getting his 'trading relations' right so that other managers' demands on him are realistic and can be negotiated in an atmosphere of mutual trust.

Advisory, auditing, stabilization and innovation relationships
These types of relationships have proliferated as organizations have become larger, more sophisticated, and more specialized. They are also the most difficult to handle, for a variety of reasons.

Advisory functions rely on specialist expertise in some particular aspect of work done by someone else. The classical example is work study, a much more recent one is operational research. The main problem revolves round the word 'advisory'. Taking the three stages of giving information, giving advice and taking a decision, in theory advisory functions come into the second category. In practice the distinction is often blurred and confusion results. Intended advice may be interpreted as a decision. Line managers, not having the expert knowledge of the specialist, find it difficult to question or reject the advice of the specialist and may even go further and avoid making their own proper decisions by calling in the specialist. Also because functional specialist departments, especially the newer varieties, tend to have managers who report direct to top management, line management tends to believe that they speak for top management. Indeed, top management may use the specialists to put pressure on the line. Even now we have not finished with possible difficulties. Specialists can try to circumvent line management by going above or below the correct level for the problem in hand. Line managers may find that their problems require not one but two or more specialist departments to solve a particular problem and that they then get conflicting advice.

Again it seems that we come back to correct 'trading relationships' as the key to the difficulties. The relationship between the line manager and the specialists should be such that the line manager initiates the call for help instead of its being forced on him from outside or above. The atmosphere should be such that free discussion of the problem can occur with sympathetic understanding on both sides and an ample knowledge by each party of the other's general problems. Mutual confidence in each other is essential for this atmosphere to exist. The line manager should see the problem as a way of increasing his own knowledge and skill and should get the credit for any improvement that follows. Specialist departments should be judged on their general performance in solving others' problems and not on the brightness of their own pet schemes.

In the one-man business the boss knows directly and intuitively what is going on throughout the business. In large, complex organizations top management and much middle management cannot possibly do this so auditing functions, which grow into auditing departments, have to be set up to monitor and report on performance and trends in all sorts of areas.

As this function is intended to check, assess, appraise and report upwards (usually) on the performance of others and is frequently used as an instrument for putting pressure on other people, conflict would seem to be the inevitable consequence. Each 'side' regards the other as the 'enemy'. Each 'side' is likely to have different standards in spite of the fact that they should both have the same 'company' standard.

Apart from monitoring and reporting auditing departments may possess degrees of power which vary from moral persuasion to absolute veto. The greater the number of aspects of work audited the more likely is the line manager to find himself with conflict between the different auditors. He will then have to 'trade-off' one against the other by compromise or by conforming to the pressure that, if ignored, could do him most harm.

Sayles suggests that the problems can largely be solved by resolving ambiguities into clear understanding. The obvious first area is on the differing nature of types of audit and the behaviour that is appropriate to each, e.g. veto, mutual discussion, joint interpretation. Auditing which is part of the work-flow should be under and report to the supervisor of the work-flow. Standards, methods of observation, and interpretation will involve problems that should be resolved by consultation.

Stabilization relationships arise when a manager has to get formal approval from higher authority before taking some action. This sort of machinery is set up where it is essential to ensure that some common, company-wide objective must be maintained so individual managers cannot be allowed freedom of action and where the normal controls and incentives do not lead to a proper balancing of pros and cons on a wide enough basis. Stabilization groups also are liable to cause conflict situations if they do not appreciate or cannot meet the special needs of departments when they occur and if the line manager feels, rightly or wrongly, that they are preventing him from getting his own job done properly. Overall plans and criteria which are not precise enough and very complex stabilization arrangements can lead to arguments, to unnecessary vetoes, and to discouraging line managers from going through all the trouble of fighting applications through. Again such machinery will work better if line management is brought in to help set the rules.

Innovation relationships get very short treatment. Special innovation groups are set up because it is assumed, only too often correctly, that the line manager is too close to his big problems to see them and has little time spare to deal with them even if he can see them. Innovation groups are intended to look at major problems and revolutionary change. To be able to see and work with possibly entirely new concepts they should be isolated as far as possible from other groups, have maximum autonomy, and maximum external professional contacts to provide new ideas and viewpoints.

In concluding this section one or two things are worth bearing in mind. Few managers' job descriptions spell out in detail this whole range of contacts and areas of managerial work. Yet as the managers involved in the research openly admitted once they were set out and described, the relationships were easily recognized as a mirror of reality. In dealing with them Sayles does appear rather to forsake his pure theory of management action and to come down to the more everyday level of explaining why such relationships are often difficult to work in practice. On the basis of 'know your enemy' this may not be altogether a bad thing and he does limit himself to the difficulties caused by structure and not by personalities.

Dynamic shifts in management patterns

As mentioned earlier Sayles does seem so far to have deliberately limited himself to a more or less static situation in which the job of management is to restore equilibrium when it becomes disturbed. While this is obviously a useful tool for analysis it must eventually be abandoned for the real-life situation of constant dynamic change. Now he moves to the situation where most managers have to fulfil many management patterns and have to be able to move easily from one form of interaction to another as the situation requires. Inevitably at times this involves the manager in conflict with himself where his job includes incompatible roles, at other times it may be conflict with others.

These conflicts can lead to shifts in a manager's pattern of relationships which, according to Sayles, are predictable from the existing circumstances. A number of possibilities are given. A manager with a poor or no job description or whose senior manager is vague as to what is required will shift his relationship towards ambiguity to give himself an escape route. Where the required patterns of behaviour and relationships are too difficult to operate the manager will shift towards simpler patterns. If a manager's status is lower than he feels it should be he will improve the position by shifting towards more initiatory action on his part, towards professionalization and becoming an expert, by dropping the low status aspects of his job, by 'empire-building'. Where the dependence on service and advisory functions is felt to be too great or they are seen as unsatisfactory the dependent manager will seek to develop his own functions within his unit.

Dynamic changes such as these have considerable significance and it is important, especially for higher management, to be aware of them. Obviously they point up the dangers of static job descriptions that rapidly become out of date and worse than useless. When top management can predict and evaluate such changes it can deliberately decide which to encourage and which to suppress. Knowing these possibilities top management can recognize more easily whether trouble spots are due to one of them, to personality clashes, or to external causes. With knowledge of the cause remedial action is more likely to be effective. For the middle manager himself it is better that he should know and recognize the true cause of his own behaviour and that of his co-managers. Finally difficulties in morale and motivation are often more correctly ascribed to conflict between units arising from these shifting patterns of managerial behaviour and relationships than to other causes.

The impact of 'external' relationships on the manager's job
There are two sides to every penny and two aspects to every shift in the management pattern. A change initiated by one manager will necessarily have an impact on the work of other managers. By 'external' here Sayles means other managers and departments within the same firm so he is considering the manager on the receiving end of a change initiated by another.

Presumably the researches on which this work is based showed this sort of change to be a continuing fact because the challenges and constraints which result from it are often a crucial and major part of the manager's work-load although they are seldom recognized as a part of his work. Although the assumption is now one of dynamic change it is still assumed that the individual manager's prime concern is for stability in his own department. To get or to try to get this the manager subject to pressure is likely to negotiate with the auditing, stabilization, or service groups, although these negotiations are likely to present problems themselves. (Author's comment. Why these particular groups are involved is not quite clear.) Such negotiations will consist of bargaining, compromise, give and take and may fail, leading to open or concealed hostility with which the manager must be prepared to live. Perhaps the most useful knowledge a manager can have is to know which pressures he can safely resist or ignore.

The idea of consensus and unity as vital factors in successful operating simply does not match reality. 'The manager must anticipate that more than one team will be playing in his organization and not find this immoral or upsetting.'[3]

Management as leadership
This topic must, more than any other, arouse controversy. To the psycho-sociologist it will be mostly heresy. To the practical manager it will be realism unadorned. The reader must decide for himself and the author must do his best to present the material without bias of any kind.

Negotiation and mutual compromise between a manager and his subordinates may not be necessary as they are, in general, measured by the same reward–sanctions system. Even so, the manager today must do more than tell or give orders to get compliance with his wishes.

According to Sayles the most important element in leadership is 'control' in its narrow sense of assessing results and intervening if necessary. 'What the leader does will be seen primarily as a function of how things are going, not of abstract and static conceptions of "democratic" or "autocratic" ways of dealing with people.'[4]

Leadership in an organizational setting cannot operate on the basis only of pair, man-to-man, relationships. The simultaneous influencing of a number or group of people by one person (the leader) is essential to effective functioning. Where this situation is established it is claimed that the people influenced will develop co-operative patterns of behaviour towards each other which will be directed towards the work process. This one–many relation, also called 'direction' by Sayles, is usually associated with the initiation of change because plans are not working out as required and the position must be restored or new plans and methods substituted. How much of this direction will be required depends on the variability in the system and the manager's ability to recognize the need for change.

The manager should have available a number of techniques to bring about this group response:

(i) Drill, conditioned reactions due to practice.

(ii) Legitimization of his authority through expertise, social distance, status symbols, association with people and causes to which his group responds.

(iii) Insulating the group from initiations from outside.

(iv) Early detection of possible non-response by the group.

(v) Ensuring the group is adequately trained.

(vi) Using 'lieutenants' or informal leaders in groups.

(vii) Ensuring that his influence is felt right to the lowest ranks in the group but without by-passing intermediate ranks.

(viii) Taking direct action only when it is necessary and ensuring that it is then prompt and effective.

But leadership is not simply a one-way downward process. The leader must respond to initiations by his subordinates and represent their views to other members of the organization. Within the group the interrelationship between leader and led must be a two-way balanced one. As the led respond to the leader so must he respond to them by providing help, assurance, and giving them at least some control over their own environment. It is suggested that a lack of close supervision will lead to feelings of neglect among group members but there seem to be mutual contradictions here. Close supervision has been amply shown by Likert and Argyris among others to reduce the degree of assurance within the group. If on the other hand, Sayles really means close contact rather than supervision, this runs counter to his suggestion of social distance as a help to leadership.

L. R. Sayles

Monitoring techniques and control theory

For the individual manager his total environment will include not only the technology of the firm, but also the state of the firm and his superiors, peers, specialists and subordinates. Monitoring for him should be a constant evaluation of the total situation in relation to his group and to take action to ensure that the system characteristics of his group are maintained. 'As we have indicated organization success or effectiveness depends on increasing the routine nature or regularity of the work-process.'[5] Again it looks as if we are going back to a static view of the organization where the manager's job is to correct deviation and return to the *status quo*. Sayles is, of course, writing about middle and lower management where innovation may be difficult and, in practice, not expected. But, in a total environment in which change is a 'given', managerial intervention must surely at least mean adaptation and possibly involve initiation and innovatory behaviour.

Monitoring is a specifically managerial activity and should be concerned with relating the actual behaviour of the manager's group with the behavioural requirements of the situation. It has secondary functions such as letting people know how they stand, relating rewards and sanctions to performance, identifying and curing once and for all problems that could be recurrent in nature, and locating strengths and weaknesses in the group so that they can be taken into account in future planning. Effective monitoring involves decision on the forms it should take, how much of it should be delegated to subordinates, and on the criteria which determine when the subordinate should come to the manager for help.

After the insistence on the manager's function of minimizing disturbance and developing 'predictable and repeated patterns of interaction'[6] it is perhaps a little surprising but comforting to find Sayles turning to stability and change. Complete stability, while it is the ideal, will never be attained. Interruptions, both external and internal, constantly face the manager. Some of them will require short-term remedies to restore the position. Others will involve dynamic changes in the form of new methods or new personnel. So the manager's objective becomes modified from a static system to a 'dynamic stability' or an equilibrium that responds to changes in the environment.

Monitoring or control systems seldom are, although they should be, integrated systems. Their real purpose is to identify quickly and accurately situations, events, and trends at the time they occur so that management action can be taken before it is too late. To do this the system must have a pattern of how often checks are made and with whom. They should cover both technical performance and measures of organizational relationships within the group. Management by results may have its exponents as a superior control system elsewhere. Sayles produces six reasons why it is a fallacy. Like many other things it is probably a case of how it is used.

At higher levels in the hierarchy where a manager will have as his group a number of subordinate managers each of whom controls one or more systems, the senior manager runs into greater problems of monitoring. This applies also to managers who have to monitor individuals, e.g. specialists, who move through and work with several or many groups intermittently. The answers lie in monitoring the boundary regions between the groups and sections. Failures of co-ordination in these regions indicate poor performance by the subordinate managers. Specialists are by their very nature focal points of the demands for their services. If the senior manager watches for significant departures from the normal pattern at these points these departures will identify shifts in the parameters of operations requiring attention.

Finally there are the behavioural techniques for monitoring. The traditional ones are the manager contacting other people, others contacting him, observation, and review of numerical records. These are not condemned out of hand but are criticized on the grounds of not being sufficiently programmed, frequently being non-discriminatory, and, so far as records are concerned, being essentially past history. A more important criticism in line with other developments in the 1960s is that most current methods lack statistical validity and fail to distinguish between random variation about a norm which in the long run is normal and significant deviation which shows a system out of control or moving towards it.

Introduction of long- and short-term changes
Now it is clearly stated that a major responsibility of management is to detect when change is needed and to initiate it. Short-term change, also known as corrective action, is dealt with first.

Short-term change is defined as change that lasts only as long as the manager intervenes in the situation. It occurs within a sub-system and to ensure that it does not upset the overall operation of the whole system the manager initiating it should notify his superior and the managers of other sub-systems whose operations are likely to be affected by the change. Only if he does so can corresponding or compensatory changes be made to avoid strains and stresses in the larger system. The initiation of change has considerable implications for managerial behaviour. For one thing he is bound to require changes in the behaviour of his subordinates and some colleagues. These may be obtained by his own previous behaviour which has built up a 'bank of favours' given and created a moral obligation to help him, by selling the idea, by offering complementary help, and by putting pressure on by indirect routes. Appeals to rules or to higher authority are discounted as practical methods. Negotiation between pairs or with successive individuals is the more usual strategy between managers. To be effective it requires knowledge of the correct sequence to use.

An accumulating pattern of disturbance or underlying structural problems in the organization can only be dealt with by long-term, fundamental change that is a function of the higher and top levels in the hierarchy.

Problems of this nature arise from stresses and strains that cannot be solved by short-term changes and so recur again and again, from problems and new factors in the outside environment, and from internal aspects of the organization such as personalities or incompatible demands in the work situation. It is suggested that many major needs for change arise because middle and lower managers do not make marginal adjustments when these are necessary so that situations build up and deteriorate to the point where drastic action is the only solution.

Somewhat abruptly the topic changes to the implementation and validation of change. The human relations emphasis on securing acceptance as the vital element misses the essential operations involved in the process. These involve four stages:

(i) An increase in the managerial initiative towards subordinates.
(ii) An opportunity for increased interpersonal contacts between the individuals to be affected.
(iii) An increase in the contacts from the subordinates to the manager to make comments, suggestions, etc.
(iv) Responses by the manager to these comments, suggestions, etc., which the subordinates see as rewarding.

The mere initiation of change does not ensure that it will continue. Human systems tend to revert to the previous equilibrium unless the change produces an apparent improved situation for all concerned. Increased monitoring activity by the manager is required until the new pattern of behaviour is firmly established.

The manager and the decision process
Decision-making in an organization is a dual concept. On the one hand it is an organizational process shaped by the interaction patterns between individuals. On the other hand it is also a contemplative, cognitive process carried out by individuals. Most managers' problems have a composite generalized form but the manager concerned will be at the centre of converging, specialist interest groups. He cannot safely rely on any one

of these converging pressure groups. A somewhat similar conflict situation arises when a manager moves through the organization trying to persuade others to support his point of view. Again he will run up against incompatible views. From this Sayles concludes that two managers with the same job programme can quite easily act differently in the same situation as they may accord different values to the pressures and aspects of conflict. The job programme does not completely determine the course of action.

Further, as decision-making for the manager will involve other individuals and groups it must present the manager with situations where to reach a decision he must 'trade' with others, giving something here in return for support there. Such 'trading' decisions are crucial to the final decision and they will be very personal to the manager concerned. His estimates of risk, emotional feelings, previous conditioning, likes and dislikes are some of the factors influencing him to a greater or lesser extent.

In the large organization the individual manager can never satisfy everybody. In that sense he can never win. Give and take, rules that can be 'bent', flexible standards ease decision-making but involve the need to live with the insecurity of possibly being in the wrong (and being found out!).

This leads to a tightly argued conclusion on decision-making. It must be given in Sayles's own words.

'The implication of this analysis of administrative decision-making as an organization process, not essentially as cognition, is in the area of change. If decisions are unsatisfactory, the answer most often lies in shifting the patterns by which various interest groups converge on a given manager. In a sense decision-making is a flow process. There is an observable sequence in which individuals come together when a problem emerges. Their relative impact is also a function of the type of administrative pattern each exercises, which, in turn, relates to the organizational position of the group or manager. All these must be taken into account in order to shift in some predictable fashion the quality of decision-making.'[7]

In terms of Sayles's system, as distinct from the personalities of the occupants of positions in the system, decision-making is 'playing the organization'. As he detects changes in the pressures and allegiances of his own group, other groups, and externally the manager modifies his behaviour. He constantly balances and modifies his trading with one group against the actual or potential hostility of others. This balancing consists of marginal adjustments to the situation resulting from earlier decisions rather than the 'all-or-none decisions envisioned by the student of traditional management theory'.[8] It may appear that the decision is made by the individual but '. . . most prices [in trading-off terms] are the resultant of the actions of many decision-makers, no one of whom can be said to have made the decision as to what price will prevail'.[9]

(Author's comment. In terms of orthodox decision-making theory Sayles's argument is shattering. In its defence it must be said that it is derived from direct observation of middle and lower managers in a large complex organization. We are told that the managers themselves agreed afterwards that the descriptions and the conclusions drawn were recognizable as their own experience. The conclusions seem to have close similarities with much of W. H. Whyte's *Organization Man*, another study of middle managers in large organizations.

But is the argument completely watertight even at middle and lower levels? A two-manager, face-to-face trade-off must occur sometimes as must a manager–subordinate situation. The final 'agreement' or decision is one of three things. First it can be the outcome of individual decisions by each party on their areas of indifference, the points on which they are prepared to trade. If these areas overlap then a decision is possible within the areas of indifference of both parties. If the areas do not overlap in the superior–subordinate decision the superior can decide to take the risk of enforcing his point of view against any resistance. He may not win but at least *he* has decided. In the two-manager situation if a trade-off is impossible the initiator may decide to drop the matter and do nothing, or either or both may decide to retrench, shift their positions or search for allies.

Even on the point of marginal adjustments arising from shifts in the environment Sayles seems to be on the horns of a dilemma. The manager must first detect the change and then decide whether to react to the change or ignore it. If, of course, it is forced on him by other parties whom he cannot afford to ignore, it is somewhat different. When other managers approach him first he must, surely, decide himself whether and which others he should approach for help. As pointed out in Chapter 19. Simon considers that each decision is made up of sub-divided decisions at different points.

Sayles's apparent argument, which seems to border on determinism rather than free-will in decision-making, must be given credit for explaining the mechanisms which put restraints on middle and lower managers' choices, but determinism surely goes too far.

One final intriguing possibility remains. Have top managers greater freedom in decision-making than middle managers or are the pressures and trade-offs with the larger environment equally restrictive and decision determining on the larger scale?

Summary: the systems concept of managerial behaviour

Styles of management, e.g. democratic or autocratic, are not valid in the middle management field of large organizations. The behaviour of the manager is a function of the organization and sub-division of work, the complex pattern of relationships, the compatibilities and conflicts inherent in his organizational position. It must match the requirements at the interface, the areas of contact in which behaviour takes place.

Generally the manager works on the basis of making marginal adjustments to his situation to restore equilibrium. Only when this fails will he go for major, structural change.

Each manager is a point in an open system subject to external and internal changes that impinge on him and require some reaction from him. At the same time his actions impinge on other parts of the system. Under these circumstances neatly labelled job descriptions and job boundaries will be inaccurate to the point of irrelevance.

Within this pattern of changing circumstances and inter-relationships, 'The one enduring objective [of the manager is] the effort to build and maintain a predictable, reciprocating system of relationships, the behavioural patterns of which stay within reasonable physical limits. But this is seeking a moving equilibrium since the parameters of the system are evolving and changing.'[10]

Management is not a heroic job. It means dealing with ambiguity and uncertainty. To succeed the manager must fight well in battles which he can never win, must be able to survive frustration. This is the price of large size, complexity, and specialization in organization.

In conclusion Sayles claims some unique features for his systems model. It makes change and stability, competition and co-operation real and all acceptable at the same time. For unitary leadership and consensus it substitutes and encompasses the realities of incompatible interests, all forms and sources of influence and leadership, bargaining, negotiating and trade-off in decisions, alliances, revised and reversed decisions. Is it fair to suggest it substitutes reality for the fairy story? It could well be.

References

(1) Sayles, L. R. *Managerial Behaviour* (New York: McGraw-Hill, 1964), p. 28.

(2) Ibid, p. 47. (Quoted from Chappell, E. D. and Sayles, L. R. *The Measure of Management* [New York: MacMillan, 1961), p. 39].

(3) Ibid, p. 141.

(4) Ibid, p. 143.

(5) Ibid, p. 157.

(6) Ibid, p. 161.

(7) Ibid, pp. 217–18

(8) Ibid, p. 218.
(9) Ibid, p. 219.
(10) Ibid, pp. 258–9.

Bibliography

BOOK BY L. R. SAYLES
Managerial Behaviour (New York: McGraw-Hill, 1964).

23

J. D. Thompson—II
1967

The first half of Thompson's book *Organizations in Action* has already been dealt with in Part I of this book. The second half deals with behaviour as conditioned by organization structure. This bringing together of that which had previously been quite discrete approaches to management and organization is possibly a very significant development for the future. For the moment, as Thompson has separated his ideas into the halfway mark of two Parts within one cover, it seems sensible to split his book between two Parts of this book.

One of the major problems in the more advanced, recent theories of organization has been how to discuss its nature and effects without giving the impression that it exists in its own right as a separate entity, apart from the people who compose it. This idea of reification of the organization is flatly rejected by Thompson at the very start. 'They (organizations) do nothing except as individual members within them act.'[1] The difficulty is to some extent a question of language, of trying to express ideas without being unbearably cumbersome. How difficult it is is shown in the first of the two aims set out for Part II by Thompson himself. This is to set out the extent to which *organizations achieve* (my italics) certainty or predictability about the conduct of their members, and of others in the task-environment. On the face of it this is pure reification, the organization on one hand, the members on the other. But when we recall that the organization is an intangible structure made up of patterns of action and relationships determined by the results of interaction between members themselves and between them and the task environment, by the aims and objectives that arise from this interaction, by the modifying effects of uncertainty, of real or contrived relative certainty, by technology, by past events and actions and by the many varied attributes and contributions which members have or make, the use of the one word 'organization' is an essential shorthand. It is essential, however, always to bear in mind that the term is shorthand.

The second aim is to consider the administrative (or management) process that has to cope with the fact that technology and the task-environment very seldom completely determine what should be done in every particular case. This means that discretion has to be exercised, judgements made and decisions promulgated. What effect does organization have on the distribution and exercise of the right of discretion?

We are, therefore, dealing with behaviour and its conditioning by and effect on organization.

The variable human

Each person is an individual and in the ultimate, unique. He or she has different heredity, experience, behaviour patterns, and attitudes. It is, and is likely to remain, impossible within an organization to understand fully every or even any member, and organization itself could not function if every individual exercised every facet of his or her individuality in the workplace.

Instead a simple theory of human action is put forward as a base from which to work. It arises from the interaction between the individual possessing aspirations, standards, and knowledge or beliefs about cause and effect in the world around him and the situation facing him which presents opportunities, constraints, and costs. This interaction may be modified to a greater or lesser extent by perception and knowledge both of which may be imperfect, biased and misleading. But with this modification the individual will act in the way that seems best to meet his aspirations and standards within the recognized constraints.

The individual is brought up and exists within a social culture which in many, but not all, ways prescribes some forms of action and proscribes others. This produces a homogenizing process which ensures that in a considerable number of ways the individuals within a given culture will be reasonably alike. Typical areas for this process are ways of perceiving reality, cause and effect relationships, attitudes to authority, what is worthwhile in life, what constitutes success. (Author's comment. It can be dangerous to take this too far. For example, broadly it can be said that there is one social culture in the United States and another in Great Britain. In some ways they are alike, in others they differ. But also within each broad social culture there are sub-cultures that form people's immediate backgrounds and that will differ very markedly within each country and, perhaps even more, between the two countries. It is dangerous to assume, for example, that management practices in the United States can be applied lock, stock, and barrel, without any modification to the sub-cultures of Great Britain!)

Having said that, however, it remains true that within a given society the culture does predetermine fairly large areas of behaviour so administration can take these for granted and its problem becomes one of matching limited diverse needs with the diversity within the organization structure. In addition the structure of society and, to a considerable extent, the immobility between one stratum and another have the effect of preforming aspirations, attitudes, and expectations.

Complete homogeneity remains impossible until Huxley's *Brave New World* or Orwell's *1984* become established fact. Personal differences of age, sex, experience, ability, and so on remain and must be taken into account.

Thompson draws on Barnard (1938), Simon (1957) and March and Simon (1958) for the basis that the decision to participate in an organization and the corresponding decision to employ a person constitute a contract with implicit or explicit expectations of and constraints on behaviour and the promise of rewards for compliance. As a result there is a 'zone of acceptance' (Simon, 1957) or 'zone of indifference' (Barnard, 1938) within which management has discretion to specify modes of behaviour. The prospects of promotion or a career are also determining factors in this area of acceptance.

The actual content of the contract depends on the relative power positions of the parties, power, as previously, being taken as the existence of dependence of one on the other. The different dimensions of different jobs provide the holders with different possibilities, e.g. opportunity to learn skills that may be useful for promotion or another (better) job, or the opportunity to be noticed by others with power in their hands, or the kind of assessment to which the job-holder will be subject.

Obviously the technology behind the job will influence possible patterns of behaviour. At the one extreme is the fully determined, microscopic routine job on the assembly line where anything other than purely conditioned behaviour would lead to organizational chaos and the individual is regarded as completely interchangeable with any other individual. On the face of it such conditions should cause individuals to leave. Instead, as opportunities for change are not all that obvious, the tendency is towards joint action to protect and improve the job. In such joint action carried out by joint negotiations both sides are concerned with setting up recognized practices that define the boundaries and rules for collective bargaining. In this power for one side depends on the degree of dependency of the other, e.g. the 'closed shop' enhances the power of the Union.

At the other end are the boundary-spanning jobs with variations according to whether the task-environment is homogeneous or heterogeneous. The extreme is the heterogeneous task-environment which gives the job-holder great discretion, wide power of action, high visibility to others and individual power over the organization when he can handle effectively the organization's dependence on his sector of the task environment.

Managerial jobs are usually such that the entry qualifications of skill, knowledge, and aptitudes can only be stated in very wide terms, values and loyalty are regarded as very important aspects and performance is very difficult to measure.

Discretion and its exercise

While the need to exercise discretion is essential to the functioning of an organization its distribution around the structure of an organization is by no means uniform, neither is the ability to exercise it. Again it is a matching job of needs and resources.

The motivation of the individual comes into the picture at two stages. first in the decision to seek or accept a job that entails exercising discretion and secondly in the decision whether or not to exercise it when he has the right and power to do so. The appeal, or lack of appeal, of status, prestige, and rewards influence the first. Tolerance for and the risk of ambiguity are thought to be possible factors in the second.

Thompson may possibly oversimplify with his statement that 'Individuals exercise discretion whenever they believe it is to their advantage to do so and seek to evade discretion on other occasions'.[2] It is not just a case of personality or objective factors but a subjective assessment of the negative and positive factors in the situation as the individual concerned sees them.

So far these are generalizations which hide the real complexity shown in the following summary of propositions. Where an individual believes that he cannot trust his capacity to bring about the required effect with the means at his disposal he will resort to methods other than the use of discretion. Inappropriate organization structures hinder the exercise of discretion as do extremely diffuse interdependence, and inappropriate assessment criteria for the individual's actions. The greater the risks involved in an error in decision the more the individual will delay and try to find other values by which to assess the situation. Multiple, incompatible criteria for assessment of the individuals will produce a bias in the exercise of discretion. The exercise of discretion especially in complex organizations may involve considerable personal sacrifice to the individual. But even these propositions are generalizations and cannot be used for prediction in an individual case. Exercise or evasion also depend on individual character, individual beliefs on causation, levels of aspiration, and norms of belief and conduct.

The right to exercise discretion may confer on the individual, at least for a time, the power to exceed his permitted scope and to use criteria not in line with organizational objectives. In order to guard against this the organization uses policing methods which tend to be resisted or at least resented by the people being checked.

Both unused discretion and incorrectly used discretion cause problems for the organization. In addition there are doubtful areas where it may be extremely difficult to decide what was the right decision and who gained or lost by it. It is, therefore, very important to have organization norms for what is correct conduct.

While work-loads ideally should be manageable it often happens that managers are overloaded. Where this happens and the manager has any options he is likely to concentrate on those areas that he believes will count most in any assessment of his performance. Similarly, if he has the alternative, he is likely to report his successes to his superior and suppress evidence of his failures.

For those at the top of the hierarchy, where the widest discretion exists, the exercise of this discretion may improve or worsen the spheres of action of other people, especially those nearer to them.

Within the range of discretionary jobs there will be a power struggle. Those with the greatest amount of discretion will try to increase their power by reducing their dependence on others. Another whose power is less than his discretion will try to increase his power by forming a coalition with others having similar problems. The behaviour of coalitions of this type is an extremely vital factor in the understanding of the behaviour of complex organizations. Status within coalitions depends on the values which the respective members represent. Coalitions may extend beyond the boundaries of the organization if the occupants of boundary-spanning jobs feel that by initiating such coalitions they will increase their power. Finally on coalitions, changes in organizational dependencies, either between sub-units within the organization or between the organization and its task-environment, will increase the power of some coalitions, reduce that of others and possibly leave some unchanged.

Again the assumption is implicit in these propositions that the behaviour patterns given assume action under norms of rationality.

Discretion and goals

Thompson does not approve of either the reification of the organization so that it can set its own goals or of the organizational goals being a complicated summation of individual goals. In Chapter 7 it was suggested that the organization's goals were the outcome of the interactions within the organization's domain, the boundary transactions with the task environment, and the organization's core technology or technologies. From the point of view of its effect on organization this almost pre-determined treatment was adequate but it is also obvious that the fourth factor in that interaction is the exercise of discretion in making decisions at various points. For instance the decision to extend the organization's domain or not, the decision as to which alternative boundary transaction to put into operation are only two instances where discretion will influence goals. At this point emphasis is put on the fact that management is always acting in the future, it may be only seconds or it may be years. So goals for the organization are desired states for the future, desired future domains. They will be determined by the exercise of discretionary power in making decisions by the dominant coalition. For this purpose the dominant coalition may include people outside the organizational struc-ture, e.g. especially important customers, or bankers in times of financial stringency. The people within the coalition have sufficient control collec-tively to decide the direction in which the organization will be committed. Under present conditions of complexity and diversified ownership of the firm's resources the tendency will be towards survival and growth for the organization and, as a by-product, for the power of the dominant group as well.

Power structure variations
The number of bases for power within an organization depends on such things as the number of sources of uncertainty and contingency. Internal politics or struggles for power among competing groups are a common feature of complex organizations. More complex organizations with more power positions and a heterogeneous task environment tend to increase the scope for political manoeuvre but, on the other hand, decentralization by limiting interdependence dilutes the power structure.

Both dynamic task-environments and changing technologies lead to more frequent changes in goals, more internal politics, more changes in the interdependence of units leading to variation in the make-up and strength of coalitions.

The power of an individual holding a boundary bridging position will increase, if the resource for which he is responsible becomes relatively scarce.

Members of the dominant power coalition are presumed to monitor or at least be aware of changes in existing coalitions and of the need for changes that have not occurred. It is also safe to assume that an individual whose power had been based on a strong dependency on him by other members of the coalition will try, when that dependency diminishes, to hide the fact from the other members of the coalition.

Powerful coalitions which on behalf of the organization commit future resources to courses of action in order to resolve present difficulties will at the same time create limitations on the future power of the organization to adapt to changes in technology and task-environment.

Control of complex organizations

At any stage beyond modest complexity in the organization the single all-powerful boss cannot retain control effectively except to the extent that he is not dependent on others. The rational model approach to organization theory would seem to confirm the correctness of the idea of an all-powerful single control, for example, Fayol with his scalar chain. And, in fact, it can work in tightly closed-system technical cores and, in small subsidiary companies where the dependence involved in obtaining resources is absorbed by the parent company.

But in the vast majority of cases the single boss just cannot cope with all the complexity of technology, cannot obtain single-handed all the resources required, and cannot keep under surveillance all the contingencies in a heterogeneous task-environment. He must be dependent on others to carry some or much of this load. Depending on the situation some or all of these people will, with the boss, become the dominant coalition in which final power rests. How powerful this or any other lower coalition is will depend on its ability to manipulate the bases for decision or policy guidelines for the next lower level in the hierarchy.

Processes of decision

Thompson attacks the decision process from a rather unusual standpoint. Taking the two major dimensions of decision-making as beliefs about cause and effect relationships and preferences as to possible outcomes he gives each two possible values – certain and uncertain. This gives a sort of matrix of types of decision thus:

Cause/effect beliefs	Desired outcome	Decision type
Certain	Certain	Computational
Uncertain	Certain	Judgement
Certain	Uncertain	Compromise
Uncertain	Uncertain	Inspiration

The distribution of decision-making power will depend largely on the types of decision required within the organization. Where the dominant coalition is able to specify more or less fully the cause/effect relationships and the desired preferences for the levels below them the coalition will be very powerful and the lower levels will only be required to make computational decisions. This, of course, implies very good two-way communication with the dominant coalition, all important variables to be under the organization's control, and full agreement on what the main objectives are.

The size of the dominant coalition, which in any case must have the last word, depends on the circumstances of decision. The more the decisions come into the second category of judgements the larger the coalition will be. The core-technology will be represented in it if the technology is not perfect as will the task-environment specialists with a heterogeneous task-environment.

A small dominant coalition is only likely under conditions of a standardized technology, a standardized product and a standardized market, i.e. very largely computational decisions. The more the decision process moves towards the judgemental type and beyond, the larger the coalition must become to include representatives of areas where judgemental decisions are required.

In order that control should be effective there must be some constraints on the possible range of preferred outcomes. A strong dominant coalition could, if it wished, set up and enforce any preference at all but to do so could ruin the organization's future. Rationally, only outcomes for which sensible instrumental approaches are thought to exist and which are probable results of organizational action will be considered. This does not necessarily or even probably mean complete consensus. Compromise between the core technology and boundary-spanning activities, between the dominant coalition and controllers of scarce resources, and between people with different professional standards are all possible. The greater the interdependence of the members of the coalition and the areas they represent the greater will be the likelihood of compromise.

These propositions supply confirmation of and reasons for the virtual inevitability of conflict within the large, extremely complex organizations of today. Taking just the three main themes of large areas of judgemental decisions, a heterogeneous task-environment, and high interdependence between members of the coalition the chances of consistent unanimous agreement are negligible.

For survival of the organization one or both of two solutions are required. The first possibility is an inner super-dominant ring within the dominant coalition. This may be elected or informally and tacitly recognized. Each member of the inner ring will represent a subgroup of interests from the dominant coalition. This makes effective compromise possible where a much larger group could only work by majority rule. The second possibility, usually in conjunction with the first, is the central power figure, the individual leader. He symbolizes the power of the whole organization but is only effective as final arbiter if he is recognized by and has the consent and the approval of the dominant coalition.

The administrative process

It is unfortunate that the most important question in management literature is 'What do you mean by . . .?' By 'administrative process' Thompson seems to imply an overall concept of the total direction and control of the whole organization.

He suggests that we have been too busy making complex organizations work by trial and error to study them and find out the true laws that govern them. We are faced with the paradox of complex purposive organizations that are natural systems being administered almost by rule of thumb derived from inappropriate rational-model assumptions that do not fit the facts. He says 'complex purposive organizations are natural systems subject to rationality norms . . . and the significant phenomena of administration arise precisely because of the inconsistencies of that duality'.[3] Purely rational models could be designed so that they would operate automatically. Purely natural systems would develop spontaneous procedures to cope with their problems as an essential to survival. We have neither completely. Instead one is almost tempted to suggest that we have an unholy alliance of both.

Cautiously but wisely Thompson goes no further than to offer some suggestions to be built into a better understanding of administration.

Organizations must have a viable technology to meet the needs of a task-environment that may be stable or changing, homogeneous or heterogeneous. Somehow that technical core must be protected from the disastrous effects of environmental change but, at the same time, must be capable of change under controlled conditions. Major environmental problems can be met by deliberate changes in domain and/or structure. Somehow all this must be consistent with the logic of the core-technology closed system and the multiple variety of input and output requirements. With the unavoidable interdependence in organizations of high complexity the difficulty of achieving all this is very great.

There is, says Thompson, no spontaneous mechanism for correlating combinations of interdependence with co-ordination. The assessment of the organization as a whole and of its component parts cannot be handled by closed-system logic. The adjustment of inducement/contribution ratios to attain desired results and co-ordination is extremely difficult in complex organizations. These are the supreme tasks of management. They involve not the one-thing-at-a-time approach but the handling of many problems simultaneously while keeping a proper balance between them. In broader terms they are the problems of co-alignment, of maintaining a balance and emphasis in time and space between individuals and streams of action to ensure survival, a viable domain and an appropriate structure design. All this is to be achieved in an environment that almost by the day becomes more complex and more dynamic.

But management often does not simply adapt to its environment. It can and does innovate to the extent that innovations are acceptable to those inside and outside the organization on which it must depend.

Another task of management is to convert the uncertainties of the environment and relations with it to the relative certainty essential to the technological core. Conversely it converts the stability of the lower end of the hierarchy to the flexibility needed at the top end.

Together these tasks constitute not the job of an individual but an ongoing process flowing through the actions of members, spanning and linking levels, incorporating interaction between levels, components and individuals.

There is, of course, a proviso that this is all a theoretical ideal, to be hoped for, strived for, but never reached. Real life is Cyert and March's (1963) problemistic search and Simon's satisficing behaviour. At the highest levels administration should be surveying the environment looking for new opportunities, but this, says Thompson, is a relatively scarce activity.

Other limitations, too, occur in reality. Mostly these arise because men and managers are not infallible. Managers tend to regard management simply as holding a secure job in a sheltered and protected organization; they prefer a dubious certainty of doubtful validity to the reality of uncertainty; they prefer short-term to long-term views; their knowledge of the design and structure of the organization in which they work is imperfect; they insist on such diffusion of power that no effective institutional level or inner circle appears to perform the essential top level jobs.

Modern industrial society is, in fact, on the horns of a dilemma. It has committed itself to very large scale, extremely complex forms of organization using so many resources that it cannot do other than depend on their operation for survival. Yet Thompson suggests that top management is essentially different from core technology and from middle management and is the vital component about which we know least and for which we do little, if anything, to train people. This was the problem he posed in 1967.

References

(1) Thompson, J. D. *Organizations in Action* (New York: McGraw-Hill, 1967), p. 99.

(2) Ibid, p. 118.
(3) Ibid, p. 144.

Bibliography
BOOK BY J. D. THOMPSON
Organizations in Action (New York: McGraw-Hill, 1967).

24

A. S. Tannenbaum
1968

Tannenbaum's book, *Control in Organizations*, is itself a summary of some twenty books and articles giving accounts of and conclusions from field research projects and experiments. These have had as their main emphasis the subject of control in organizations, its influence and the factors that, in turn, influence the form and nature of control. It is an important book in that it draws together so many different sources and shows where the trends are towards congruence. Equally, if not more importantly, it shows where differences still exist and where there are still areas of uncertainty.

To summarize a large book that is itself largely a summary of a score of other books would be an impossible and irrelevant task. The purpose of this chapter will be to try to extract Tannenbaum's own ideas on the overall situation at the time he wrote the book and to ignore the details of the individual researches, however interesting they are in themselves.

The concepts of control and total control

In broad terms Tannenbaum's thesis is that the Classical concepts of control in management theory are based on outdated experience and are no longer applicable to the typical large scale complex organization of the second half of the twentieth century. More general and more realistic concepts are emerging which form the basis of Tannenbaum's ideas. For a start he suggests that the idea of control being a limited quantity which can be shared in different ways but only so that what is gained by one party must be lost by another is completely out of date. There must be in modern theory a clear-cut distinction between the distribution of control and the total amount exercised. The latter is always at least potentially capable of being increased. So in a two-party situation both can increase the amount of control they exercise at the same time or either one can increase its amount without the other having to lose in absolute terms. Despite the rejection of Classical ideas this particular aspect, like so many others, was surely foreshadowed by Mary Follett with her ideas on 'power-with' and on 'control'.[1]

The importance of control in modern society rests on two facts. Almost all men and many women are for a large part of their waking hours involved in and committed to one or more organizations. These organizations are links between the individual and the larger society. They affect the individual's motivation, aspirations, and way of life. If people are to survive they must belong to some organization. If the organization is to survive it must have control over its destiny and activities and, hence, over the people who belong to it. Conformity and integration are vital to the concept of organization. This presents a dilemma that has not yet been solved. Through control the organization provides (relative) order, security, and abundance. These could, and do, provide for the individual some opportunity and choice, in a word, some freedom. But the social order and organization needed do themselves restrict freedom.

The centralization of power and control in the hands of the few brought about by industrialization and Scientific Management has meant that for the vast majority initiative, freedom, and control no longer exist at work. Only recently has research and management practice shown the beginnings of a reversal of this trend. It is with these recent trends that Tannenbaum is concerned.

The term 'control' as used by Tannenbaum is 'any process in which a person, or group of persons or organization of persons determines, that is, intentionally affects, the behaviour of another person, group or organization'.[2] Further 'authority . . . refers to the formal right to exercise control'.[3] Tannenbaum shows this as a closed loop in which the intention of A leads to his attempt to influence B and this attempt results in behaviour by B that fulfils the intention of A. Although this is given as a closed cause–effect loop it is recognized that many other factors will be involved such as the assumptions and values of both A and B, the power situation, the relationships between A and B and between them as individuals and other people, and the technology in which both are involved. A's intentions may not be his own. They may have been passed to him from some other source for onward transmission. B's behaviour may be overt and direct or covert and indirect.

Tannenbaum conceptualizes the amount of control as the difference between the probability that B conforms after A's attempt at influence and the probability that B would have performed this particular act without any influence from A. This cycle of control is held to be a basic unit of organization structure and if the cycles break down regularly then the organization itself has broken down.

A review of the traditional bases of control and of recent developments can be summarized to illustrate the meaning that is here attached to the term. Its early forms were tyranny, authoritarianism, conflict, the strong-willed leader and the ignorant mass. Early industrialization enshrined it in the possession of the means of production. This concept was backed up by economic theory. Weber's bureaucracy transferred it to an hierarchy based on merit and rules. More recent changes in society, education, and social culture have cut across the traditional bases of charismatic, traditional, and rule-based authority and introduced such new bases as social approval, expert knowledge, and mutual power.

It would be clumsy to use the phrase 'the effective use of power, authority or influence in order to produce a desired result' as Tannenbaum's fundamental topic but this seems to be the spelling out of the meaning implied in 'control' here.

Two relatively new ideas are central to the theme. The first is the distribution of control throughout the organization. The old idea that control was vested in the higher echelons of the hierarchy is abandoned in favour of the concept of variable distribution. Control can exist at any level or, rather, can be spread between all levels. While it is still more general for a relatively greater amount of control to be vested in the higher levels, in so far as the lower levels can directly or indirectly exercise influence upwards on their superiors or on their own working surroundings they will have their share of control. The second idea is that the total amount of control in an organization is not limited. Increase in the total may mean more for everybody or just more for certain groups while not decreasing that of others. This expansion in the amount of control may arise from the organization extending its influence further out into the environment. It may also come about internally provided certain conditions exist or can be brought into being. These are that the organizational structure is favourable to an increase in the interaction and influence between members and that the motivation and attitudes of members lead them to become interested in exercising more control themselves and, at the same time, to accept more control from others. It is possible that increased opportunities for exercising control may lead to greater involvement and desire to use these opportunities.

Half a dozen sources are quoted for a somewhat different slant on control. This is based on 'exchange of resources'. One person (or group) exchanges some valued resource in return for the compliance of the other. It brings in the idea of an increase or decrease in the total of valued resources as the determinant of the amount of control. It also extends valued resources from purely material things to such things as social approval, like or dislike between parties, and common interest.

Yet another approach to increasing total control comes from changes in the psychology of work. It was, and often still is, a fact that the work situation only involved a very limited sector of the individual's talent, skills, and personality. Bureaucracy is deliberately designed to exclude 'non-relevant' aspects. Where the working environment has been expanded so as to involve a greater proportion of 'the whole man' it has generally increased commitment to and involvement in the organization and so increased the total of control.

In all systems the natural tendency is towards entropy, that is, the running down of the system from a state of relative order to one of complete randomness. Control in the organization can be taken as one input of energy which maintains or increases the amount of order and so creates negative entropy, the opposite of running down. To put this in more everyday terms a collection of people behaving as individuals will behave in a much more random fashion than would the same people as members of an organization that is subject to managerial control.

Tannenbaum quotes Harvey's concept of graph theory which is a means of showing the social network between individuals and between groups. In effect this says that groups of individuals or groups of sub-groups will tend towards having more ideas, attitudes, and behaviour in common as the amount of inter-relatedness between them becomes greater. Cross-fertilization of ideas, standards, and norms can be expected to produce more common patterns.

A dozen or so authorities ranging from Selznik in 1953 to Argyris in 1964 are quoted to show that increased personal involvement, increased participation, higher skills, sophistication and sensitivity, lower conflicts, and resistance all lead to better organizational performance. But Tannenbaum insists on adding one condition and it is one that does much to explain the failure of many experiments and research projects in the late 1950s and 1960s to produce this better performance. The condition is this. All these schemes for greater participation, etc. will only succeed if, and so far as, they lead to greater total control in the system. This must act to reduce the conflict and tensions in the overall system. It must produce more effective control by more influence being exercised by all and not necessarily by more orders being given.

Relating this for a moment to Likert's interaction–influence ideas greater (i.e. tighter) control by management alone can produce better performance over relatively short periods of, say, up to two years, but long-term improvement is likely to be obtained only by increased influence and control being exercised by all ranks right down to the shop floor through effective interaction. It is at points like this where an increasing number of different approaches seem to be coming together.

Returning to Tannenbaum, reaching this high level of control through participative, organic models (Burns and Stalker) involves:

(i) Strong inter-connectedness between sub-units (Likert);

(ii) High total, not partial, inclusion of individuals' personalities and skills (Argyris);

(iii) Large stock of resources over and above physical and material ones, such as social approval, inter-personal skills (Simon);

(iv) Low rate of run-down or entropy through the reduction of misunderstandings, conflicts and resistance (Simon).

While the measurement of the degree of control in existence would be an important conceptual tool in analysis Tannenbaum admits that no really satisfactory method of doing so had been found by 1968.

As a last word before turning to a detailed analysis of research projects and findings Tannenbaum remakes the point that the concept of total control and the possibility of increasing it does not necessarily imply that any increase is always desirable. However, the concept draws its importance because of the implications it seems to have for the psychological adjustment and welfare of members of the organization and for its possible effects on overall performance by the organization.

Research findings

It is not intended at this stage to go into an analysis of the findings and conclusions of the work quoted. Two things, however, do seem to be reasonably certain.

The first is that Tannenbaum is extremely objective in his reporting and conclusions. It is undesirable to draw conclusions from researches which he has not quoted in relation to his general thesis. But he certainly does not baulk at including and analysing work that does not appear to support his ideas directly.

The second is the conclusion that, by now, should be reasonably apparent. Nowhere in management theory or in practice is it tenable to assume a one-cause/one-effect relationship. Increased total control, however spread, will not of itself produce more effective organizational performance. There are too many other variables in the situation which will have influence on the result to claim a direct cause/effect link. But in a very complex situation the amount of total control and its distribution will influence the result positively if other important factors (in the particular situation under consideration) are congruent with it. If they are not then its effect may be negligible or even negative.

Individual adjustment and organization performance

Tannenbaum concludes his book with a chapter in which he seems rather to be thinking aloud. He suggests that the research that he has quoted at some length points to the conclusion that the way control is exercised, or the amount that is exercised has significant effects on the adjustments of organization members and on the performance of the organization.

With regard to personal adjustment there are five factors involved:

(i) Every act of control within an organization has two aspects. One is the pragmatic aspect in which the act says something about what the individual must or must not do, under what conditions or what restrictions. At the same time the act of control carries symbolic interpretations such as superiority or inferiority, dominance or submissiveness, guidance and help or criticism and reprimand. The symbolic aspect involves an emotional charge to a greater or lesser extent.

(ii) For most members of an organization the right to exercise control has a positive psychological value and is preferred to a situation of powerlessness. Generally speaking workers, and often managers, have been found to have less control over their working situations than they would like or feel they are entitled to. This preference for more control or power may arise from the positive psychological value that an increase in it would have, or it may come from the pragmatic view of being more able to adjust the situation and environment to one's own ends.

(iii) The right to exercise control with its effect of increasing involvement in and identification with the organization is a powerful factor for integrating the individual into the organization.

(iv) The actual exercise of control is not simply a satisfying experience, it may, and usually does, involve frustrating consequences for the person exercising it but with which he must learn to live. The opposites are powerlessness with alienation and power with more or less frustration. (Author's note. There is a school of thought developing that seems prepared to accept alienation or, at least, non-involvement as the price of industrial progress and a condition with which management must live.)

(v) An increase in control for one invidivual may be matched with increases in control elsewhere so that the individual may at one and the same time be more controlling and more controlled. As his loyalty to and identification with the organization increase he may well find himself bound to accept influences over him which, with less loyalty, he would have refused.

So far as organizational performance is concerned Tannenbaum is a little more cautious. Variations in control patterns have important effects psychologically on members which are sometimes predictable. They *may* also have effects on organizational performance but, until more positive direct measures become available, there will remain some controversy over this. The measures used in the researches may not be sufficiently objective but there seem to be reasonable inferences that control and effectiveness are related, at least as perceived by the members involved.

From the researches Tannenbaum is prepared to make a number of 'statements':

(i) Organizations with influential lower levels can be as effective as those with relatively uninfluential lower ranks. Power at lower levels does not necessarily involve anarchy.

(ii) Organizations with powerful autocracies can be as effective as those with less influence at the top.

(iii) Of two organizations with similarly influential lower levels the one with the more powerful or influential upper levels is likely to be the more effective.

(iv) Of two organizations with similarly influential top levels the one with the more influential lower levels is likely to be the more effective.

(v) Organizations with influential leaders *and* influential members are likely to be more effective than any other combination involving less influence in either group.

(vi) Variations of power between ranks within the normal range of variations are not likely to correlate with criteria of performance.

(vii) Total power or control exercised is a better explanation of the functioning of an organization than relating participation with power equalization or considering some fixed system of differential power.

Conclusion

The dichotomy of having increased efficiency at the cost of reduced individual freedom or having individual freedom frustrated by the industrial anarchy that would result can only be resolved by some middle way. Essential to this 'middle way' becoming operative is a widespread belief that the individual and the mass are or can become capable of accepting and working in a social organization that provides both adequate personal satisfaction *and* adequate industrial and commercial efficiency. It involves a new view of control as something which can be increased in many ways rather than as a fixed quantity involving squabbles as to who should have how much. It assumes more total control, it assumes self-respect and respect for others in the individual, it assumes greater significance to the individual and to the group of the importance of success and failure.

Tannenbaum does not say so, but this seems to imply, not a far off and impossible millennium of perfection, but a distant goal where every step, however small, towards it could leave an organization in a better state than it was before.

References

(1) Metcalf, H. C. and Urwick, L. *Dynamic Administration* (London: Pitman, 1941), Chapters 4 and 9, and
Pollard, H. R. *Developments in Management Thought* (London: Heinemann, 1974), Chapter 12.
(2) Tannenbaum, A. S. *Control in Organizations* (New York: McGraw-Hill, 1968), p. 5.
(3) Ibid, p. 5.

Bibliography

BOOK BY A. S. TANNENBAUM
Control in Organizations (New York: McGraw-Hill, 1968).

Conclusion

Conclusion

The earlier companion volume to this book, *Developments in Management Thought*, ended at about 1960 when significant changes in thinking seemed to provide something of a watershed. But any idea that this book might produce the outline of a definitive theory of management was shown very early on to be completely unrealistic. Instead of a definitive theory we have a selection of two dozen or so works out of a number that is staggeringly large, a second instalment of an apparently never-ending serial.

Behind every word of this book and behind the two to three million words which it purports to represent two questions lurk and remain almost unanswered. The first is 'How can Western civilization *manage* to survive?'. The double meaning of *manage* here is absolutely intentional. The second may seem old-fashioned today but is probably more vital as the answer to it will condition ultimately the answer to the first. It is 'Why? What is the central ethic, the purpose behind modern organized society?'. The old values appear as tattered rags of symbols seen by most people as irrelevant to the late twentieth century, whatever lip-service they may pay to them. On every hand can be seen the near frantic search for some new value to give meaning to modern living.

At the centre of this maelstrom lies modern organization, industrial, commercial, governmental, and social. According to March and Simon it is the most pervasive factor in modern life and it is difficult to refute their point of view. At the very centre of organization lies the process of management, the mass of managers, the individual manager. Whether he realizes it or not, whether he likes it or not the individual manager is adding his mite to the answers to these questions every day of his working life. He must have more than the myths and folk-lore of previous generations of managers to guide him.

The answers to the search for a new ethic or purpose must be moral value judgements on ultimate ends. As such they cannot be judged as correct or incorrect. They could be reached in a number of ways – by democratic processes which could be well- or ill-informed, by power blocs or groups, by dictatorship, by a 'managerial elite' as suggested by James Burnham in *The Managerial Revolution*.[1]

But, while we wait for answers to 'Why?' which, by their nature, will be longer in coming, we must have better answers to 'How?'. Here for the moment we might be on safer ground but it is ground where greater knowledge has, at least for the time, produced greater controversy.

At one extreme lies Lawrence and Lorsch's concept of the very limited number of extremely large, viable firms which will have crushed or absorbed all the smaller ones and will tower over nations, governments, groups and individuals as the all-powerful determiners of the quality of life. But have we, or shall we have, the men with the qualities and the ability to manage these mammoth corporations? And would they be really viable anyway? Is it just coincidence that both American and Russian organization is beginning to back-track to smaller self-controlling units? Simon suggests that aggregative (policy) decisions at the top level have to be converted down the organization into specific, detailed decisions. He doubts whether, as the organization gets larger, the specific decisions will be the best responses to the aggregative decisions and whether any adequate means of checking and controlling them can be found.

It is, presumably, inevitable that theories and, for that matter, empirical research must be influenced to some considerable extent by the environment in which they occur. The seemingly endless growth and prosperity following the end of the Second World War nearly to the mid-1970s must have done something to encourage the cult of size in organization, backed up, as it was, by the needs of developing technology. At the same time it hid the dysfunctional effects of size, growth and complexity. Etzioni's suggestion of self-adjusting organizations appears to be somewhat over-optimistic in the light of the difficulties, problems and apparent lack of real control at the top of almost all large public and much of larger private industry in the mid-1970s.

Sayles's study of middle management in a large corporation is factual rather than prescriptive. If his conclusion of determinism at middle and lower levels of management is correct he is saying 'here is what is' not 'here is efficiency and success'.

The psycho-sociologists as a whole seem to have consolidated their position. Empirical evidence and gradual extension seem to be the order of the day. But this is not to suggest wholesale agreement and unity. Two or three pointers seem to be of particular significance.

Miller and Rice seem to suggest that human needs and organizational needs must necessarily be in conflict. From this it follows that human needs will be constraints on the organization and must be studied to minimize their effects. It is a very short step from here to the conclusion that managers should organize for conflict and sub-optimize below the level that could be obtained if both sets of needs could be made to coincide.

It is a short step, too, from our question of 'How?' to the prescriptive answers of the psycho-sociologists. So easily can they be assumed to be saying 'This is what the manager *should* do'. The Ahmedabad experiment was said to be possible only because top management was self-critical, open-minded, and willing to change itself before asking others to change.

With a different approach Likert and Herzberg seem to be suggesting an impossibility and at the same time a sinister, if outside possibility. On the face of it they ask for a perfect world of perfect people – that is the impossibility yet, at times it has been seen to work. Blake and Mouton go further with a theory *and* a method. On the other hand if managers really understood and had the abilities to employ these theories unscrupulously they could create a manipulated but satisfied work-force. But manipulated to what end? George Orwell and 1984? Blake and Mouton, on the other hand, seem to be quite happy to say, 'Here is what we should do' and to back up their claims.

We have with almost inevitability come full circle back to the question 'Why?', 'To what end?'.

It was Weiner in an early book on Cybernetics who suggested that the loss of sensation and hence of understanding was greater from having a thumb amputated than from losing a leg from the hip down. As an experiment I blindfolded myself, covered my right thumb with my other hand and felt and tried to use familiar objects with the remaining four fingers. Quite familiar objects became two-dimensional instead of three, often almost unrecognizable and generally unusable.

It is ironic that in trying to present a summary of further dimensions of management thought we seem at first sight to have got further away from rather than nearer to the realities the manager faces every day. But it is Weiner in reverse. Previously flat objects have become three- or more dimensional. Appearances are deceptive. Complexity cannot be truly represented in simple terms and analogies, and there can be no doubt about the complexity of the typical modern organization. So a viable theory must, of necessity, become more complex, and the manager in his day-to-day practice must be able and willing to recognize the complexity of reality rather than the simplicity of mythology.

The preceding chapters are no more than a summary, probably a highly personal one, of a very limited cross-section of a decade of vast increase in our knowledge about management. It must be my hope that they will be useful summaries that create enough interest to lead readers on to the original sources and to other material, and from there to their own answers to the questions 'Why?' and 'How?'.

In Richard Bach's story of Jonathan Livingston Seagull Jonathan says, 'Look at Fletcher! Lowell! Charles-Roland! Judy Lee! Are they also special and gifted and divine? No more than you are, no more than I am. The only difference, the very only one, is that they have begun to understand what they really are and have begun to practice it.'[2]

Conclusion

The path to understanding lies through the question honestly asked. If this book helps to raise the questions it will have served its purpose.

References

(1) Burnham, J. *The Managerial Revolution* (Harmondsworth: Penguin Books, 1945).

(2) Bach, R. *Jonathan Livingston Seagull* (New York: Avon Books, 1973), p. 114.

General Bibliography

This bibliography is divided into sections, three of which relate directly to the three parts of this book. Beyond that it includes sections relating to Classical theory, to Systems theory and to some of the books on management practice which appear to have a reasonably sound theoretical base.

The sources quoted are much wider than the books specifically dealt with in the text. It must not, however, be assumed that the list is fully representative let alone comprehensive. The items are arranged in date order of publication under each heading. Books dealt with in the text have not been included.

CLASSICAL

Taylor, F. W. *Shop Management* (New York: Harper and Bros., 1911).

Taylor, F. W. *The Principles of Scientific Management* (New York: Harper and Bros., 1915).

Gantt, H. L. *Organizing for Work* (New York: Harcourt, Brace and Howe, 1919; London: Allen and Unwin, 1920).

Rowntree, B. S. *The Human Factor in Business* (London: Longmans, 1921, 1925, and 1938).

Sheldon, H. *The Philosophy of Management* (London: Pitman, 1923).

Mooney, J. D. *The Principles of Organization* (New York: Harper and Row, 1947).

Urwick, L. F. *The Elements of Administration* (London: Pitman, 1947).

Gilbreth, F. B. and Gilbreth, L. M. (Eds. Spriegel, W. R. and Meyers, C. E.) *The Writings of the Gilbreths* (Homewood, Ill.: Irwin, 1953).

Brech, E. F. L. *Management. Its Nature and Significance* (London: Pitman, 3rd edn., 1953).

Fayol, H. *General and Industrial Management* (London: Pitman, 1957).

Urwick, L. F. and Brech, E. F. L. *The Making of Scientific Management. Vol. I Thirteen Pioneers* (London: Pitman, 1957).

Gantt, H. L. (Ed. Rathe, A. W.) *Gantt on Management* (New York: American Management Association, 1961).

ORGANIZATION – STRUCTURE

Jaques, E. *The Changing Culture of a Factory* (London: Tavistock, 1951).

Brech, E. F. L. *Organization. The Framework of Management* (London: Longmans, 1957).

Brown, Lord W. *Exploration in Management* (London: Heinemann, 1960).

Boulding, K. *The Organizational Revolution* (New York: Harper, 1963).

March, J. *A Handbook of Organization* (Chicago: Rand Macnally, 1965).

Woodward, J. *Industrial Organization. Theory and Practice* (London: Oxford University Press, 1965).

Bennis, W. G. *Changing Organizations* (New York: McGraw-Hill, 1966).

Bennis, W. G. *Organizational Development* (Reading, Mass: Addison Wesley, 1969).

Dalton, G. W., Lawrence, P. R. and Lorsch, J. W. *Organizational Structure and Design* (Georgetown, Ont: Irwin-Dorsey, 1970).

PSYCHO-SOCIOLOGICAL

Follett, M. P. (Eds. Urwick, L. F. and Brech, E. F. L.) *Dynamic Administration* (London: Pitman, 1941).

Rothlisberger, F. J. and Dickson, W. J. *Management and the Worker* (Boston, Mass: Harvard University Press, 1947).

Mayo, E. *The Social Problems of an Industrial Society* (Boston: Harvard Business School, 1945; London: Routledge and Kegan Paul, 1949).

Homans, G. C. *The Human Group* (New York: Harcourt Brace and World, 1950).

Urwick, L. F. and Brech, E. F. L. *The Making of Scientific Management. Vol. III The Hawthorne Investigations* (London: Pitman, 1952).

Eysenk, H. J. *The Uses and Abuses of Psychology* (Harmondsworth: Penguin Books, 1953).

Brown, J. A. C. *The Social Psychology of Industry* (Harmondsworth: Penguin Books, 1954).

Maslow, A. H. *Motivation and Personality* (New York: Harper and Row, 1954).

Whyte, W. F. *Money and Motivation* (New York, 1955).

Argyris, C. *Personality and the Organization* (New York: Harper, 1957).

Landsberger, H. A. *Hawthorne Revisited* (Ithaca: Cornell University Press, 1958).

Leavitt, H. J. *Managerial Psychology* (Chicago: University of Chicago Press, 1958).

Sayles, L. R. *Behaviour of Industrial Work Groups* (New York: Wiley, 1958).

Herzberg, F. *et al. The Motivation to Work* (New York: Wiley, 1959).

McGregor, G. *The Human Side of Enterprise* (New York: McGraw-Hill, 1960).

Likert, R. *New Patterns of Management* (New York: McGraw-Hill, 1961).

Costello, T. and Zalkind, S. *Psychology and Administration* (Englewood Cliffs: Prentice Hall, 1963).

Leavitt, H. J. *The Social Science of Organizations* (Englewood Cliffs: Prentice Hall, 1963).

Trist, E. L., Higgin, E. W., Merry, H. and Pollack, A. B. *Organizational Choice* (London, Tavistock, 1963).

Blauner, R. *Alienation and Freedom* (Chicago: University of Chicago Press, 1964).

Vroom, V. H. *Work and Motivation* (New York: Wiley, 1964).

Zaleznik, A. and Moment, D. *The Dynamics of Interpersonal Behaviour* (New York: Wiley, 1964).

Bass, B. M. *Organizational Psychology* (Boston, Mass: Allyn and Bacon, 1965).

Bennis, W. G. and Schein, E. H. (Eds.) *Leadership and Motivation* (Chicago: University of Chicago Press, 1966).

Fiedler, F. *The Theory of Leadership Effectiveness* (New York: McGraw-Hill, 1967).

Etzioni, A. W. *A Sociological Reader on Complex Organizations* (New York: Wiley, 1969).

Argyris, C. *Intervention Theory and Method. A Behavioural Science View* (Reading, Mass: Addison Wesley, 1970).

Argyle, M. *The Social Psychology of Work* (Harmondsworth: Penguin Books, 1972).

Luthans, F. (Ed.) *Contemporary Readings in Organizational Behaviour* (New York: McGraw-Hill, 1972).

DECISION THEORY

Hodnett, E. *The Art of Problem Solving* (New York: Harper and Row, 1955).

Simon, H. *A New Science of Management Decision* (New York: Harper and Row, 1960).

Gore, W. J. and Dyson, J. W. *The Making of Decisions* (New York: Macmillan, 1964).

Kaufman, A. *The Science of Decision Making* (London: Weidenfeld and Nicholson, 1968).

Cyert, R. M. and Welsch, G. A. *Management Decision Making. Selected Readings* (Harmondsworth: Penguin Books, 1970).

Rappaport, A. *Information for Decision Making. Quantitative and Behavioural Dimensions* (Englewood Cliffs: Prentice Hall, 1970).

Moore, P. G. *Risk in Business Decisions* (New York: Longman, 1972).

Schleip, W. and Schleip, R. *Planning and Control in Management. The German R P S System* (London: Peter Peregrinus, 1972).

SYSTEMS THEORY

Weiner, N. *Cybernetics* (New York: Wiley, 1961).

Beer, S. *Decision and Control* (New York: Wiley, 1966).

Beer, S. *Cybernetics and Management* (London: English Universities Press, 2nd edn, 1967).

Beer, S. *Management Science* (London: Aldus Books, 1967).

Buckley, W. *Sociology and Modern Systems Theory* (Englewood Cliffs: Prentice Hall, 1967).

Carzo, R. Jr., and Yanouzas, J. N. *Formal Organization. A Systems Approach* (Homewood Ill: Irwin, 1967).

Johnson, R. A. *et al. The Theory and Management of Systems* (New York: McGraw-Hill, 1967).

George, F. H. *Cybernetics in Management* (London: Pan Books, 1970).

Lee, A. M. *Systems Analysis Frameworks* (London: Macmillan, 1970).

MANAGEMENT ACTION

Barnard, C. I. *The Functions of the Executive* (London: Oxford University Press, 1938).

Drucker, P. *The Practice of Management* (London: Heinemann, 1955).

Newman, W. H. *Administrative Action* (London: Pitman, 1958).

Granick, D. *The Red Executive. A study of Organization Man in Russia* (New York: Doubleday, 1960).

Whyte, W. H. *The Organization Man* (Harmondsworth: Penguin Books, 1960).

Falk, R. *The Business of Management* (Harmondsworth: Penguin Books, 1961).

Burnham, J. *The Managerial Revolution* (Harmondsworth: Penguin Books, 1962. 2nd ed).

Kerr, C. *et al. Industrialism and Industrial Management* (London: Heinemann, 1962).

Stewart, R. *The Reality of Management* (London: Heinemann, 1963, Pan Books, 1967).

Drucker, P. *Managing for Results* (London: Heinemann, 1964).

Flanders, A. *The Fawley Productivity Agreements* (London: Faber and Faber, 1964).

Kahn, R. L. *et al. Organizational Stress. Studies in Role Conflict and Ambiguity* (New York: Wiley, 1964).

Blake, R. R. and Mouton, J. S. *The Managerial Grid* (Houston: Gulf Publishing, 1964).

Blake, R. R. and Mouton, J. S. *Managing Intergroup Conflict in Industry* (with Herbert A. Shepard. Houston: Gulf Publishing 1964).

Scott, W. G. *The Management of Conflict* (Homewood, Ill.: Irwin, 1965).

Sloan, A. P. *My Years with General Motors* (London: Sidgwick and Jackson, 1965).

Blake, R. R. and Mouton, J. S. *Corporate Darwinism* (with Warren Avis. Houston: Gulf Publishing, 1966).

Drucker, P. *The Effective Executive* (London: Heinemann, 1967).

Blake, R. R. and Mouton, J. S. *Corporate Excellence through Grid Organization Development* (Houston, Texas: Gulf, 1968).

Blake, R. R. and Mouton, J. S. *Diary of an OD Man* (Houston: Gulf Publishing, 1976).

Blake, R. R. and Mouton, J. S. *The New Managerial Grid* (Houston: Gulf Publishing, 1978).

Glossary

AMBIGUITY (Social sciences): unresolved differences in the ideas, aims and expected conduct forming the social and organizational situation in which the individual must exist.

ANALOGUE (Systems approach): something which, in broad principle, is sufficiently similar to something else to be used for comparison and analysis although the details may be quite different, e.g. a thermostat controlling temperature may be an analogue of a production control system.

CAUSAL VARIABLES (Social sciences especially Likert): the factors and actions that are the initial causes of activity and that are largely under management's control, e.g. organizational structure, managerial practices, capital investment. Likert also includes needs and desires of members.

CLASSICAL MANAGEMENT (Management theory): applied generally to most writers before about 1940. In general they tended to regard management as an art with a systematic rather than a scientific base and as something that could be studied in isolation.

CLOSED SYSTEM (Systems approach): a system that is self-contained and can function independently of the environment in which it exists (*see* System).

COLOURING INFORMATION (Communication): the person passing on information does it in such a way that its true meaning is distorted to a greater or lesser extent in the hope of making it more acceptable to the recipient.

CORE ACTIVITIES (Social sciences especially Argyris): the essential activities that are fundamental to the continued existence of an organization, i.e. achieving objectives, maintaining the internal system and adapting to the environment.

CORE ACTIVITY (Systems approach especially Thompson): the central (manufacturing) activity of the firm that is geared to operate essentially as a closed system.

CULTURE (Social sciences and organization): the generally accepted ideas, values and standards in a group, organization or community which tend to guide conduct and behaviour patterns.

DIFFERENTIATION (Organization): the result of specialization and division of labour. Implies not only differences in jobs and in the functions of sections and departments but also the resulting differences in aims, outlook and attitudes.

END-RESULT VARIABLES (Social sciences especially Likert): the final outcome, in whatever form, of activities. Includes not only tangible results such as production, stock, sales, and financial costs but also intangibles such as hidden costs, strikes, grievances, complaints, etc.

ENTROPY (Systems approach): the inevitable tendency of all organized systems to run down to a completely random distribution of their parts if left to themselves, i.e. when there are no further inputs of energy to maintain the system.

EVOKED SET (Social sciences especially Katz and Kahn): every individual has an extremely large store of knowledge, facts, memories, attitudes, standards, etc. In any particular situation only a part of this store will be in the conscious mind and only part of it will be seen by the individual as relevant to the situation. This relevant part is his evoked set. (*see* UNEVOKED SET and SET).

FEED-BACK (Communication): the response by the recipient of communication which shows what he understands the communication to mean. May be by words (spoken or written), by gesture, by facial expression, or by actions.

FEED-BACK (Systems approach): a procedure by which information on the actual results of activities (human and/or mechanical) are passed to a control point for comparison with the planned or desired results.

FILTERING INFORMATION (Communication): the conscious or unconscious withholding of parts of information because they are expected to displease or annoy the recipient.

FORMAL ORGANIZATION (Organization): originally a Classical Management term. It assumed the division of labour, authority, responsibility, and decision-making and the deliberate allocation of these to individuals to produce a pattern or structure of posts, duties, and relationships which were the formal organization. The detailed preciseness of this concept has come under question in more recent times (*see* INFORMAL ORGANIZATION).

HIDDEN COSTS (General): costs of operating which, either because the accounting system does not allow for their separation or because they cannot be directly measured in financial terms, do not appear as separate cost items in the accounts, e.g. falling morale, a strike, or poor supervision all involve extra costs in the form of lower or less effective production which do not appear directly as cost.

HIERARCHY (Organization): the pattern of structure in an organization whereby the supervisory and management posts are arranged in ascending order of importance and responsibility.

HOMEOSTASIS (Systems approach): the condition of a system or organization which has built-in controls that ensure that when changes occur in the environment the system or organization remains unchanged or adapts to produce an unchanged result.

HOMEOSTAT (Systems approach): a 'mechanism' or control device that ensures stability in a system in spite of changes in its environment.

INFORMAL ORGANIZATION (Organization and social sciences): the pattern of relationships between groups and/or individuals which arise more or less spontaneously within a larger organization either to meet psycho-sociological needs that are not met by the formal organization and/or to cope with deficiencies in the formal organization which prevent effective operation (*see* FORMAL ORGANIZATION).

INTEGRATION (Organization): literally 'to bring parts together into a whole'. Tends to be used as the complementary process of differentiation and is the management activity for ensuring that sections and departments work towards overall objectives and that their various sub-objectives fit together. Called co-ordination by most earlier writers.

INTER-PERSONAL COMPETENCE (Social sciences especially Argyris): the ability of people (especially at managerial level) to work well together in spite of differences that may exist, to communicate effectively and to handle conflict constructively.

INTERVENING VARIABLES (Social sciences especially Likert): the internal factors within the individual and the group which modify in some way the effect of the causal variables and consequently the end-result variables of activity. The chief ones are personality, perception, past experience, orientation towards job and surroundings, group traditions and aims, expectations, attitudes, motivational forces, and behaviour patterns. Generally they are much slower to change than causal variables and so confuse the link between causal variables and end-result variables (*see* CAUSAL VARIABLES and END-RESULT VARIABLES).

JOB ENLARGEMENT (Psychology): the attempt to remove the worst effects of extreme sub-division of work, monotony, apathy, etc., by combining several units of work into one wider job.

JOB ENRICHMENT (Psychology): the extension of job enlargement arising from the realization that the job not only had to be wider but had to be so designed that it provided an appropriate degree of psychological satisfaction from its performance.

LINK-PIN (Social sciences especially Likert): relates to the pattern of formal organization in which the leader of a lower group is, with other similar leaders, a formal member of the next higher group. This next higher group has as its leader the immediate superior of its members.

The pattern is repeated right up the organization to the highest group which comprises the top man and his immediate subordinates. It has been extended to include members of specialist groups who are also members of operational groups at their appropriate level. The man with dual membership is the 'link-pin' with the functions of communication and representation in both directions.

MECHANISTIC (Organization especially Burns and Stalker): the term used to describe the typical form of organization which is relatively formal and stable occurring in conditions where change of any kind is relatively slow. It tends to rely heavily on the hierarchy, on rigid procedures and rules and on high level decisions (*see* ORGANIC–ORGANISMIC).

MENTAL HEALTH (Psychology especially Argyris): the state where the individual's capacity, attitudes, aspirations, and hopes are matched by his achievements and surroundings. It may include stress and conflict provided the individual is able to cope with them satisfactorily. The important thing is the balance not the level which will vary from one individual to another.

NEGATIVE ENTROPY (Systems approach): the reversal of the process of entropy or running down of the system. The system is maintained or improved by the input of new resources and energy (*see* ENTROPY).

NORMS (Social sciences): generally accepted and expected standards and items of belief and conduct prevalent within a group.

OPEN SYSTEM (Systems approach): a system that is influenced by and has to react to changes in its environment.

OPTIMIZATION (Decision theory): finding and obtaining the best possible solution among alternatives.

ORGANIC OR ORGANISMIC (Organization especially Burns and Stalker): a flexible form of organization which matches a rapidly changing environment. It is characterized by the minimum of formality, much direct contact between individuals at all levels and a high degree of adaptability.

PSYCHOLOGICAL ENERGY (Psychology especially Argris): the will to make an effort arising from some psychological tension due to the difference between what *is* and what the individual would like. It is assumed to exist to explain why purely physical, biological energy may be under-used and why, on other occasions, effort may be expended when physical reserves appear non-existent.

RECEIVED ROLE (Sociology especially Katz and Kahn): an individual's interpretation and view of the actions, behaviour and attitudes other people expect from him (*see* ROLE and SENT ROLE).

REGRESSIVE BEHAVIOUR (Psychology): behaviour that is below the level of maturity which would be expected from the individual concerned. Usually defensive behaviour where the individual feels unable to cope. Often gets and deserves the epithet 'childish'.

ROLE (Organization): the formal duties, functions, and relationships involved in occupying and operating a formal position in an organization.

ROLE (Sociology): the function(s) assigned to or adopted by an individual in a group, e.g. leader, counsellor, peacemaker, resource man. In this sense usually applies to informal groups and the individual's role may change according to time and circumstances.

SATISFICING (Decision theory especially March and Simon): setting certain minimum criteria that a decision must meet and adopting the first solution which meets them (Contrast OPTIMIZATION).

SELF-CONCEPT (Psychology): a person's generalized idea of himself, his ability, aptitudes, physical and mental make-up and his orientation to his surroundings.

SELF-ESTEEM (Psychology): a person's evaluation of his own self-concept.

SENT ROLE (Sociology especially Katz and Kahn): the pattern of actions, behaviour and attitudes expected by one person of another as seen and communicated by the person expecting it (*see* RECEIVED ROLE).

SET (Psychology): a recognizable pattern of behaviour or ideas regularly resulting from a given stimulus (contrast EVOKED SET and UNEVOKED SET).

SOCIO-TECHNICAL SYSTEM (organization/psychology especially Miller and Rice): a view of organization which recognizes that the sociological needs of individuals and groups and the needs of technology must both be met simultaneously.

SUPPORTIVE RELATIONSHIPS (Social sciences especially Likert): relationships and actions of others towards him which the individual sees as being helpful, maintaining his self-respect and self-esteem and furthering his own aims.

SYSTEM (System approach): a blanket term for a 'whole' which comprises a collection of inter-connected and inter-related parts that interact in such a way as to attain the objectives of the 'whole'.

UNEVOKED SET (Social sciences especially Katz and Kahn): that part of a person's total knowledge, etc. which is not used in a particular situation (*see* EVOKED SET).

Index

Index